George Rooper

Flood, field and forest

George Rooper

Flood, field and forest

ISBN/EAN: 9783337113384

Printed in Europe, USA, Canada, Australia, Japan

Cover: Foto ©Andreas Hilbeck / pixelio.de

More available books at **www.hansebooks.com**

FLOOD, FIELD, AND FOREST

Frontispiece.

"IT WAS PLEASANT TO SEE THE BENEVOLENT AND GRATIFIED EXPRESSION WITH WHICH SHE WOULD REGARD US."

FLOOD
FIELD AND FOREST

By GEORGE ROOPER

AUTHOR OF "THAMES AND TWEED," "TALES AND SKETCHES," ETC.

FOURTH EDITION

WITH ILLUSTRATIONS BY G. BOWERS AND J. CARLISLE

W. ISBISTER & CO.
56, LUDGATE HILL, LONDON
1874

PRINTED BY TAYLOR AND CO.,
LITTLE QUEEN STREET, LINCOLNS' INN FIELDS.

CONTENTS.

AUTOBIOGRAPHY OF THE LATE SALMO SALAR, ESQ.

CHAP.		PAGE
I.	I Volunteer the Story of My Life, and Commence it before I was Born	
II.	My Infancy—the Perils that attended it—My Enemies — I Moralise, and Marvel for what End they were permitted to Exist	5
III.	Having Donned my Silvery Coat, I go forth into the "Wide, Wide World"—I pass a Modest but Candid Opinion on my own Appearance and Attributes	13
IV.	I Encounter my First Great Peril—I Escape therefrom, and, Proceeding on the Journey of Life, Seek the "Vast Unknown"	20
V.	The Goal is Reached—The "Treasures of the Deep"—I become Surfeited with Pleasure, and long to Revisit the Scenes of my Youth	28
VI.	I Return—My Reception—My Second Great Peril	35

CHAP.		PAGE
VII.	The Baillie's Misadventure in Search of "Saumon-Roe"—Mode of Fishing with that Prohibited Bait	39
VIII.	The Ascent of the River—I find again to my cost that "All is not Gold that Glitters," and afford a Practical Illustration of "The Biter Bitten"—My Third Great Peril	44
IX.	I Foregather with a Kelt, whose Gallant Struggle and Ultimate Capture I Witness	53
X.	"Thou Rash Intruding Fool! I took thee for thy Betters"	61
XI.	My Faithful Companion is Torn from my Side and Ruthlessly Slain—I Moralise thereon, and Proceed Upwards—The Waterfall—The Spawning Beds—Mortality among the Kelts—I commence my Return to the Sea	69
XII.	"The Sea, the Sea! the Open Sea! the Blue, the Fresh, the ever Free!"	80

A FOX'S TALE.

I. Vixen and Cub	87
II. Life in the Haystack	92
III. Life in the Gorse	101
IV. Cub-Hunting	110
V. The Meet	119
VI. The Run	130
VII. The Frost	145
VIII. The Finish	153

BOLSOVER FOREST.

CHAP.		PAGE
I.	Master B.'s Youthful Reminiscences	171
II.	Pupil and Preceptor	180
III.	Dog-breaking	190
IV.	Boyhood's Pleasures	203
V.	Birds'-nesting	215
VI.	School days	230
VII.	Ratcatching	245
III.	The Badger	261
IX.	Fen-shooting	275
X.	Wild and Tame Animals	290
XI.	A Quarrel and its Result	302
II.	The Condemned Cell	313

THE BAGMAN.

I.	The Bagman	331
II.	The Meet	336
III.	The Run	341

LIST OF ILLUSTRATIONS.

"It was pleasant to see the benevolent and gratified expression with which she would regard us." . . . . *Frontispiece*

                                                                          PAGE

"Then the kingfisher would dart down like a plummet from his roost." 5
"It's of no use putting it back, parr or not, it's dead." 21
"The first intimation Piscator had of the escape of his prey." 66
"We sink back one by one to the pool below." . . 69
"More than once a puzzled hound jumped over her back." 87
"I see her now, creeping, crawling, crouching." . 94
"The first Monday in November." 120
"I scrambled up the sloping trunk and lay completely hidden." 142
"Oh! Johnny saw the fox." 143
"Come, old fellow, where's our fox?" . . . 166
"I'll take him home, and chain him up to the old barrel under the lime tree." 167
"She took wing and flew strongly and rapidly away." 223
"What ails old Vic?" . . . 257
"The badger." 261
"As I crawled along the horizontal bough at a giddy height, the sharp-billed creatures continually dashed at me." 274
"You should not have fired, Master." . . 286
"Truly, my lord was avenged." 313

AUTOBIOGRAPHY OF
THE LATE SALMO SALAR, ESQ.

CHAPTER I.

I VOLUNTEER THE STORY OF MY LIFE, AND COMMENCE IT BEFORE I WAS BORN.

" I was born, or rather—"

"Bless my heart!" said I, somewhat startled, "*who* are *you*? How did *you* get here?"

No wonder I was surprised. I had that morning quitted the Edinburgh station of the Caledonian Railway, and, with the accustomed selfish liberality of a young man, had bribed the guard to lock me up in a compartment to myself, in spite of which I now found myself accosted, without preface or apology, by a queer-looking old gentleman, dressed in a straw-coloured paletôt, with a short pipe in his mouth, sitting, with his legs tucked under him, on the opposite seat to mine, as much at his ease, apparently, as if he had as much right there as I, who had paid two-and-sixpence for the privilege of appropriating six seats to myself.

"Or rather—" he proceeded.

"I really must beg, sir," I began; but somehow his manner overawed me, as it were, into listening. I felt like the wedding-guest in the presence of the Ancient Mariner. He went on in the same tone, without noticing me, or even taking his pipe out of his mouth.

"Or rather, I struggled into existence, for the egg from which I sprang had lain, with countless others, for well-nigh four months in one of the tributary streams of the Upper Tweed. My life, if life it could be called, had hitherto been a dreamy, monotonous, uneventful one, a gleam of sunshine quickening my pulse and increasing the natural yearning I felt for release and liberty, a passing cloud or a chill wind driving me back to somnolency and partial oblivion. But now the garish beams of the late February sun had called me forth into a new world, and I felt myself, with a proud sense of independence, launched, free from trammels and control, upon that wild waste of waters, henceforth my habitation and my home.

"Queer little mis-shapen creature that I was! With head and eyes frightfully disproportioned to my size, a little tail, and almost invisible fins, my appearance presented to the unpractised eye rather that of the tadpole, the progeny of the wide-mouthed waddling frog, than that of the noble Salmon, the monarch of the waters.

"Still, Nature, careful of her worthiest offspring, had not neglected the means of preservation during its helpless infancy. I found myself furnished, beneath my embryo fins, with a little sac of nutriment, which I felt would sustain me for many days, until my growing strength should enable me to seek the abundant food which the surrounding waters contained, and to escape the numerous enemies that sought to make a prey of me.

"When I burst forth from the bed of gravel in which I had so long been buried, very many of my brethren accompanied me, and, as we eyed each other's grotesque forms with astonishment, not unmixed with admiration, we, one and all, urged by the promptings of Nature, scuttled away and hid ourselves, each under some projecting pebble or stone, over which the waters rushed harmlessly, and in which quiet haven, fed from the sac I have before mentioned, we lay safe, happy, and in full enjoyment of our new life, making observations on the, to us wide, wide world, which now opened to our view."

CHAPTER II.

MY INFANCY.—THE PERILS THAT ATTENDED IT.—MY ENEMIES.—I MORALISE, AND MARVEL FOR WHAT END THEY WERE PERMITTED TO EXIST.

"LABOUR is the lot, not only of man, but of birds, beasts, and fishes. We must all work for our living, and I for one have a natural inclination to swim against the stream; but I own to looking back to this part of my life as one of unmixed happiness. Fed without the trouble of seeking, or even opening my mouth to swallow, my food — sheltered by an overhanging stone, and lulled by the pleasant ripple of the stream around me—I passed a dreamy, happy existence, without care, or thought, or trouble, and, as the sense of life quickened within me, it brought with it only a deeper sense of enjoyment. 'Where ignorance is bliss, 'tis folly to be wise,' and I may be thankful that I remained so long in blissful ignorance of the dangers which surrounded me. The power of reflection was not given to me, and, although I saw numbers of my brothers and sisters daily destroyed before my eyes, it never occurred to me as possible that a similar fate might await me. My ignorance, however, was my protection; careless of what was passing around me, I lay under my stone, motionless and fearless, and thus escaped danger until Nature had given me the means of avoiding it.

"When I look back on the number of our enemies, I can only wonder that even one out of our numerous progeny should be left to tell the tale. Even the insect tribe was in arms against us; I have seen a huge water-beetle seize an embryo samlet by the throat, and carry it off to devour at his leisure; and the larvæ of sundry insects fed upon us while we were in the egg, or newly hatched, more especially those of the dragon-fly, which, goggled-eyed, misshapen, repulsive, the hideous face furnished with a pair of unnaturally elongated eyebrows, and the mouth with sharpest teeth, would destroy, in the course of a few days, thousands upon thousands of eggs. There was a little brown-coated bird,* with a white waistcoat, the neatest, pleasantest-looking creature imaginable, who would *walk* † deliberately into the stream, and, setting at defiance all laws of gravitation, peck away at marine insects, floating morsels of spawn, and I have heard, though I never actually witnessed the atrocity, and do not believe it possible, little samlets like myself.‡ There was a company of black-headed gulls,§ who, with loud laughing cry, perpetually hovered over the stream, and, though their professed object was to feed upon the March-brown fly which, dead or alive, in countless myriads lined the shore or covered the face of the waters, they never let slip an opportunity of snapping up some little brother or sister of mine who had carelessly left the place of refuge. Then the kingfisher, with rufous breast and glorious mantle of blue, would dart down like a plummet

* The Water Ouzel—*Cinclus aquaticus*.
† Waterton doubts this, but I have seen the operation, times and oft.—*Ed.*
‡ The correspondence in 'Land and Water' and my own observation have convinced me that this interesting little bird is absolutely guiltless of the destruction of salmon spawn.—*Ed.*
§ The Laughing Gull—*Larus ridibundus*.

from his roost, and seize unerringly any little truant which passed within his ken. The appetite of this bird was miraculous; I never saw him satisfied. He would sit for hours on a projecting bough, his body almost perpendicular, his head thrown back between his shoulders; eyeing with an abstracted air the heavens above or the rocks around him, he seemed intent only upon exhibiting the glorious lustre of his plumage, and the brilliant colours with which his azure back was shaded; but let a careless samlet stray beneath him, and in a twinkling his nonchalant attitude was abandoned. With a turn so quick that the eye could scarce follow it, his tail took the place of his head, and, falling rather than flying, he would seize his victim, toss him once into the air, catch him as he fell, head foremost, and swallow him in a second. This manœuvre he would repeat from morning till night; such a greedy, insatiable little wretch I never saw! A huge, melancholy heron, sometimes accompanied by her mate, would station herself knee-deep in the pool near at hand. She was held in terrible awe by me in later days, but at this time I think she despised such 'small deer' as we were; I have seen her though, kill a rat with a single stroke of her powerful beak, transfix a frog, or swallow an eel in spite of his writhings and struggles, and not unfrequently, to my infinite delight, kill, and carry off to her distant nest, those most hated and destructive foes to our race, our cousins the yellow and bull trout. Yes! our own blood relations are our direst foes, and I have witnessed the destruction, by a hungry old kelt, of fifty of his own progeny for breakfast.*

" Artificially-bred samlets, confined in large ponds, and daily stuffed with food, escape most of these perils; but, I think, the system is carried too far. Protected from all danger, the young fry are ignorant of its appearance, and they lose the natural instinct which would otherwise prompt them to avoid it. They are like home-bred boys, who, having been brought up under the surveillance of parents and tutors, only sent forth into the world at an age when other lads, less carefully attended, are fully capable of taking care of themselves, become the easy prey to the sharks and cormorants, and cold-blooded slimy eels, in the shape of usurers and others, whose vocation it is to prey upon them. The grand loss to

---

* This is denied by Mr. Buckland and others, whose opinion is deservedly of weight, but I cannot doubt the fact. The kelt is as voracious as the pike.

our race is in the first stage, that of the egg; save these, protect these, hatch these, and leave Nature to do the rest. The nursing ponds, the restrictions as to the time when we should migrate, the chopped bullock's liver, and the two years' attendance are useless, and worse than useless, expenses.

"I increased gradually in size; my form developed; the little sac was absorbed, and, with a new-born appetite, I felt was given the power of supplying it. I began to make excursions from my place of refuge, seizing with avidity the minute insects which swarmed in the waters around me, and even rising at times to the surface and seizing some unconscious midge-fly or preoccupied gnat, that had alighted to drop her eggs on the water. If danger arose, we (for in these excursions I was joined by numberless fry of my own standing) at once rushed for shelter beneath the stones, or sought it in the shallows where our enemies, the great trouts, could not follow us. I remember on one occasion, though it was somewhat later than the time of which I am now treating, how I saved myself, by a desperate manœuvre, from the jaws of a hungry trout. The savage brute singled me out from among all the rest of the shoal, and, hunting me round and round until

I was well-nigh exhausted, was on the point of making me his prey, when a bold and happy idea occurred to me: springing out of the water, six inches or more upon the dry shingle, I lay gasping and half dead with fear, but out of the reach of my enemy. The refraction of the water enabled me to see him, though he could not see me; he beat up and down the spot at which I had disappeared, with much the air of a retriever puppy, when the squirrel he has chased for the first time takes refuge in a tree. His search being in vain, he retired, and I had just strength left to squatter into the water again, and soon regained my accustomed haunt beneath the stone.*

"There seems something very shocking, and contrary to the benevolent design of nature, in the fact that creatures so helpless and so capable of enjoying life are exposed to these incessant attacks. Why are we not allowed to enjoy life in peace and happiness without fear or danger?"

I broke in here upon the old gentleman's narrative. "Why, sir, did you not tell me just now that *your*

---

* This anecdote was related to me by a lady who witnessed the occurrence, and on whose power of observation, as well as veracity, implicit reliance may be placed.

great enjoyment was to devour all the little insects on or beneath the surface of the water that came within your reach?"

"What, sir," said he testily, "has that to do with the matter? Those miserable animated atoms were, doubtless, created expressly to feed us beings of a noble order. If you compare a wretched gnat, or a miserable—"

I assured the choleric old gentleman I had no such intention, and begged him to proceed with his interesting narrative.

CHAPTER III.

HAVING DONNED MY SILVERY COAT, I GO FORTH INTO THE "WIDE, WIDE WORLD."—I PASS A MODEST BUT CANDID OPINION ON MY OWN APPEARANCE AND ATTRIBUTES.

"TIME rolled its ceaseless course; days melted into weeks, and weeks into months; more than a year had passed since I—a small, helpless, mis-shapen embryo—had hidden myself under some casual pebble or fragment of a rock. I was then scarcely an inch long, my body marked with transverse bluish-grey lines, the 'badge of all our tribe,'* and my head an eyes altogether out of proportion to my body. I was

* The young of the Salmonidæ amongst fishes, like those of the Felidæ amongst beasts, are invariably barred or striped.—*Ed.*

now some five inches long, trim, well-shaped, and vigorous, marked from shoulder to tail with distinct dusky bars. Although still haunting the waters in which I had first breathed the breath of life, I had long since extended my rambles, and, in company with my brethren, sought the more rapid streams. We rejoiced in our new-born strength to stem the torrent, and vied with one another, while poised as hawks in mid-air, in seizing the small insects which were borne along the stream above us. Although there was a sameness in this life, it was not monotonous. We had become sufficiently cognisant of the dangers around us, but, with the buoyancy of youth, we felt more pride in our cleverness in escaping them than gratitude for the escape. Then the changes in the mighty river herself were subjects of perpetual interest. Sometimes while stealing along in a quiet deep channel but a few yards wide, worn through the rock, or between it and the green bank opposite, the spectator would marvel at the broad expanse of shingle or barren sand. Little would he wonder, if, after a week's rain, he sought the same spot, when Tweed was coming down in her might, and every tributary stream, transformed for the nonce into a river, swelled the mighty flood. Then, timber trees, sawn wood, dead animals, farming implements, even haystacks, would come floating down, and the very channel of the river would be diverted, sometimes never to return to its ancient course. Sad was the havoc occasioned among the embryo spawn; torn from its bed, it would be carred down the stream, to be devoured by the trout or the eel, or to perish amid the waste of waters.* We felt on these occasions pretty safe. Our principal enemies were dispersed: the gulls sought worms in the ploughed uplands; the kingfisher and the solitary heron flew away to the smaller streams, where the less turbid water permitted them to see their prey. The cold, slimy, cruel eel, alone of all our enemies, was then to be dreaded. Crawling along at the bottom of the water, his flat wicked head pressed against the gravel, so as to escape the force of the stream, the wily beast would insinuate himself into every crevice or corner where a small fish might have taken shelter, or a drowned worm be lodged, and all was prey to him. But, as I said, these perils passed lightly over, and

* This most serious cause of destruction might be greatly lessened by the removal of the spawn from beds exposed to the force of the flood to selected spots unaffected by it, and equally adapted for hatching.

were forgotten as soon as passed; 'we had health and we had hope,' and, so that the day passed pleasantly away, we had little care or thought for the morrow.

"A change was, however, to be wrought upon us. I had long observed in my companions, and could not but be conscious within myself, of a striking and beautiful alteration in our external appearance. Without losing the dark blue stripes, the distinctive marks of the salmon tribe, they became gradually coated over, as it were, with bright and silvery scales, as though we had been subjected to the process of electrotyping. I would not be thought vain, but I look back, even now, with feelings of pride and delight, at the image memory conjures up of the beautiful appearance we presented. Glancing through the water, we glittered like fire-flies in the air. Our strength had increased in the same ratio as our beauty, and, when I say that our form was nearly as possible that which I now present, I need hardly say it was faultless."

"Really, sir!" I interposed, "for a gentleman who disclaims vanity———"

"Sir! I assert that the form of a salmon, fresh run from the sea, *is* faultless. Could the vigour he displays, could the strength he possesses, be lodged in any form short of faultless? Could he ascend the cataract—could he stem the roaring torrent—could he——" The old gentleman was getting into such a state of ebullition that I hastily checked him with a torrent of profuse apologies, not unmixed, I fear, with a *soupçon* of flapdoodle, the stuff which Mr. O'Brien informed Peter Simple they feed fools on. Somewhat pacified, he proceeded:—

"With my increasing vigour, a strange feeling of restlessness came over me, a longing desire to wander forth into some unknown world of waters. The wide river seemed all too narrow to contain me; and one glorious May morning, when the heavy rains which had fallen on the mountains had swelled the river some foot or two, the migratory impulse became irresistible, and, accompanied by *millions* of my companions, actuated by the same impulse, I dashed away down stream, seeking 'fresh fields and pastures new.'*

"When the prisoner of Chillon looked out through

---

* This is the invariable misquotation. Milton says "fresh woods;" but let S. S. have his wáy, especially as "woods" would not do.—*Ed.*

the barred hole, which did duty for a window in his dungeon wall, upon the waters of Lake Leman, the fish 'were joyous one and all,' but never so joyous as we—escaping, as it seemed to us now, from a hated monotonous existence, though Heaven knows we had been happy enough in it for many a month—as we dashed along the rolling, rapid waters of fair Tweed. The Peel Burn foot is soon passed, and now we float down the bright stream known as Yair Water. Ettrick gives forth her contingent of thousands upon thousands of shapely silver-coated fish, and in their company, we proceed on our happy pilgrimage. Together we traverse famed Glen-mein, and breast the rapid whirling waters of the Hart's Pool. Poisonous Gala drives us, sickened and choking, to the other side of the stream, and Abbotsford, with its wooded banks, planted by the hand of Scott; the Brig-end stream, where churlish Peter refused a passage to Father Philip; the 'fathomless pool,' whence the Kelpie arose, to 'grin and glour' at him; the 'haunted glen,' 'fair Melrose' itself, are left behind ere comparatively pure water is reached. How merrily we swam, we leapt out of the water, we raced through the water, we dashed at the flies which settled on the surface; we would have shouted, but that speech was denied us; and, exulting in the pride of form and beauty and strength, felt as though fate had no power over us. Alas! pride goeth before a fall."

CHAPTER IV.

I ENCOUNTER MY FIRST GREAT PERIL.—I ESCAPE THEREFROM, AND, PROCEEDING ON THE JOURNEY OF LIFE, SEEK THE "VAST UNKNOWN."

"As thus buoyant, elated, and self-confident, I proceeded onwards, I observed a boat, with a young man in it, anchored in strange fashion a little on one side of the main stream down which I was passing. The anchor consisted, in fact, of another person, older than the occupant of the boat, who, standing in the water as deep as his long legs enabled him, leaned his weight upon the stern of the boat, and so held it fast in its position. I passed them carelessly, and when I was but a few yards in advance, my attention was attracted by a small, struggling, brown fly, which had apparently just dropped into the water. Rushing towards it, and rising suddenly to the surface, I greedily seized, and was preparing to swallow, the delicate morsel; but scarcely did it touch my lips when I felt a slight but smart sensation, as of a thorn pricking my mouth, and found myself dragged by some invisible but irresistible force against the stream, until, half choked, I approached the boat, into which I was instantly lifted in a light net. I found myself clasped by a painfully warm hand, and held firmly, in spite of my struggles, until the hook attached to the treacherous fly I had seized, was extracted, not untenderly, from my wounded jaw. I was already more than half dead, limp, faint, and bleeding.

"'It's just a wee parr beastie,' said the elder of the two, preparing to slip me into the water.

"'It's of no use putting it back,' said the other; 'parr or not, it's dead.'

"'It may dee and be dom'd; I wash my hands of it,' was the reply with which my profane friend placed me in the water carefully enough. I felt sick and helpless; without power to maintain my proper position, I floated, with my back downwards, until I rested against some long floating grass, to which the eddy of the stream had carried me, a few yards from the boat. Although too weak to move, I retained my senses, and heard the younger man say to his companion—

"'Why, John, what made you throw that poor little dead beast into the water again?'

"''Deed,' was the reply, 'yon beastie's just a smolt, an' there's a fine for killing sic like.'

"'But you killed a parr just now?'

"'Ay.'

"'But you call this a parr?'

"''Deed, an' it's the fau't of those who gie the same name to twa different fishes.'

"'What do you mean?'

"'A mean that there's a wee fish ye killed just noo ca'ed "the parr," an' it's a fish of itself,* an' has melt an' roe as ilka ither fish has, an' ye'll find it in

---

* I have opened hundreds of the *Burn Parr*, *Salmo Salmulus*, male and female. I have seen them on their spawning beds, and taken them out of burns where salmon never yet ascended, nor could by possibility ascend. I have baited hooks with the tough little beggars, and released them alive after they had towed a trimmer for six hours about a loch; the salmon parr being as soft as a pat of butter, and endowed with about as much power of sustaining hardships. Doubtless the young salmon is a parr, but a parr is not *always* the young salmon. —*Ed.*

"IT'S OF NO USE PUTTING IT BACK—PARR OR NOT, IT'S DEAD."

Page 21.

rivers an' burns, an' abune waterfalls, an' in mountain tarns, where no saumon ever yet was seen or could get, an' it's streekit an' barred all the same as the young saumon-parr; and it's just the confusion of ca'ing the twa by the ae name that's raised a' the fash that's made about the "edentity," as they ca' it, of the parr with the young saumon.'*

"'Then you believe that the parr is not the young of the salmon?'

"'If ye ca' the young saumon the parr, the parr is the young saumon; but there's anither parr that has a better right to the name, an' it's a pity that twa fish should be bund to hae but ae name betwixt them.'

"At this point of the conversation, feeling myself somewhat recovered from the effects of my immersion in the uncongenial air, I struggled from my resting-place, and, after one or two unsuccessful attempts at swimming, which resulted in a circular aimless movement, I found myself carried out of earshot down stream. By the time that I had quite

* Since this was written I have taken immense pains to convince Mr. Buckland of the fact that the *mature* barred S. Fano is *not* identical with the *immature* barred Salmo Salar, but, I fear, in vain, though the fact is absolutely indisputable.—*Ed.*

recovered myself, and, with the careless and elastic spirit of youth, had already forgotten the severe lesson I had experienced, I found myself on the brink of a precipice, over which, to what unknown depths I could not guess, the great river was hurried in ceaseless flow. This was the cauld, or dam, that by the supernatural agency of the wondrous wizard, Michael Scott, 'bridled the Tweed with a curb of stone,' just above the beautiful old abbey of Melrose. Pausing for a second to collect my energies, I instinctively turned my head up-stream, and, swimming with all my power against it, allowed myself to be carried over the rock, and down into the foaming water below. The shock was much less in reality than in anticipation; I speedily recovered my senses, and, blithe and free, resumed my downward course. I may mention here, that this manœuvre of swimming tail first was invariably practised by us whenever the stream was at all rapid. Our movements were eccentric but graceful; darting at intervals ostensibly upwards, but always yielding, and, like the snail in the problem, descending ten feet for every one we ascended. By yielding to the might of the river, we were carried more safely and pleasantly on our destined course.

"Passing the noble ruins of Dryburgh Abbey—scarcely, if at all, inferior to those of Melrose—I speedily reached another—the Mertoun—cauld, and, passing it with equal ease and less fear than the former, swam along the Bernersyde water, by woody Makerstoun through one of the narrow channels called the 'Clippers,'* by the magnificent castle of Floors, and, tarrying but to taste the sweet waters of the Teviot, on through Kelso Bridge and Sprouston Dubs, through the Edenmouth and Carham Waters, Lady Kirk and Collingwood, to Coldstream Bridge. In this neighbourhood I escaped, by pure good fortune, a danger that I afterwards learnt proved fatal to thousands—nay, tens of thousands—of my young companions. The stream had apparently divided, and whilst I followed the course of the right-hand one, the greater number passed down the wider but less rapid left-hand division. Here they speedily encountered a terrific mill-wheel, and, dashing on one side, they found their progress stopped by a small net, which being passed under them, they were landed literally by bushels. My informant, who

---

* Tweed is so confined by rocks at this point, an active man may cross it by jumping from one to the other.—*Ed.*

escaped by passing under the mill-wheel at the imminent risk of being crushed to death, assured me that the bodies of our unlucky brethren were used as manure! And, degrading as the suggestion is, it seems not impossible, for the numbers taken could not be sold or used for food. The water-bailiffs, a useless crew—who, at the time the river chiefly requires protection, usurp the places of the private keepers—connive at or refuse to notice this wholesale destruction, and content themselves by seizing and bringing before the magistrate the wretched urchins who, with a long stick and a long string, a schoolboy at one end and the most questionable semblance of a fly at the other, fill their breeches' pocket with smolts, and run home to broil them for 'daddy's supper.' Doubtless many thousands are destroyed in this way, but what is that when our prolific nature is considered? Every female of our wondrous race lays, on an average, eight thousand eggs; and, so long as we have only our natural enemies to contend with, the rivers we affect will be stocked to repletion in spite of all the schoolboys birched betwixt Peebles and Berwick. It is now as it was of old, we strain at the gnat and swallow the camel, we screw at the tap and pour out at the bung-hole; we permit the slaughter of the teeming mother, and preserve the barren kelt; we connive at the infamous pollution of the rivers, the poisoning of men, beasts, and fishes by millions, and we punish a child for catching a smolt."

CHAPTER V.

THE GOAL IS REACHED.—THE "TREASURES OF THE DEEP."—I BECOME SURFEITED WITH PLEASURE, AND LONG TO REVISIT THE SCENES OF MY YOUTH.

CONSCIOUS that the latter portion of my excited companion's diatribe was, if not unanswerable, quite beyond my powers to meet by any argument I could adduce, I prudently ignored them, and referring to his previous remark, I said, "You think then, sir, that the water-bailiffs are useless?"

"By no means," said he, in a more argumentative and less dictatorial tone than he had hitherto used; "but they should be supplemental to, and not in the place of, the 'fishermen' or private keepers. These men know every pool, and rock, and haunt of a fish, spawning or otherwise, on their respective waters. They are directly interested in the increase of the fish, and they generally know and are *not* connected with the poachers. Yet on a certain day, as a rule, the keepers, one or more of whom are attached to each water, are *functi officiis*, and their place supplied by water-bailiffs, to one of whom are frequently entrusted three or four miles of river, and who is somehow invariably at the farthest part of the beat, while his kinsmen, and possibly former comrades, are netting the ascending or leistering the spawning fish."

I have always doubted whether the above lucubrations emanated in reality from my strange companion, or whether they were not in fact the embodiment of my own dreamy notions; for, truth to say, my friend had become somewhat prosy, and an "exposition of sleep" had come over me. I roused myself, however, and listened with marked attention as he proceeded in his natural tone:—

"At last, then, we had attained the goal of our hopes, the unknown object of our yearning aspirations; and never were wishful anticipations — offspring of the promptings of Nature—more abundantly satisfied. Not only did the novel element in which we found ourselves—for, so unlike was it to that which we had hitherto inhabited, that it might properly be so called—brace and invigorate our frames, rendering us keenly sensible of the delight of wandering at will through what seemed to us boundless space; but the waters absolutely teemed with life,—marine insects and molluscs, shrimps and prawns, young crabs and lobsters, herring and other fry, sea-worms, embryo creatures of lower organization in millions, all destined doubtless for our sustenance and delectation, and for the gratifying (satisfying seemed out of the question) our appetite, which 'grew with what it fed on.' And we grew too; how could we otherwise, consuming as we did almost our own weight daily of the most nutritious and palatable food?

"I have heard wonder expressed that so small a fish as the smolt should, in a few short months, increase from the weight of three or four ounces to that of frequently twice as many pounds. But where is the wonder My mother, who was murdered on the spawning beds before half her eggs had been deposited, weighed twenty pounds; the noble kipper, her companion, half as much again. What would be

The late Salmo Salar, Esq.

the weight at more than two years old of a dog, offspring of parents such sizes? And was ever puppy fed as we were fed? No! *Fortes creantur fortibus.* Large fish, like other large animals, especially when the females are large, produce large offspring, and when I left the sea and again ascended my native Tweed in July, I weighed nearly seven pounds;* but I anticipate.

"Although the world of waters was all before us where to choose, we never of our own accord wandered far away from the land. Coasting along, we hugged the shore, and thereby not only secured a greater abundance of food, but escaped many dangers to which those who were driven by accident or fear away into the unknown depths of remoter waters were exposed. True, danger even in the humble path we had chosen for ourselves met us at every

---

* A suggestion offers itself here, which I put forward with great diffidence. Instead of putting back the undersized fish, the necessity for doing which is now so strongly advocated, suppose the angler were to return those monsters of the deep whose capture and dimensions we occasionally find recorded in the sporting newspapers—the females especially. Would not the probable result be an increase in the *size* of the fish? After all, small fry are pleasant eating, and exist in such numbers that the effect of rod-fishing upon them is absolutely inappreciable.

turn; dog-fish and cod-fish, and porpoises, and seals, and otters preyed upon us remorselessly, but the numbers of the first four were greatly increased as we increased our distance from the shore; besides which, we lost those landmarks which had afforded us confidence that we should one day be able to retrace our steps, and saved us from the bewildering sensation of being utterly lost. Few fish, once driven out to sea, ever returned to our company; they were devoured, or perished from want of proper food; or, if haply they reached some unknown shore, they wandered listlessly and helplessly along it, seeking a stream or river suitable to their wants, and, finding none, perished miserably.

"Great indeed is the wickedness and heavy the responsibility of that greedy, selfish class — thank Heaven! now at last a limited one—which, having acquired in some incomprehensible manner the legal right of privately destroying what ought to have been the most cherished, as it is the most valuable, public property, planted those accursed engines, the stake-nets, along the coast and in the tideways known as the highways most frequented by our persecuted race. Nor is the fatal result that of chance only. As the shoal of salmon and grilse feel their way along shore, they run against the guide-net, stretching far away into the sea, turning to avoid the danger seaward, they are exposed to the attacks of ravenous hakes and dog-fish, approaching in size to sharks; these, with the seals, watch the entrance to the nets in murderous numbers, having learnt by experience the rich banquet afforded by the terrified fugitives.

"However, these and many other dangers, which in the course of twelve months left scarcely one in five hundred of my original companions alive, affected such of us as escaped no more than the unknown perils of our childhood. 'Heaven from its creatures hides the book of fate.' My life was passed in one continued dream of sensual enjoyment.

"But all such pleasures, even to the brute creation, are of short duration. I had for some little time become aware of a feeling of satiety, a desire for change; and it was, I think, about the middle of June that this feeling rose into an impulse strong as that which, in May of the previous year,* had driven me

---

* I have here, to some extent, waived my own opinion in favour of that of scientific and trustworthy men whose experiments appear to establish the fact, that the Salmon Parr remains *two* years in the fresh water. I still believe that the early hatched fish go down to the sea, as smolts, the same year in which they

down into the sea. As to Lord Lovel, 'a longing wish came over my mind' to revisit my early haunts, and to taste again that sweet fresh water I had so gladly left. Besides, while I had been wandering through the waving groves of sea-weed in search of my prey, certain sea-lice had detached themselves from the sapless stems, to browse upon my 'fair pasture.' They swarmed beneath my gills, and other parts of my body, to my great annoyance. Instinct told me that these creatures could not exist in fresh water; so, in company with a few stragglers, the remnants of my early companions, and many elder fish, I turned my head, and resolutely commenced my homeward journey."

are born. This is, I think, the general opinion of the local fishermen, and I have great faith in the accuracy of their observations.

CHAPTER VI.

I RETURN.—MY RECEPTION.—MY SECOND GREAT PERIL.

"Although the time spent in the sea was really considerable, and the experience acquired appeared to our youthful imaginations illimitable, the actual distance passed in our wanderings was not great, and a few days found us at the broad estuary into which fair Tweed empties herself.

"Here, after tarrying a short time to accustom our palates to the change from salt to fresh water, and impelled by the sweet taste of an unusual flow of the latter, we ran at once into the mouth of the river, prepared to ascend with the flowing tide of that night. Little indeed did we calculate upon the destructive power of men, whose living was our death. We had collected, as I said, by hundreds, still in the sea, but close to the mouth of the river. Suddenly a boat, manned by two stout rowers, put off, and, whilst they rowed quickly round us, a third paid off an immense net of apparently endless length, and deep enough to sweep the bottom. So rapidly was this effected, that, notwithstanding a strong feeling of imminent danger, we found ourselves surrounded, and, the two ends of the net being joined on the shore, entrapped and confined within a circle becoming, as it was hauled in, gradually of smaller dimensions. In vain, swimming wildly about and around, we sought some outlet of escape—there was none; slowly, but surely, the mighty circle lessened and still lessened, until we found ourselves dragged to the very shore, and there, heaped together, we lay, a mass of helpless, struggling fish, gasping, flapping, choking, suffocating, rolling over one another, and exhausting our little remaining strength in futile jumps, or vain endeavours to hide ourselves beneath the doomed victims. Already the dull, heavy thud of the short club, used by the fisherman to despatch those fish that came readiest to hand, sounded in our ears; already hope had given way to despair, and I, like the rest, felt the desire of life departing with the hope; when a cry arose among our captors that the net was breaking! Such indeed was the fact; the net had been pulled somewhat too high upon the shore, and the vast weight of more than three hundred fish, aided by the struggles of some of the heaviest, broke the meshes, and in a moment we were free! Many of my companions were nevertheless seized and killed; but by far the greater number, myself included, rushed through the wide opening, and dashed back again to the friendly sea we had so lately left. What became of my companions I know not—many doubtless were lost, many devoured: for myself, I lingered sadly about the spot, and should have in all probability shared their fate, but that I was accosted by a female of my own race, bright and beautiful, but twice my size and age. She told me she was seeking the spawning-beds above, and I, as youth ever does, felt an instinctive love and veneration for one so much older and grander than myself. She told me of the dangers she had escaped, almost by miracle, the year before; how, after being twice all but taken in the drag-nets, from which I had just escaped, she had entered the river; how for some miles as she ascended, when her back or that of her larger companion was seen above the surface of the shallow water, there had been a cry of 'Fash! Fash!' and then a net had been hastily dragged across her path, while another was stretched below to prevent her return; how men with loud shouts or splashings of the water had driven the devoted fish into the toils before them; how at each projecting rock, forming still water where the struggling fish might rest, a net was placed;* how the deep pools affording a more permanent harbour were dragged; and how, when at last the shallow spawning-beds were attained, many of her race were 'gaffed' for the sake of the spawn within them. Such had been the fate of the baggit from which I sprang, some particulars of which I learnt in after-times. I may as well relate them now."

* These nets are now prohibited by law.

CHAPTER VII.

THE BAILLIE'S MISADVENTURE IN SEARCH OF "SAU-MON-ROE."—MODE OF FISHING WITH THAT PRO-HIBITED BAIT.

" I was lying listlessly one day in summer thirty feet beneath the surface, beyond the influence of the rapid stream above, in the fathomless pool called The Pot, some half-mile below Merton Bridge, a boat, kept in its place by two light oars, floating above me, when the fragments of a conversation reached my ears, and by degrees absorbed my attention. A river-keeper was detailing to his employer the circumstances connected with the capturing of a poacher.

"'Ay, sir,' he said, 'but that saumon-roe is a sair temptation; mony a guid mon has been beguiled by it, ar ken ane, a baillie; a took him mysel'.'

"'How came that? Tell us all about it,' was the reply.

"'Ar was watching, aiblins six months syne, up in the Pavilion Water; the fish were thranging sair upon the spawning-beds, and weal ar kenned they were thrang on the bank abune the Whirlies. Ar was hidden in the wee brae just abune the brig, and a hadna' been there mebbe twa hour, when ar see a mon come daintily alang. Lookin' carefully this way an' that, an' seein' naebody, he just out wi' the gaff, an', screwin' it on to the end of his walking-stick, stepped lightly into the water. It wouldna' be mickle abune his knee, an' the back fin o' mair than ae great fish was plain to be seen on the bank before him. 'Deed, but he wasted little time in selection, an' wi' vara little ceremony he treated 'em. In a second the gaff was in a puir half-spawnit beastie, an', luggin' her ashore, he started aff het foot towards Melrose. Ar up an' after him, an' for a weighty mon he made mickle runnin'. When he saw me he dropped the fish, but no' stoppin' to pick it up, ar just kept on under the railway brig, doon the meadows, by Ailwand Foot, under Melrose Brig, an' there, as he was creepin' up the steep bank, a grippit hold of him ahint; ar grippit hard, an' he turned and said, "Sandy, lad! dinna grip sae hard; ye'll reeve ma breeks." "Ay, Baillie," said I, "*is that you? How cam' ye to do it?*" And he said quite solemn-like, "Sandy!" he said, "it was neether the need nor the greed, but *joost the saumon-roe!*" "Ech, Baillie," ar said, "a wadna' have believed it of ye, but it will be dear saumon-roe to ye." And sae it proved, for he was fined five pund, and ither harm cam' of it.'

"'And served him right,' said his companion; 'a man ought to be hanged who kills a spawning fish on its bed. Why! the very Jews by divine command spared the sitting bird, the nursing mother; and what is the value of a flavourless bird laying half-a-dozen eggs at most, to that of the noble salmon which lays eight thousand!'

"''Deed, ye speak true, sir,' said the other voice; 'an' its aye a strange thing to me, that ony ca'ing themselves sportsmen can condescend to fish wi' roe. It's just no sport ava, an' the best trouts that are killed, though the biggest in the haill river, are no worth the killin' at that time o' year.'

"'Indeed, I believe you; but I never saw the operation of fishing with roe. How is it performed?'

"'Aweel, ye require neither rod, nor line, nor gut, nor reel, nor onything, but just a strong stick—a stake out of the hedge is aboot as guid as anither—an' a bit of cord, no matter how thick, and a heuk with a bittock of lead to sink her, an' a lump of roe as muckle mebbe as a marley is put intil it; an' ye tak' the highest flood and the darkest water, an' ye stan' on the bank, an' the spent trout that have spawned, ye ken, seek the still waters close in shore, an' they're varra empty and hungry belike, an', when ye feel they swallow the roe, ye just fling 'em ower your head; an' a' the best trout in Tweed are caught that way.'*

"'By Jove!' said his companion, 'your friend, the baillie, deserved a ducking for his snobbishness, as well as a fine for his wickedness! I wish I had

---

* There are those who think that the common trout should be annihilated, on account of the injury he does to the salmon-roe. I differ; but, with that object in view, no more efficient instrument exists than angling in spring with roe. After all, trout only eat that portion of spawn which, from two females in succession occupying the same spawning-bed or from other causes, has been dislodged and floats down the stream, and which under any circumstances must be lost. The insidious attacks of the dragon-fly larvæ are a thousand times more destructive, and, what is worse, impossible to be guarded against.

the power, and I'd make it felony to fish with salmon-roe."

"Sinking down to the quiet depths below, and pondering what I had heard, I fully concurred in the sentiment last uttered, on general as well as selfish grounds."

CHAPTER VIII.

THE ASCENT OF THE RIVER.—I FIND AGAIN TO MY COST THAT "ALL IS NOT GOLD THAT GLITTERS," AND AFFORD A PRACTICAL ILLUSTRATION OF "THE BITER BITTEN."—MY THIRD GREAT PERIL.

"DANGERS, fears, and perils forgotten, the next morning found my companion and myself again at the mouth of the river. The scarce-ebbing tide brought with it the smell and taste of a freshet, the result of the last night's rain, and we stemmed the retreating tide more boldly as we felt the assurance of good swimming-water above.

"It was Saturday morning; from then to Monday the river is free; so for thirty hours at least our persecutors were restrained from crying 'Havoc' upon our devoted race. No net, no boat stopped our way; we swam joyously up stream, and by noon that day had passed the well-remembered Norham Bridge. Here we met a little crowd of frightened fish, returning to the sea, dismayed and disheartened, as well they might be. This sparse band, scarce half a score in number, were all that remained of some five hundred noble fish who had attempted the passage but the day before. They had escaped the long sea-nets, and the more deadly drags used in the river; they had been hunted in the shallows, and pelted in the streams, and when they might fairly hope for rest and safety, they had found themselves debarred from the goal they sought by a long, deep, heavy net fastened right across the stream, sunk a little below the water, and intended to keep the fish from passing upwards during the short interval from Sunday to Monday, when net-fishing ostensibly ceases, until they could legally be dragged out of the pool on Monday morning. They urged us to return,* and seek the com-

---

* Running fish, especially grilse, are frequently turned back by meeting others which, having been scared by the nets, are again returning to the sea, thus affording a double chance of capture to their vigilant enemies.

parative safety of the sea, swarming as it did with our natural enemies, in preference to placing ourselves within the power of those short-sighted, unprincipled scoundrels who disgrace the name of fisherman! Had I been unsupported, my natural timidity, enhanced by the remembrance of the dangers I had gone through, would have induced me to accompany them, but my more experienced and bolder companion overruled their counsel. She told them how, by swimming on the surface of the water, instead of the bed of the river, on which, to escape the force of the stream, our course had hitherto been held, we should escape the danger, and how essential it was to our health, and the preservation of our race, that the upper waters, where alone fitting spawning-beds could be found, should be reached; she pointed out how even yet the sea-lice clung to our gills and bodies, and promised us that twenty-four hours' sojourn in the fresh water would relieve us from every one: finally, taunting us with timidity in proposing to go back after daring so much and advancing so far, she succeeded in persuading us to risk all chances and follow her lead. For myself, I dashed recklessly after her over the net of which we had already taken stock, as we advanced towards it. Many of our companions followed, and a few hours brought us, without further let or hindrance, to the Cauld Pool, below the well-remembered ruins of Dryburgh Abbey, where all that is mortal of the great poet and novelist of Scotland lies interred. Here, taking advantage of the comparatively still water behind a large submerged rock, we rested motionless and silent, and though 'we, like mortals, never sleep,' enjoyed that perfect rest which cessation from labour, and total oblivion from cares and troubles, ever bring with them.

"This, and a portion of the following day were thus serenely spent. The sea-lice which had clung to our scales dropped off, unable to exist in the fresh water, and no care or trouble was present. A restless feeling had, indeed, arisen within me, and I was on the point of suggesting to my companions a movement higher and still higher up the stream, when my attention was attracted by what appeared to me a familiar object—a shrimp or prawn, or some other small native of the ocean so lately quitted, such as had furnished me with many a satisfactory meal. It floated gently over my head, not particularly bright in colour, but showy, and its hues, which were dispersed uniformly over its body, blended together, and formed one harmonious whole. Its movements were short and rapid, such as are those of the insects—'Crustaceæ,' I think, is the proper term—I have referred to, and it seemed to be striving, with doubtful result, to stem the somewhat rapid stream. What induced me I cannot say; I was not hungry; indeed, I had felt no desire to eat since I entered the fresh water; I was hardly in the mood for play, for I felt that the serious business of life was before me; but, impelled by some unaccountable impulse, I rose from my resting-place, and attempted to seize it in my mouth. The motion was rapid, but still too slow to be effectual; the creature vanished ere my lips could close on it. Whilst turning slowly round to seek my former station—somewhat sulkily, too, for the object I had failed to attain had, in consequence, acquired a value it had not previously possessed—I heard a voice say—

"'Ay, but that was a bonny grilse! Ay, but it was a grand rise he made, too! Ye were ower quick in striking.'

"'I think I was,' was the reply, 'but we'll try again.'

"'Bide a wee, sir; bide a wee; give him time to return to his old station before you show him the flee again.'

"Utterly unconscious of the meaning of these words,* and in no respect connecting them with myself or my doings, I saw with some surprise, not unmixed with pleasure, the little jerking figure again passing within three feet of my nose. There was a band of silver round its throat that excited my cupidity, and I was, moreover, somewhat nettled at the failure of my previous attempt to seize it. Without a moment's pause, I dashed at it, and, seizing the bright wings between my lips, was prepared, at least, to carry it down with me, to be swallowed or not, as I might choose; when, to my amazement and alarm, ere I could as much as turn away after my spring, the creature snatched itself from out my very jaws, and vanished as it had previously done. Sulky and annoyed, I sought again my resting-place, and again I heard the same voice which had before spoken,

"''Deed, sir, ye were just ower hasty again; ye dinna let the fash tak' a grip of the flee before you snatch it out of his mouth.'

* I trust the young reader may not be equally so; it is a golden rule.—*Ed.*

"'Never mind, Sandy; we'll try again.'

"'A'm thinking I'll just change the flee; mebbe he's seen ower muckle of this ane.'

"Read by the light of after experience, these words were plain enough; but, young and inexperienced as I was, they conveyed no meaning, no warning, and it can hardly be wondered at that, tantalized as I had been, no sooner did I see a creature similar in form and colour to the other, but somewhat smaller and brighter, apparently striving to stem the stream a little above me, than, again dashing at it, I seized it firmly, and, turning round, was going back to my lair, when I felt a sharp smart, a convulsive shock thrilled through my frame, and I found myself madly struggling against some great unknown, invisible power, which controlled my will, and, for a time at least, rendered me helpless—almost hopeless.

"Willing to realize the worst, and anxious to learn something certain respecting my condition, I rushed upwards, and, jumping high in the air, saw two men standing on the bank, the connection of whose movements with my own position I had no difficulty in tracing. The one with a long rod in his hand, the line from which restrained and controlled me, stood motionless; whilst the other, with a horrible hook attached to the end of a stick in his hand, seemed to be aiding and advising him.

"'Canny, lad,' I heard him say: 'canny, noo; he is but light heukit; I ken by his jumpin'. Canny, noo; he's just a fresh-run grilse, an' his mouth unco saft.'

"I had heard enough; and by this time my terror had somewhat abated, and my natural energy returned in aid of the strength with which I was gifted. No longer coursing about the pool with aimless rapidity, or wasting my strength in fruitless jumps, I dropped back gradually into the deep pool behind, and, sinking to the bottom, lay motionless behind the big rock I had so lately quitted. My companion kept ever beside me,* and, though she could render no assistance, her presence was an aid and consolation to me, and I felt cooler and stronger for her sympathy. Aided by the weight of water above me, I defied the power still exercised by my persecutor to move me. I felt but little pain, and, but for the choking sensation occasioned by the interference of the free passage of water through my gills, little annoyance; and it was only on observing a

* A fact of constant occurrence.—*Ed.*

huge stone, thrown for the purpose of dislodging me, descending directly upon my head, that I started from lair. Rushing wildly away, my escape was brought about by the very means intended for my destruction. Impeded by the line, my movement was slow, and the stone, barely missing me, fell upon the line itself, released the hook from the slight hold it had in my mouth, and I felt that I was free! Joyous, exulting in my deliverance, I again sought the surface, and, as I jumped two or three times out of the water, I had the satisfaction of observing visible marks of disappointment and regret on the countenances of my friends on shore. The one stood with his rod straight upwards, his line floating down the stream, himself in the precise attitude in which he had maintained that dead, strong pull against me, which, by exhausting my strength, had so nearly proved fatal; the other was apparently solacing himself with a pinch of snuff, and the only words I heard him utter were—

"'Ay, but you was a bonny grilse! Deil tak' the stane!'"

CHAPTER IX.

I FOREGATHER WITH A KELT, WHOSE GALLANT STRUGGLE AND ULTIMATE CAPTURE I WITNESS.

"The Cauld Pool, so lately a pleasant haven of rest, was no longer an abiding-place for me. The dread and terror I had endured were associated with every rock and stone about me;* and, had I stayed there for a month to come, I am certain that no gaud, however cunningly devised, would have tempted me so much as to look at it. The freshet, however, still continued; there was good swimming-water, and that very night, my faithful companion by my side, I

---

* It is a singular fact that fish which have got off the hook, although consistently refusing the fly in that pool or stream, will take it without distrust in another.

ascended the heavy fall of water which rolled over the dam, and proceeded onwards towards those faintly but dearly remembered scenes of my early youth, the waters of Upper Tweed.

"I may here correct a very common error as to the manner in which we salmon ascend a rapid. In many pictures, in many books, we are represented as leaping over a rapid some fifteen or twenty feet in height; in some of ancient date, we are depicted as taking our tails in our mouths and springing upwards, like skip-jacks, by the force of liberated tension; this is simply absurd. Excepting in the exuberance of animal spirits, the exultation arising from escaped danger, or under the peculiar influence caused by a change in the weight of the atmosphere, we never *jump:* we *swim* upwards, and the effort carries us beyond the surface high into the air; we *swim* up a rapid, and what appears like a jump is nothing more than the abortive result of a misdirected effort; an attempt, in fact, to swim in a perpendicular direction up a stream, which descends more or less horizontally.

" One or two failures occurred, but with little difficulty we surmounted the obstacle, and, passing rapidly onwards by the low green meadows and woody banks above Melrose, we made no further pause till we reached that long extent of unrivalled water, where may still be seen the foundations of the old bridge, the gate of which, in the days when 'the Monastery' was still itself, was kept by the churlish Peter, the bridgeward. Here, again, choosing our station behind a projecting stone, we rested; and, whilst many of our companions passed onwards, a considerable number, and those of a large size, took up their position around us. Indeed, the place was, in every respect, satisfactory, and adapted to our requirements. The bed shelving gradually from the southern side, the force of the stream increased proportionately to its depth, so that, with the least trouble, we could seek such depth and strength of water as suited our tastes for the time. Excepting a few large stones, behind which we usually lay, the bottom of the stream was perfectly level; and, as the river made a considerable angle on the opposite side, beneath the steep, wood-crowned bank, we could at any time bask in the sun, or exchange its sultry beams for the cool shadow beyond.

"In addition to the companions of our voyage, and many others who had previously ascended with the same object—to deposit their spawn on the gravelly beds, so common in the upper waters—our pool contained a large number of kelts : * fish, that is, which during the preceding winter and early spring had successfully deposited their spawn, and were now sinking downwards by easy stages towards that land, if I may use an Irishism, of plenty, the sea. These kelts were the jolliest of fish; they seemed like married men escaped for a short time from the cares of a family and the troubles of housekeeping. They ate minnows, and parr, and the late samlets of the previous year, water insects, flies, worms, and slugs, and, in fact, whatever came uppermost. Though thin and emaciated when they left the spawning beds, good cheer told upon them, and I have rarely seen a handsomer specimen of our race than a grand eighteen-pound kelt, with whom I struck up a passing acquaintance as we sheltered behind adjoining stones in the Brig End Pool. He was, perhaps, a trifle longer in proportion to his

* I have constantly observed in the *Field* pungent gibes directed against the slayer of the kelt. In the same paper, too, I occasionally observe diatribes upon battue-shooting, which is likened to slaying cocks and hens in a farmyard. Now, I am no friend to over-preserving, and fully admit that battue-shooting may be carried too far; but the man who can stand at a cross-ride and toss four out of six rocketing pheasants dead ten yards behind him, or can land "weel mendit" kelts in Tweed, in the month of May, is *not* a muff!

depth than a fresh-run fish; his back had a bluish tinge, and he was less thick about the tail; but the scales beneath were of silvery white; he was well-proportioned and well-favoured; and his strength was manifested by the ease with which he poised himself, like a bird in the air, even in the rapid part of the stream. What fun it must be, thought I, to be hungry! as I saw him dash playfully upwards at a gaudy-winged butterfly which, after hovering a moment above us, had dropped apparently exhausted into the stream, and was now, despite its struggles, drowning, as I thought! I had seen my friend the day before, when the water was somewhat muddy, absolutely gorge himself upon dead worms, and other not over-delicate *débris*, that floated down the stream. The butterfly was more to my own taste, and, as he rose at the painted fly, he rose in my estimation. But what is this? Scarcely had he, with a sweep of his mighty tail, reached the surface, when he descended again, rushing by me in evident horror and alarm, and seeking, with a rapid but rather constrained motion, the dark depths below. The facts of the case were apparent to me instantly. My poor friend, in the buoyancy of his spirits, had seized, more in playfulness than in greed, the treacherous imitation of a fly, cast by one of the deadliest foes to our race on Tweed. No hope of release from a friendly misdirected stone was here: if a stone were thrown by him it might startle, but never loose, the fish; and, confident in the strength of his tackle and the delicacy of his touch, little did the fisher heed the poor kelt's attempt at sulking. Not, as in my case, was the strain upwards, giving me the advantage of the whole weight of water to increase the resistance; sideways was the force exerted, at an angle which deprived the devoted fish of all help from that source.* Indeed, the run of the stream was in the direction of the slow, strong, steady pull, persistently kept up, to which, at first slowly, but eventually with a rush, like that of a hawk through the air, the kelt was constrained to yield. Dashing up stream, with a velocity still comparable to that of the bird, he sought the rough pass above the railway bridge, where haply he might cut the line against the sharp edges of the rocks, or rub the cruel hook from the jaw in which it was too securely fixed; but this was not allowed. The strong, pliant rod was in no

---

* The only mode I have ever found efficacious for moving a sulking fish is here described. The leverage applied at the proper angle, it is impossible the fish can long resist it.

tyro's hand, and the maddest efforts of the fish were controlled by a power which could never be measured or met by opposed strength, and was felt to be irresistible. In vain, rushing upwards, did the poor kelt leap three feet from the surface of the water into the thin air, hoping to fall upon the line in his descent, and so disengage the biting hook; in vain, I say, for rod, and eye, and line, and hand seemed guided by one impulse alone, and that derived from the struggling fish. As he jumped, the hand yielded, the rod bent, the strain of the line loosened; and the quiet eye twinkled with exultation, as, gaining nothing by the exhausting effort, the poor fish sought again his native element. Weakened and failing, unable to drag the weighty line against the rapid stream, the fish now turned his head downwards, and with a simulation rather than reality, of strength, dashed away at his former pace. But swimming down stream, with a hook in one's mouth, is a game that cannot be long played. Breathing, as fishes breathe, becomes impossible; and with pain I speedily beheld my poor acquaintance turn on his side, and approach, with no will of his own, the low shelving bank of shingle, where the shallow water left half his huge body exposed. A large net was passed under him, and while, as he was dragged ashore, the exulting 'whoo whoop!' of his captor rang in my ears, I naturally concluded that I had seen the last of my gallant, handsome, ill-fated friend; such, however, was not the case; and the conversation that reached me before he was returned to the water, as to my great surprise he was, explained the cause of his good fortune."

CHAPTER X.

"THOU RASH INTRUDING FOOL! I TOOK THEE
FOR THY BETTERS."   *Hamlet.*

"'Hurrah! hurrah! A clean fish at last! And what a beauty! What do you think of *that?*'

"'Hoot! It's no fash ava! It's joost a kelt beastie.'

"'A kelt! Why, now I look at it, it is a kelt; but it is a grand fish, and the sport it showed first-rate.'

"'And what for no'? A fish that's fattened in the river, wi' guid, wholesome food, is just as strong as ony fattened in the sea, an' it kens, mind ye, every hole, and stream, and rock in the pool, an' it's no' sae frightened at the bauk's side as a fash fresh-run from the sea, where there is no bound on ony side.'

"'And about the eating?'

"'Weel, I'll no' say that the eating is sae guid as a clean fresh-run saumon: 'deed, there's naething in nature can beat that; the fash caught in the nets are no' to be compared to it; but it's guid, wholesome food for a' that, an' dainty eneuch. I was up to London ten years syne to gie evidence, as they ca' it, anent saumon and sich like, an' ech! the evidence I heard gi'en! There was ae lad swore that *his* fish were bred in the sea, an' had no necessity to come to the rivers at a'! There was anither swore that it was the Saturday's slap that destroyed the fish, for it just allowed those who would have returned to the sea, there to spawn in safety, to gae up the river to be kilt by the poacher! I saw on the stalls of the fishmongers, as ye ca' them, mony mair kelts than clean fish; an', though they were a thought paler in colour, an', I kenned weel, vara inferior in taste, they seemed to sell t'ane as well as t'tither.'

"'Then you think kelts ought to be killed?'

"'Hoo', not at a'! But a kelt that is fit to be kilt an' eaten should be kilt an' eaten. What for no'? Ye'll tak' aiblins twal or aughteen fish in a morning, an', out of them a', twa, or four mebbe, are weel mendit; a'd gie *them* a tap on the head, an' they're just the fash that gie the greatest sport, an' mony ane dees from exhaustion when putten back into the river, the rest might swim away an' be thankful, an' if some of them dee, what are they after a' but single fish ?'

"Whilst speaking, my friend had carefully disengaged the hook from the gasping fish, and, with one hand below its body beneath the water, and the other grasping its tail, had launched him, as it were, into the deep pool. As it felt itself loosed from restraint, a convulsive effort of the tail drove the sickened, half-alive beast some five feet diagonally across the stream, and then it helplessly resigned itself to the force of the water, floating unresistingly down stream. Whether the good fish lived or died I know not; but if it died—and many that have been hooked, and fought well, I know have died—it were better that it should have furnished food for human beings than for the foul-feeding carrion-crow, or the slimy ravenous eel.

"Time passed on, and still found me a denizen of Brig End Pool. Fish came and went, and some tarried beside me, and some passed upward. The kelts, one and all, dropped down the stream by degrees, and by the end of May not one was left. In August,

I found myself surrounded either by fish of my own standing, which had passed months in the water, or fresh-run salmon, the early kelts of the preceding year, which had now returned from the salt water.

"During my sojourn in the pool, many and many a lure passed over me, and many times I felt half inclined to seize the tempting bait, but I always restrained myself; every rock, and ripple, and cliff, and stream reminded me of the struggles of my friend the aforesaid kelt, or some other doomed fish, for many a gallant struggle was I witness to between the fisherman and the credulous fish, the victim of his perfidious art. Of these some escaped, but the majority were, after more or less resistance, dragged ashore and killed. Of the various wiles practised by those fortunates who did escape, it may be interesting to make some passing mention. One, I remember, a grand fish of some eighteen pounds weight, at the first touch of the hook dashed with lightning speed down stream, turning neither to the right nor to the left, running out a hundred yards of line. The fisherman having neglected to tie a knot at the end, there was nothing to stop it, and the great fish sailed away seawards, dragging in his wake two pounds' worth of excellent tackle. No doubt a few hours relieved him from the encumbrance, and his would-be captor paid not too dearly for a lesson he was unlikely to forget. One very extraordinary escape I witnessed was precisely analogous to my own when a smolt. The fish was hooked from the north or high shore; terrified apparently beyond the influence of instinct or reason, he dashed madly up the shelving bank on the opposite side, and lay gasping three feet beyond the shoal water. Taken aback by this utterly unexpected manœuvre, the fisherman slackened his hold, and the fish, with the same effort that restored him to his native waters, shook the hook out of his mouth. I have seen fish escape by running rapidly round a rock, obtaining either for themselves a dead pull, and so wrenching the barb from their jaws, or, leaving a dead pull against the rock to the fisherman, afford him an excellent opportunity of breaking his tackle and releasing his prey. I have seen a fish spring three feet out of the water, when struck, and contrive in his descent to fall on the line, so as to break the hold of the hook. I have seen many, when but slightly hooked, by a violent and continuous effort *shake* the hook out of their mouths; and I have seen others, well hooked but too tightly held, break the strong line like pack-thread, or straighten the hook itself as though it were made of pin-wire. But perhaps the most efficacious, and to the fisherman annoying, mode of escape, was one not uncommonly practised by a clean-run vigorous fish. Indeed, I must own that, though the kelts showed more craft and cunning, and had great physical power, the fresh-run fish, for a clean rush and a stand-up fight, beat them hollow. The dodge they practised was as follows: swimming near the surface, and rushing down stream some thirty or forty yards, they suddenly sought the bottom, and returned upon their tracks with scarce diminished speed. The weighty water bagging out the line, gave the fisher, more especially if a tyro, the idea that his intended victim's course was still downwards, and, paying out line rapidly, he enabled the fish to bring such a weight of water upon it as eventually to necessitate its breakage. The first intimation Piscator had of the escape of his prey was the exulting bound of the salmon some fifty yards above the spot which in his imagination it occupied attached to his line. This mode of effecting an escape I have heard designated as *drowning*, and certainly I have seen fishermen, after the manœuvre had been practised at their

"THE FIRST INTIMATION PISCATOR HAD OF THE ESCAPE OF HIS PREY WAS THE EXULTING BOUND OF THE SALMON."
Page 66.

expense, look as though drowning were an enviable escape from their mortification. Another most successful manœuvre resorted to by a hooked fish, especially if a long line were thrown, was the running in of the salmon right to the feet of the fisherman. In vain the rod was held aloft, in vain the reel was wound with reckless haste, in vain its holder receded from the river bank; the line *would* become slack, and a shake and a scuffle at once got rid of the hook, unless it had penetrated more than ordinarily deep, or had struck upon some soft part of the fish's mouth. Happily, however, for us, there are few such parts in our mouths; if fresh-run the palate is soft, but the bone is hard beneath, and, if we have been long in the water, it is hard throughout; whether or not a regular, firm, and equal strain must be kept on the hook, or the fish escapes; if the strain be too strong, the rod, or the line, or the gut, or the hook, or the hold in the mouth is broken; if it be slack, it is at once, and with ease, shaken out. There is, in fact, no sort of sporting in which the quarry has such odds in his favour as the salmon. I allude, of course, to fair fishing with the rod and line · it were a blithe day for the salmon when they had no worse enemies than anglers to contend with.*

* I should think so! In a water I once rented, I killed during six weeks, at an expense of a hundred pounds, forty fish, and was considered to have had good sport. Out of one pool on the same water, *eighty* fish have been taken at a single haul of the net! I have since rented one of the best waters on Tweed, and continue to do so. The fishing-book would show that a hundred fish have never been, for the last ten years, killed in any one year, yet a hundred pounds, at least, is spent, in addition to rent, solely in preservation of the fish. The "lower proprietors," who owe all to us, grudge even this poor return for our outlay.

CHAPTER XI.

MY FAITHFUL COMPANION IS TORN FROM MY SIDE
AND RUTHLESSLY SLAIN.—I MORALISE THEREON,
AND PROCEED UPWARDS.—THE WATERFALL.—THE
SPAWNING BEDS.—MORTALITY AMONG THE KELTS.—
I COMMENCE MY RETURN TO THE SEA.

"The seasons wore on; summer had melted into autumn, and the breath of winter had blown icily on the woody banks of the beautiful river. Strange colours were reflected from the banks in lieu of the dark green that had so long prevailed, and the dead leaves, whirled around by the eddies of the fitful wind, were deposited by millions on the bosom of the water, floating down stream, as though they, like the swallows, were bent on migrating to some happier land. It was high time to seek the spawning-beds in the upper waters, towards which our course had been all along directed, and, though with somewhat impaired vigour, with an equally strong will, we recommenced our ascent.

"I think there is no creature on whom the lessons of experience are more completely thrown away than upon one of our race. Continually, for weeks past, we had observed with anxious eye the wiles practised for our destruction. But the moment we left the scene of our temptation, and the associations connected therewith, it seemed that all previous knowledge and caution, acquired by experience, had left us also. We had proceeded scarcely a mile on our upward journey, and were tarrying in the Boldside Water, when my companion, rising, in pure wantonness, at the semblance of an errant butterfly whose white-tipped wings,* apparently failing from weakness, seemed to have precipitated it on to the surface of the water, found herself securely hooked, and, rendered weak by her condition, was dragged, as I had seen many a good fish before, helplessly resisting to the shore. I was not, however, hopeless as to her fate. Surely, I thought, these men who respect

* No more killing fly on Tweed than the "white tip."

a solitary kelt, because, in time to come, he or she may become a parent, will be most careful of the teeming mother, about to produce thousands after her kind at once. But I was wrong. To my horror, I saw a dreadful instrument, called a gaff,* stuck into her side, and in a moment, bleeding and helpless, she was laid on the shingle, where a blow on the head from a round stone speedily released her from her pain. To some indistinct proposition of putting her back into the water as useless, a muttered answer was returned to the effect that she would be equally useless there, 'with that muckle hole in her wame.' Frightened and horrified, I left the spot, meditating sadly on the inconsistency of sparing the single fish, and slaying the one about to produce thousands.

"The water had again risen, and very many fish

---

* The use of the gaff is, I believe, now prohibited during the autumn months, but is frequently used nevertheless. Hundreds of fish full of spawn, which would otherwise be returned to the water, are killed for no better reason than that suggested in the text. A *barbed* gaff should be prohibited under any circumstances and at all seasons; it is essentially a poacher's weapon, and a deadly one. It is the instrument by which three-fourths of the fish are taken from the Usk in October. A *plain* gaff, such as a sportsman uses, would be almost useless to them, the fish would struggle off it. I have in vain urged this self-evident proposition on the authorities.—*Ed.*

were thronging upwards on the same errand. Some, like myself, had come up in pairs; many, like 'Hal of the Wynd,' on their own hand; and I observed that the predominant feeling was cordial dislike and jealousy between the individual members, at least among the kippers—the male fish—of the ascending crowd. For myself, I shrank moodily in the rear. I was no match for many of the great fish I saw around me; and I, like them, had what would have been a disadvantage in the event of a fight, for a great horny substance like a beak had gradually grown up from my lower jaw, and fitted into a corresponding aperture in the upper. It seemed as though we could scarcely open our mouths to feed, much less to bite; though I afterwards found by experience I could do either on provocation. However I was sad and sorrowful and lonely, and shrank from the companionship of my fellows. Still I struggled onwards. Sorrow abideth not with youth—grief fadeth away, and joy, as of old, cometh in the morning. One morning, a freshet breathing through my gills inspired me with all the vigour, if not the buoyancy of the days of my early ascent, and I strenuously urged my striving upward way towards the spawning-grounds, the goal of our hopes.

No jumping now, no springing out of the water, as in the exuberance of our young elastic spirits at our early entrance into fresh water; but we swam strongly, steadily, soberly along, moving principally at night, and making about three miles an hour. The falls between the cauld-pools of Mertoun and old Melrose are passed, the bright, rapid streams above ascended; and we deem ourselves within easy reach of the gravelly beds and shallow aerated waters beneath which the hopes of a future race are to be deposited, when an obstacle apparently insurmountable opposes itself, in the shape of a nearly perpendicular fall of water over a rugged rock some twelve feet in height. Now commences a wild and in some cases fatal dance amid the baulked crowd: all rush boldly forward; some essay to swim, but the white treacherous water aids them not. Some attempt to jump, but the height is far beyond their powers; beaten, exhausted, bleeding from contact with the sharp points of the rocks, we sink back, one by one, to the pool below."*

The aspect of my narrator here suddenly changed, presenting either a real or fancied resemblance to

* The fish ladders and passes invented by Mr. F. Buckland have, in many rivers, effectually remedied this evil.—*Ed.*

that of the old river-keeper, under whose guidance I had lately fished with signal success some of the waters described above. Nor was it his aspect only that was changed, for, raising his voice to a petulant, almost menacing tone, and speaking in a new dialect, he resumed:—

"Why, mon, what dom'd eternal fules ye a' be! Ye write anent saumon in a' the papers—in the 'Sporting Gazette' and 'Bell's Life,' in the 'Field' and in 'Land and Water,' which is, far away, the best of the whole; ye claver anent saumon at your clubs and your dinners, at hame and abroad, at market—aiblins at Kirk; ye leegislate about saumon, and ye persecute puir fisher bodies wha dinna ken reet frae wrang, nor hardly their reet hands frae their left, an' your writers an' your talkers an' your leegislators joost ken naothing mair about the matter than the puir bodies ye send to gaol for takin' a few fash—not ower bright mebbe, but guid an' wholesome—at the ony time of the year they *can* tak' them; an' ye save the kelts in spring, an' kill the baggits in autumn. There's but ae mon in braid England that kens onything about the matter; that's Frank Buckland, an' he's mickle to learn yet. Why don't ye leegislate for the ripe baggits? The savin' of the kelts was a grand straik, and mickle gude thereby; but why dinna ye save the ripe baggits that are worth ilka ane a thousand kelts? Why dinna ye encourage the rod-fishers? puir fule bodies that spend hundreds an' thousands of punds sterling joost for the chance, an' aiblins a bad ane, of takin' an odd fash or twa now and again. The rod-fishers are the real preservers of the water I say, an' I wish they were on frae January to December. Why dinna ye mak' siccan passes up the weirs an' falls as fash can *swim* up? We dinna want stairs or ladders or gimcracks; we want black water, such as a fash may *swim* in. We care na how steep or how high, so they can *swim*; a fash is no' an Irish hodman, an' he canna *walk* up a ladder of white water. Why dinna ye buy up the mills an' the mill-dams,* which are joost fash traps? Why—"

"Sir!" interrupted I, half stunned by his rapid utterance and threatening tone — when suddenly

---

* This query of our choleric friend applies with equal force to mills and mill-dams throughout the country. On the banks of the Ouse, the Welland, and other sluggish rivers are thousands of acres of valuable land utterly destroyed by the constantly-recurring floods caused by the successive mill-dams on their course. The increased produce of a single year would pay twice over the purchase money of existing rights.

the fire faded from his eye, he sank back on the seat, and resumed the placid appearance of the quiet, grey-coated, somewhat prosy traveller, who had so long engrossed my attention.

"For days we lingered disheartened in the pool; but a heavy flood came at last, and with comparatively little difficulty we surmounted the hitherto impassable barrier, and speedily arrived at the spawning-beds — a broad expanse of water a few miles above the falls, with a bottom of deep gravel, over which the river flowed at depths varying from six inches to three feet. One or two tributaries on either side added weight to the stream, and deposited at their mouths additional banks of gravel, on which and on those more in the centre of the stream the female fish, after a few days' rest, commenced making their redds, digging great troughs in the gravel by working ther fins and the lower part of their bodies against it. There was a wild scene meanwhile among the kippers, the larger driving the smaller away and fighting madly among themselves, swimming in circles around the redds. The wounds inflicted by some of these great fish were terrible, and many a lusty young kipper was killed outright.

"The spawning over, and the eggs destined to

produce young safely buried beneath a mass of gravel, partly placed by the spawning fish and partly deposited by the action of the water, we revenged ourselves upon the great kippers, now weak, exhausted, and defenceless, by biting at their fins and tails, and otherwise maltreating them. Hundreds died, and were swept downwards by the rapid stream, furnishing food as they went to insects and carrion birds and foul-feeding eels, and, strange to say, when washed ashore, occasionally to cows and other beasts, until, swept out to sea, the remnant was finally devoured by those general scavengers of ocean, shrimps, prawns, crabs, and lobsters. Millions of light eggs were carried down by the water and devoured by hungry trout waiting below on purpose to intercept and feed on them. And why not? All-bounteous Nature provides nothing in vain; and when one female produces from five thousand to twenty thousand eggs, it may be fairly inferred that a part was intended for other purposes than hatching.

"Sinking gradually backwards, offering scarcely more opposition to the hurrying waters than was required to keep my head up-stream, I floated rather than swam downwards till I reached the

Cauld Poole above Melrose. Here I rested, and here, my appetite growing with the increasing days, I glutted myself with food of the most nourishing, if not of the choicest description. I wish those wiseacres who assert that we salmon never feed in fresh water could have seen our daily bill of fare,—worms, flies, water-insects, small trout, smolts by hundreds, nothing came amiss, and we throve on our varied fare. When I entered the pool I was large-headed, lank in body, poor in spirit, and flabby in flesh, almost white in colour throughout, and with just strength enough to keep my head towards the stream: this was in February. When I left on the top of a rolling flood in the beginning of May, I was strong in body, bold in spirit, and bright in colour. True, my shoulders were not so thick as they might have been, and the dark colour of my back bore something of a bluish tinge; but I was silvery white beneath, and my flesh, if not red, was no longer white, but pink and wholesome.* I felt that

* I would not imply that all kelts are equally " weel mendit," but the description above is true of a very large number; and it is a pity that all should, without exception, be returned to the water when caught. After a certain time, say the 1st of April, a discretion as to killing, or returning to the water, a kelt, might fairly be left to the fisherman.

were a hook again within my jaws—which I took good care it should not be—I could make a good fight for my life; and a good fight I surely would have made. This, however, was not to be; experience had made me cautious, and a fortnight later found me again a denizen of the mighty deep."

CHAPTER XII.

"THE SEA, THE SEA! THE OPEN SEA!
THE BLUE, THE FRESH, THE EVER FREE!"

"THE boundless, bounteous sea! If as a grilse I revelled in the prodigal supply of food she afforded, how much more did I now! Rude health and vigour returned to my frame, the parasitic suckers fell from my gills at the first taste of the wholesome salt water, my colour darkened and brightened, my form developed, my power of swimming increased, and I felt the confidence of safety which arises from the consciousness of strength, moral and physical. The number of my enemies decreased as my relative powers and proportions increased; and from such as I was unable to cope with I could now readily escape. In addition to the food I had formerly taken, I now swallowed fish of a goodly size, full-grown herrings, sand eels, young haddocks, and many others, that came in my way. My second sojourn in the sea was, if possible, a season of more unmixed happiness than my first, just as a boy's latter school days are happier than his earlier ones. Still, as of old, I never wandered far from the shore; food was more plentiful in its vicinity, and when my long holiday had passed I again sought the fresh water, I readily coasted back to the well-remembered Tweed mouth. I linger not to describe the various dangers again in succeeding years encountered, and again escaped. Instinct and such reasoning as experience taught but partially protected me. I was hooked once and again; I tore the barbed instrument of torture from my mouth, I broke the strong line, I cut it against the sharp edge of the rock, I straightened by main strength the curved steel, I wore out the hold on my flesh by constant dogged resistance, I shook the hook from its hold, in short I escaped.—*I was a salmon!!!*

"Another, and yet another year, and heavier, stronger, nobler than ever, I went down each recurring spring to the sea, and each time tarrying longer than before, I ascended at last a huge beast full thirty pounds in weight, thick in the shoulder, firm in the flesh, greyish in colour—for age will not be denied—

'Nec certus manet color,'

slower in my movements, but mighty in my strength. I reached the great pool below Mertoun Bridge. I never got further. I need not tell you why. You know best by what vile arts——"

———

Another change, a misty consciousness, the sound of a bell. "Tring! Tring! Tring!" sounded in my ears. I awoke from my long dream to a consciousness of my real position. I was still in the North-Western train—the friendly guard had not played me false—five pounds' worth of seats had been at my disposal for half-a-crown—and my talkative intruder, the elderly gentleman in the straw-coloured paletôt, resolved himself into the straw-enveloped salmon, the victim of my prowess but yesterday afternoon. His pipe had changed into the beak he had referred to. I proceeded to London, if not a sadder, a wiser man; for though, doubtless, the history to which I had listened was but the expressed result of my own reflections and experience, I could not but feel, with some gratification, that I had reduced them—vague, and possibly in some places erroneous, as they might be—into form and shape; and as such I offer them, with much deference, to that kindest-hearted and most liberal body of men, the followers of the " gentle art."

The Narrator was killed by the Author the latter end of October; he was a fine, firm, well-shaped, wholesome fish, deep red in colour, and of excellent flavour. I attribute his greyish complexion partly to his prolonged residence in the sea, partly, as he himself did, to the effects of age; our own locks are not so bright or so dark as in the days of our youth. I consider him to have been six years old, reckoning " ab ovo," thus:—

Egg deposited, December 1865.

Hatched, February 1866.

Went to sea as a smolt, May 1867.

Returned a six-pound grilse, June 1868.

Went to sea April 1869; returned a twelve-pound salmon, September same year.

Went to sea April 1870; returned a twenty-pound salmon, September same year.

Went to sea April 1871; and was captured as a thirty-pound salmon in October of the same year.

PART II.

A FOX'S TALE.

A FOX'S TALE.

CHAPTER I.

VIXEN AND CUB.

"Tally-ho! Tally-ho! Tally-ho! Where did he cross, Ben? How long since?"

"By the big hoak, my Lord, just as I 'ollered;" and disappearing down a blind path, in a marvellously short time, Ben's cheery rate was heard "putting the hounds on" to the noble master, who, with more zeal than effect, was making frantic efforts to produce notes from his recently-acquired horn. Tweek! tweek! tweek! Toot! toot! toot!

"Confound the horn! Get for'ard! Get for'ard, hounds. Loo over, loo over, good hounds!" shouted his Lordship, leaning well over his horse's neck, and waving his cap on the line the Fox had taken.

"'Old 'ard, my Lord! 'old 'ard!" roared Jem Carter, the huntsman, as, galloping up at this moment, he pulled up alongside of his Lordship, and right in front of Jumper and Jester, who were feathering at the spot indicated by Ben as that at which the fox had crossed.

"It's a vixen, my Lord."

"How do you know, Jem?"

"See'd her, my Lord; she's got a cub in her mouth, too."

"A vixen—a cub. Oh, dear! oh, dear! *will* nobody stop those hounds? Why on earth was not that yelping terrier left at home?"

"Tally-ho! Tally-ho!"

"*Pray*, sir, stop that noise."

"Tally-ho!"

"*Will* you, sir, stop that —— noise?"

"You are not scaring crows to-day," muttered his Lordship more good-humouredly, for the clear, ringing note of Carter's horn, aided by the well-directed efforts of his active whips, had already recalled the body of the pack from the chase they were pursuing with less than their accustomed dash and thirst for blood.

There are times when Nature asserts her prerogative, and sustains the Mosaic interdict against taking the brooding mother with her young,* and the style in which hounds, especially old hounds, hunt a vixen about to lay up, or which has recently laid up her cubs, is very different from that in which they run a fox under ordinary circumstances.

In the meantime, I, who unfold this tale, a three-weeks'-old cub, round, brown, soft, and helpless, lay careless of danger across my mother's forepaws. Her warm fur enveloped me, her soft tongue caressed me, while, panting and breathless, but wary and alert, she crouched behind an old beech stool. Never for one moment had she lost her coolness and self-possession; never for a moment forgetful of the helpless being she had snatched at random from her litter of six, when first rudely awakened that spring morning by the deep note of old Pilgrim and the crack of Carter's heavy-thonged whip.

No, regardless of self-preservation, my devoted

* Pliny, with what truth I will not vouch, says—"Accipitres paciscuntur inducias cum avibus quamdiu cuculus cuculat."

mother in her hurried flight had encumbered herself with me, who hung from her mouth, like a hedgehog roasting at a gipsy's fire, as she grasped me firmly, but tenderly, by the nape of my neck. Now creeping beneath the brambles, now crawling along the bottom of a ditch, now crouching behind it's bank, she contrived, though often in imminent peril, to baffle her eager pursuers. So close were our enemies, that more than once a puzzled hound jumped over her back; but she never quailed, never by sign or movement betrayed herself or abandoned her helpless charge, and when at last the opportunity for doing so unobserved seemed to have arrived, she had crept stealthily, still carrying me in her mouth, across the ride. Ben's quick eye had, however, caught a glimpse of her, and, fortunately for us both, the more practised one of Jem Carter at the same moment. To this circumstance we owed our lives, the hounds, as I have before described, being stopped when further effort to escape seemed hopeless, unless I were abandoned—an alternative which never so much as crossed the mind of my heroic mother.

As we lay behind a stump, the welcome sounds of departure were borne upon our ears. "Away!

hounds, awa-ay!" Crack! crack! crack! Twang! twang! "Away! away! away!" And in ten minutes the wood was clear.

 My mother having assured herself that such was the case, took me up again, and returning to her kennel, sought the rest of her cubs. Alas! a sad sight met her eyes. Well might the master ask, "Why did they not leave that terrier at home?" The truculent little beast had discovered our lair and had slain four out of the five left there. One only was left, my little brother, Pug,—" Dear lost companion of my youthful days."—But of him and of his fortunes more hereafter.

CHAPTER II.

LIFE IN THE HAYSTACK.

OF my removal during the night I have no recollection—indeed I had no consciousness of it—but the following morning found brother Pug and myself safely and comfortably lodged in a haystack, more than three miles from the place of our birth. Our faithful, untiring mother must, therefore, have travelled at least twelve miles during the night, carrying one or other of us in her mouth. A heavy task; but it had been accomplished, and now in the grey light of the morning she was away, seeking the food she so much needed. Our own sustenance was at this time drawn exclusively from herself.

It was a charming retreat she had selected; the

haystack had been placed against, in fact touching, the barn-end, and while the intervening space afforded ready entrance and escape, we were well protected from the cold, and, both by our position and the narrowness of the approach, guarded from external dangers. Besides the main entrance, if I may so call it, my mother soon worked her way into the barn itself, and an opening provided for the cat gave ingress into a well-stocked farmyard. She excavated another hole under the stack, and almost, but not quite, through to the outside. This, however, she never used: it was reserved as a bolt-hole in case of extreme need.

Here we remained three or four months; and a very happy time it was. Every night our mother went forth on a foraging expedition, and never returned empty-handed—empty-mouthed I should say. Rabbits formed the staple of our diet; but rats, mice, and moles, nay, frogs and other reptiles, were at times found in our larder. Occasionally, too, we had game for dinner: partridges or pheasants, always hen birds, but these were of comparatively rare occurrence, and, truth to say, we cared little for them; they were dry, lean, and flavourless, as brooding birds always are. Not unfrequently, a leveret or a barn-door fowl formed portion of the feast; woodpigeons and wild ducks were not unknown—the former, wounded birds, which had been shot at and escaped to fall dead, or flutter dying to the ground—the latter my mother caught by watching, silent and motionless, at the brink of a large pool frequented by wild fowl. The birds feeding up or floating downward, would approach her lair too closely, and once within ten feet, whether in or out of the water, became a certain prey to the wily old mother who had watched for them so patiently.

Hares she would capture, even when feeding on the open Down. I see her now, creeping, crawling, crouching closely on the ground, moving silently and surely, almost as slowly, as the hands on the face of a clock. So patient was she, that the stupid old hare as she fed grew accustomed to, and careless of, the brown shapeless mass which, by imperceptible degrees, lessened the intervening distance, accommodating its movements to hers, but making five feet in advance for every three that her intended prey moved away, until at last the spring was made, and the poor squeaking victim found herself in the embrace of her deadly enemy.

In after days I became a great adept both in hare

"I SEE HER NOW—CREEPING, CRAWLING, CROUCHING."

Page 94.

and in duck hunting; and many a good meal has the lake or the common furnished me with. Rabbits, however, young or old, fresh or stale, formed, as I have said, the staple of our food, and, excepting perhaps rats, our favourite. Let no one who would preserve our noble race create a diversity of interest between those doubtful friends of ours, the keepers, and ourselves, by giving the rabbits as their perquisite. In such case the loss they sustain from our depredations is too serious for keeper-nature to put up with. Still, if so disposed, they may always compromise the matter by rats; for, much as I love a rabbit, for true *gamey* flavour commend me to the rat!

Well-fed, well-lodged, with nothing to do but to enjoy ourselves, sleeping all day, eating and playing all night, our life was a very happy one. A little snarling and snapping, no doubt, when our mother returned with the supper or breakfast; but she always checked anything like quarrelling, and divided the food she had brought equally between us.

When neither eating nor sleeping, our time was spent in play. Rolling or jumping one over the other, chasing one another round and round, under the barn-floor over the barn-floor, or in the merry moonlight round and round the stacks, in and out the streddles, catching one another by the tail, which by this time had grown somewhat bushy, or engaging in mimic fight, we were the merriest and most comical little beasts alive. By degrees we extended our rambles to the neighbouring copse, and took to hunting in a small way on our own account. A fat field-mouse, I remember, was the first victim of my prowess. Pug had previously rather prided himself on the capture of a great black-beetle, but we were still entirely dependent on our mother's exertions for our sustenance. Kind, thoughtful, considerate mother! Well do I remember that, when she had dug out a nest of young rabbits, she would bring them home, one by one, alive, and sitting demurely on her haunches, watch with delight* our puny efforts to tear them in pieces. If very young they were handed over to us absolutely; but if half-grown and strong, she would just cripple them by a sharp pinch across the loins. It was pleasant to see the benevolent and gratified expression with which she would regard us as the taste of blood roused the fierce passion latent in our nature, and with curling lip and bristling hackle, we snarled and snapped, and worried and bit with our

* A fact.

little sharp teeth until, more or less speedily, we had put an end to our squealing victims. This was sport indeed; and no meals were ever partaken of by us with half the zest and enjoyment these were.

The barn had, as I before mentioned, an opening into the farmyard, the building itself forming one of its sides. Opposite was the rear of the dwelling-house, on one side the pigsties and cow-sheds, on the other the farm-stables. Sheltered from all the winds of heaven, but open to the sun, the cribs full of fodder, and the yard itself littered with clean straw up to the animals' hocks, it was a perfect paradise for cattle of all kinds, pigs, and horses; but the part which most engaged our attention was the little hen-house in the corner, out of which every morning, just as we were retiring to sleep, some dozen or so of hens and about a score of pullets and cockerels, led by a magnificent old cock, used to issue. They generally retired to roost before we had awakened from our afternoon nap; but in the morning we either saw or heard them, as, seeking the early worm, they dispersed themselves about the yard; and feelings of a nature somewhat inimical to their safety began to awaken within our breasts.

Whether from a sense of gratitude for the protec-

H

tion afforded, or of honour, or from fear, I cannot say, but our mother had never molested these fowls, ready as they seemed to her hand. She would travel for miles, spend hours in digging out a rabbit's stop, lie watching half the night at a meuse or field-gate, until some tittupping leveret or lolloping old hare would pass within reach of her spring; she would lie half immersed in a wet ditch watching for a wild duck, and afterwards carry home her prey, a mile or more, in her mouth. To us this seemed a sad waste of labour, when the means of obtaining a full meal were at any moment open to us; but, whatever the cause, our mother not only scrupulously abstained from appropriating the good farmer's poultry, but laid her strong injunctions upon us to abstain likewise. It had been better for us had we obeyed her.

One evening early in August our mother had gone forth to forage. We had followed her, as for some time past had been our custom, to some distance, but had returned home, and, if I may use the expression, by unpremeditated concert had agreed to attack the hen-roost. Slipping through the hole in the barn-floor, stealthily crossing the yard among dreamy cattle and snoring hogs, we speedily reached the hen-house door. The hole which gave ingress and egress to the portly cock and motherly hens gave ready entrance to our lithe, elastic bodies. In a moment we found ourselves in a fox's paradise—cocks, hens, and chickens in scores above and around us. An old hen sitting on her nest was the earliest victim of my attack; seizing her by the throat, I speedily stopped her screeching, which had, however, awakened the old cock and all the inmates of his harem. I will do him the justice to say, that his first impulse was fight, and, dashing at me, he dealt me a blow with his wing, the effects of which I felt for a long time; but observing Pug, who had just slain a half-grown chicken, coming to the rescue, his heart failed him, and, followed by several of the hens and two or three young cocks, he retreated precipitately through the hole in the door. After all, a Dorking is but a dunghill enlarged; a gamecock would have left a different story to be told.

And now began the carnage! Had the stupid old hens and foolish chickens remained on their perches, they would have been safe; but, maddened by terror, they flew cackling and screaming to the ground, and offered themselves ready victims to our attack. Many escaped, but of those which huddled in the corner, apparently courting their fate, we left scarce one alive. In twenty minutes, nearly that number of carcases strewed the floor. Each one of these we conveyed through the hole by which we had entered into the yard, and there, scratching up the loose litter, we buried, or partially buried, the carcases of all, save two or three, which we dragged with us to our retreat beneath the barn-floor.

Hardly had our feast begun when our mother returned. She had been unsuccessful, and brought with her a young rabbit only. On seeing our plentiful repast she put on at first a grave and regretful air, but muttering something to herself about, " what is born in the bone," &c., she set to, and made a very hearty meal. For ourselves, we were uproarious in our delight; we ate and ate to satiety, and then curling ourselves up with our little bushy tails over our little pointed noses, we slept the sleep of self-content, if not of innocence.

CHAPTER III.

LIFE IN THE GORSE.

EARLY in the morning after our sanguinary foray, indeed, so early that we had hardly begun to sleep off the effects of the hearty meal we had indulged in, Ben Brady, or, as he loved to be styled, Mr. Benjamin Brady, first whip to the Deepdene Hounds, who was hissing violently at the small curb-chain he was rubbing between his palms, was accosted by Mr. Stubbs, the sporting tenant of the "Grange," a farmhouse some four miles distance from the Kennels. Mr. Stubbs was a fine specimen of the class which in my young days was styled the "gentleman farmer." He owned a small independence in addition to holding his extensive farm. He bred a good horse or two every year, hunted twice or thrice a week, revered the Squire, respected the parson, paid his rent and tithes like a man, and tried hard to believe that he voted according to his conscience. Nowadays, perhaps, we have too much of the gentleman and too little of the farmer; but, be that as it may, Mr. Stubbs was a good specimen of his class, a thorough sportsman, a hard rider, and greatly respected by high and low.

"Good-morning, Ben," said Mr. Stubbs.

"Mornin', sir," said Ben, stopping the rubbing, but only suspending the hissing.

"Is Mr. Carter about yet, Ben?"

"Dan!" said Ben (who seldom did anything he could get any one else to do for him) to the sharp, tight lad who acted as second whip, and who was busily engaged strapping a horse much higher than himself; "run in and see if the old 'un is off his perch yet."

Dan disappeared, and speedily returned with the information that Mr. Carter was up and shaving, or, as he expressed himself, "getting himself from behind his beard." Mr. Carter himself followed the announcement, the suds still clinging to his stubbly chin, his coat, in his haste, carried in his hand.

Life in the Gorse.

A warm greeting was followed by a pressing invitation to breakfast, which was as cordially accepted; but the farmer's face, as he seated himself at table, wore so lugubrious an expression that it was impossible it should escape notice.

"Nothin' the matter, I hope, sir?" said Carter.

"Well, Jem, I've bad news for you."

"Not about the puppies, I hope, sir."

"No; they're all right," said Mr. Stubbs.

"Nothing amiss with the colt, I *do* hope," said Carter.

"No; the colt's all right," said Mr. Stubbs.

"Not the missus or the kids?" asked Carter, putting the objects of interest in order according to their respective value in his eyes.

"No, no," said Mr. Stubbs, "they're all right enough; but the missus's white Dorkings—them darned foxes have been and killed sixteen out of thirty of them last night, and she swears that if I don't get rid of them, she'll do them a mischief, she will."

"Well, that's bad," said Carter; "we mustn't vex the missus, nohow. But what foxes be they? I didn't know you had any at your place this season."

"No more we had," said Mr Stubbs; "but an old

vixen—I expect it was the same that laid up there last year—brought a couple of cubs the day after that rattling run from Bryerly Wood, you remember, at the end of the season, when we so near chopped her, and they've been there ever since. They never did any harm that I know of till last night, and then, as I tell you, they made pretty near a clearance of my wife's hen-house."

It was, I suppose, about midday, that we were awakened by the impetuous attack of a little, wiry, grey terrier who, squeezing himself under the barn-floor, was upon us before we were aware of his approach. Our mother's first impulse was to defend herself and us, but the path was open behind her, and the devoted love which four months before would have made her "give battle to the lioness," in defence of her offspring,* had greatly cooled down of late. Waiting for but one snap at the wiry-haired terrier's upturned nose, she dashed away through the opening

---

* I was assured by a gentleman that a vixen with cubs once attacked his keeper and himself, and pursued them upwards of a hundred yards, barking and snapping. The keeper at Burton Park also told me that he, last year, saw a vixen whose lair had been inadvertently approached by a shepherd's dog, fly at and seize him, and she was with difficulty driven away by the use of the shepherd's crook.

Life in the Gorse.

I have before mentioned, under the haystack, whilst we, following the accustomed exit between it and the barn, found ourselves in a moment entangled in the meshes of a sheep-net, and, in another moment, transferred to a sack, in which, with its mouth securely fastened, we were at full liberty to tumble, or sulk, as we pleased.

We were speedily hoisted on to a horse, Pug at one end forming a counterpoise to myself at the other. The sack was old, and I managed to get my nose through a hole, and thereby obtain a plentiful supply of fresh air, as well as hear what was going on. Ben Brady sat before us, waiting for orders.

" Where shall I take 'em, sir ? " said Ben.

" To Brookside Gorse," replied Carter.

" Sure ! " said Mr. Stubbs, " they don't want foxes there."

" I don't know that," said Carter ; " there's a new owner come there, a Cockney sort of chap, who don't know much. His gardener's his keeper, and when he asked what had become of the apricots, the gardener told him the foxes had eaten them all.* That doesn't

---

* Foxes are very partial to grapes, and I do not think it improbable that upon occasion they eat other fruit. Wild berries undoubtedly form a portion of their food.

look well, does it? Besides, they're sure to get into the Bushes above; cub-hunting is just beginning, and they'll serve to blood the young hounds anyways."

"Ay," said the farmer, "but it's a bad hearing that Brookside Gorse can't find cubs enough for blooding and hunting too. Lord! what fools those keepers do make of their masters, surely."

"I wish," said Carter, "I could think as they *was* made fools of; they take to flapdoodle mighty easy, they do. 'John,' says master, 'I want a great head of pheasants in my covert; but mind, *you're not to kill the foxes*.' 'Oh, no, sir, by no means, I wouldn't kill a fox not *on no account*,' says John; and though a fox is never found where two brace or more used to be, he asks no questions, but just goes on, 'Mind, I *won't* have the foxes killed; I wish to preserve the foxes, *I* do.'"

"Ah," said Mr. Stubbs, "that's not the way my Lord did it when he was there. 'Cox,' says he to his keeper, 'the hounds will draw my coverts pretty often,' he says, 'and I expect they'll *always* find a fox.' 'Well, my Lord,' says Cox, 'I'll do my best; but the foxes, you see, my Lord, kill a deal of game.' 'But you are not to kill the foxes, nevertheless,' says my Lord. 'By no manner of means, my Lord, on'y you see they ain't *always* at home; foxes will travel, and—' 'Cox,' said his Lordship, quite solemn-like, 'listen to me: no Fox, no Cox! Good-night, Cox;' and the Gorse was never without a fox after that. Ha! ha! ah!" roared Mr. Stubbs; "that was something like, that was. I recollect—afore that it was, and while Cox was a trying it on as it were — his bringing a lot of legs and heads of pheasants in, one night, after dinner. 'Look here, my Lord,' says he, 'see what these tarnation foxes have been and done, killed all these pheasants in one night.' 'What! *all* these in *one* night?' 'Yes, my Lord.' 'By Jove,' said his Lordship, quite chuckling with delight, '*what a lot of foxes there must be!*'"

We were speedily transported to Brookside Gorse, and there, in a retired corner, shaken out of our bag by Ben Brady, who, as we scuttled away, treated us to a "view-halloo" (a sound with which I became afterwards more familiar) in his best style.

Surprised, captured, confined in a sack, and eventually shaken suddenly out of darkness into the bright sunlight, no wonder if I felt somewhat confused; but I have always had my wits about me, and even in the greatest exigencies should as soon expect my claws to drop off as my senses to forsake me. In a moment I took stock of my position, and, followed by Pug, scuttled away into the Gorse, as though I had been born and bred there; nor did we stop until, a good way in, we found a thick, brier-entangled grassy thicket, beneath which we crouched in perfect security, and speedily fell asleep.

Here we lay until the shades of evening as well as the dictates of appetite told us it was time to be up and doing. We had long ceased to be entirely dependent on our mother's foraging, and the necessity of providing for ourselves seemed to impart the power of doing so. We hunted together, and besides that, in a short time, we had killed and eaten a young rabbit, we discovered, by aid of our noses, more than half of another lightly buried in the earth. This we devoured, and, night being nearly spent, retired to sleep at the spot we had originally selected for our kennel. We slept soundly until the next afternoon, and then creeping forth made, whilst seeking our supper, a more complete survey of the localities.

The Gorse we found to be of considerable extent, stretching from the brow of the hill nearly to the brook which meandered through the meadow below.

It lay sloping to the south, and merged at the other, the upper end, in an extensive wood, "the Bushes" of which Carter had spoken.

Here, for nearly two months, we remained unmolested and thoroughly enjoying ourselves. We learned every path, and track, and meuse in the Gorse, as well as in the wood; we made, too, short excursions in the neighbourhood, more from curiosity and idleness than want of food, for there were plenty of rabbits to be had for catching; and I more than once crossed the brook, and brought home, or buried for future use, a duck or chicken taken from the farm-houses, of which two or three were within a short distance.

I may say that Pug and I, though good friends, and generally sleeping near each other, had become thoroughly independent. Except on rare occasions we hunted separately, and fed separately. We did not now even care to play together.* Still, though not a sociable, ours was a pleasant life; and I think that "life in the Gorse" was, on the whole, even more enjoyable than "life in the haystack."

* Young foxes turn even their gambols to account. So engrossed are the rabbits in watching their eccentric movements while at play by a wood or gorse side, that they allow them gradually to approach quite closely, until, suddenly separating, the one dashes at the rabbit, whilst the other intercepts his retreat.

CHAPTER IV.

CUB-HUNTING.

The days passed away, and dwindled as they passed. Summer melted into autumn; the green berries became black (we picked and ate them occasionally); the green nuts became brown, and rattled in their cups, or fell noisily to the ground; the harvest was gathered, and the ploughman was abroad in the field. At no previous time had we fared so bounteously. Birds and beasts as young, but far more guileless than ourselves, were met with at every turn, and our larder was plenteously supplied. My knowledge of the country, too, had greatly increased. I made nightly excursions, to the distance of several miles, not always returning home, but sometimes curling myself up and sleeping in the first convenient spot I came upon after a full meal. Pug was of a more stay-at-home character, but he too fared sumptuously every night, and slept as soundly at home as I did abroad.

Early one morning, about the middle of September, I was rudely awakened by noises of a most frightful description, which, as they rung in my ears, recalled with shuddering dread the fearful scene of my early escape from danger and death.

"Yoick over! Yoick over! Eleu in there, good hounds! Yoicks, wind him! Yoick, wind him there! Creep in, little bitch!" And then the boding cry of a hound fell on my ear. "Have at him there, Monitor! Have *at* him! Hark to, Monitor, hark! Get together, hounds!" At once, accompanied by the crack of whips and the long-drawn blast of a horn, the cry of some three score hounds burst upon my ear, as my poor, fat brother Pug was unkennelled.

> "A hundred hounds pursuing at once,
> And a panting '*heart*' before."

I was but little better off; for as I rushed from my lair my scent was at once taken up by about six couple of hounds, who dashed after me at a pace which tried both wind and muscle.

Instantly my mind was made up. I had confidence in my own powers, and was resolved to pit them against those of my enemies. In a moment I was outside the Gorse, and clearing at a bound the loose wall before me, jumped into the brook and swam boldly across, in full view of some half-dozen mounted horsemen stationed at the corner of the Gorse.

"Tally-ho, away! Tally-ho, away!" greeted me as I crept dripping up the opposite bank; and shaking the water from my fur, I headed boldly for Thorny Wood, an extensive covert some four miles off.

Whether my strength would have enabled me to reach this refuge in face of my pursuers, I cannot say; but the hounds, as they showed themselves outside the Gorse, were instantly stopped, and by dint of voice and whip compelled to join the body of the pack, who were closely hunting the unfortunate Pug.

Poor Pug! As I have said, he was of a domestic, stay-at-home character, and scarcely knew copse or spinney, or refuge of any kind, a mile from the

Gorse. His sole hope was, by a knowledge of the localities, to elude his pursuers, and this for a long time he did. Creeping here, crawling there, running when he had the opportunity, crouching low when he feared to run, the eager hounds were a hundred times behind him, and before him, and around him, close upon him, over him, without seeing him, until in an unlucky moment he endeavoured to cross a narrow ride cut for rabbit-shooting. Ben's sharp eye, as on the former occasion, caught sight of him, and a shrill yell brought up in a second the body of the pack. With a crack and a yelp, and a last snap at his foremost assailant, poor Pug yielded up his breath. Oh, what a row there was! The young hounds had to be "blooded," to be roused and excited not only to hunt a fox, which, as any other strong-smelling animal, they would do by nature, and to worry him, which their naturally destructive disposition would incline them to do, but to *eat* him; and eating a portion of fox for the first time is about as agreeable to a young hound as smoking a cheroot or chewing an olive is to a young Cambridge or Oxford "*man*." Indeed, nothing but the excitement of the chase, the example of the old hounds, and the belief that they are getting what some other hound wants, induces them to do it. Afterwards, no doubt, it is different, and hounds fight frantically for a portion of the dead beast. Still, no hounds will devour a "chopped" fox; it requires the excitement of the run to render him palatable.

"Who-whoop! Who-whoop! Who-whoop! Worry! Worry! Worry! Who-whoop!" And then, when the bristles of the old hounds were up, and the puppies had begun to snarl amongst themselves and to wonder what was coming next, the lifeless body of poor Pug was held high aloft, and a chorus of hunting sounds, accompanied by not unmusical blasts of the horn, filled the air. His head, brush, and pads, were cut off; and then the hounds being got together with reiterated cries of "Who-whoop! Who-whoop! Tally-ho! Tally-ho!" the mutilated carcase was thrown amid the baying pack, who speedily tore it in pieces and devoured it.

In the meantime, finding myself unpursued, I proceeded at an even, but still rapid pace towards Thorney Wood. Once or twice I sat up upon my haunches to listen; but though assured that no one pursued, I, like the guilty, fled on, and speedily arrived at my destination.

Cub-Hunting.

Thorney Wood is bounded on one side for a long mile by the turnpike-road. Opposite the furthest corner is a public-house, called 'The Fox's Hole,' and at this point I lay boldly watching the returning sportsmen. They were in high glee, exulting over the death of poor Pug, and discussing the merits of the hounds and the incidents of the chase.

"But, my Lord," said a youth mounted on a high horse, "why did you not go after the fox which crossed the brook? He took a capital country, and would have given us a run."

"But I did not go out for a run."

"For what then?"

"A lesson."

"A lesson! To whom?"

"To young hounds, young foxes, and young men."

"But a run might have imparted a better lesson to all three."

"Quite the reverse; the *moral* would have been lost to all."

"What is it, then, you would wish to teach to each of us, be we cubs or puppies?"

"The lesson I wish to teach the young foxes,"

said his Lordship, "is, that by boldly breaking and taking a line across country, they *may* escape, but that to hang in covert is death. The lesson to young hounds is, that the fox is the *sole* object of their pursuit."

"And to the young men, my Lord?"

"Well, it is difficult to say what earthly object a young man proposes to himself in getting up at five o'clock in the morning with no chance of what he would consider sport, unless to get a lesson, so I may as well give him one. He may learn first, if foxes are tolerably numerous, to view one without yelling at the top of his voice like a demented crow-keeper; secondly, that when hounds are at fault, as they must constantly be in a confined space, they must not be pressed; thirdly, that hunting and hard riding are neither synonymous nor necessarily connected with each other."

"But if we had followed the first fox, the hounds would have known what they were pursuing, the fox would have run all the farther and faster *for* being pursued, and your most instructive lesson would have been as practically and equally well instilled into our youthful minds."

"Pardon me," said his Lordship, "the fox, if he

escaped, might fairly have supposed that the pursuit was the consequence of his running away, and when real hunting begins would have tried the plan of stopping in covert; the young hounds, though hunting a fox, would not have learnt that their powers and instinct were to be directed *exclusively* towards the destruction of that noble animal; and the young sportsman would have lost the opportunity of seeing, perhaps for the only time during the season, hounds really *hunting*, and so learn when they are and when not on a scent."

"But do not young hounds hunt the fox naturally?"

"Of course they do, and they hunt cat, or a rabbit, or a sheep equally naturally; in fact, a puppy worth his keep will chase anything that runs away from him; but the cat scratches his nose, the rabbit disappears down a hole, and palpable arguments are used to prove the impropriety of hunting sheep. In cub-hunting he meets with other animals to which he is minded to give chase, and learns to abstain from so doing. No doubt, his great innate propensity is to hunt the fox, and partly by chiding, partly by ignoring his attempts to hunt other animals, he is taught to confine himself to the fox. There, I think

I have told you all about it, and if you are looking for a run, don't trouble yourself to come out cub-hunting again. The smaller the number that come out cub-hunting," added he, *sotto voce*, " the better I am pleased."

CHAPTER V.

THE MEET.

OF all the months in the year, surely November has the most reason to complain of the low estimate at which it is held. It is stigmatised as a foggy, gloomy, dreary, cheerless month,—a month in which, according to our volatile neighbours the French, suicides drop by scores over every bridge and hang by dozens on every bough. " Give a dog a bad name and hang him." " November, dark and drear," has always had a bad name. Yet November, I venture to think, is the very best of all the good months in the year. The air is keen and bracing, the days, though short, are usually bright—I do not mean in London, where frost brings fog—but in the country the tints on the woods are gorgeous, and the meadows are still sufficiently green to afford a pleasant contrast to the splendours of the woodland. It is the month of all others for out-door sports. Partridge-shooting, if you can only hit the birds, is better than ever; pheasant-shooting has really commenced; pike-fishing is in perfection; and on some rivers, the Tweed, for instance, huge salmon may be caught, affording in the swollen waters the grandest of sport; above all, it is in November that regular Hunting commences.

The "Deepdene" hounds closed their Cub-hunting season the last Friday in October, and began Fox-hunting the first Monday in November.

In the year of grace 1871, the first of November fell on a Monday, to the great delight of the eager sportsmen who had long looked forward to it; and by ten of the clock on that auspicious morning, Mr. Carter and his able assistants, Ben Brady and little Dan, radiant with delight and gorgeous in their new scarlet coats, started from the kennels in the direction of "Deepdene Grange," the first fixture of the season.

I must here introduce, somewhat more formally than I have hitherto had the opportunity of doing, the Huntsman and Whips of this celebrated pack.

"The first Monday in November."

Page 120.

Mr. Carter, or as he was commonly called, Jem Carter, one of the oldest and best huntsmen in England, was of middle stature, square-built, and wiry. His face, though somewhat wrinkled, wore a healthy, ruddy appearance, his hair was grey, his legs a trifle bowed. Walking, Jem Carter was not much to boast of, an ordinary, or less than ordinary mortal; but mounted, he was another creature altogether, seeming to realise the old fable of the Centaur—a part and parcel of the horse he bestrode; it was only when the animal fell that it appeared that they were not inseparable, and albeit on such rare occasions the horse was always allowed to come first to the ground and sustain the shock—

> " Like feather-bed 'twixt castle wall
> And heavy brunt of cannon ball,"

it was marvellous what a space Carter, while still holding his bridle, instantaneously placed betwixt himself and the animal.

He had a keen eye, a musical voice, an instinctive knowledge of the habits of the Fox, and an innate love of horse and hound. Carter was a gentleman at heart; under no provocation did he ever use foul language; even his remonstrances rarely assumed an angry form. He never flogged a hound, always saying that was the Whip's business, and, however erring, a hound should feel himself safe when he sought the Huntsman's protection. He was sixty years of age, during thirty of which he had been Huntsman to the " Deepdene" Hounds.

Ben Brady, the First Whip, was by birth a Cockney, with no great natural aptitude or inclination for the sport he was engaged in; but he had been brought up in a good school, and Mr. Jorrocks' lectures and James Pigg's double thong had worked wonders with him. Though constitutionally a coward, he had learnt to ride boldly and well, especially when there were lookers-on; he knew his business, and generally did it: on the whole, Ben, in the hands of Mr. Carter, was a not inefficient First Whip.

Dan, or Danny O, as he was commonly called, was of Milesian extraction; his full name was Daniel O'Shaughnessy, but his fellow-servants had never been able to master it, and it had gradually dwindled down to Danny, Danny O, or plain Dan. He was a good-looking youth, a light weight, with a firm seat and a bad hand, an intense love of the sport, and an equally intense admiration for Mr. Carter. He had plenty of pluck, and when not over-excited, plenty of sense; Dan had the makings of a good sportsman as well as a good servant in him.

Such were the men who on that first of November led forth the joyous pack over the paved court, through the wide gateway, and across the breezy common which separated the kennels from the winding, woody lane leading towards Deepdene Grange.

The sun shone brightly, the wind, though northerly, was not over cold, but there was a frosty feel in the air; the horses set up their backs and kicked and plunged as they felt the springy turf beneath their hoofs. The hounds clustered round Jem Carter's horse, and seemed to have no wish in the world ungratified, unless it were one for power to express their happiness, which found vent occasionally in a short bark or a long-drawn whine on the part of some old favourite hound as, looking up to Jem Carter's responsive face, he twisted his spotted carcase into the figure of an S.

Ben Brady led the way, Carter rode in the centre, and Danny O brought up the rear. In this order, joined by several farmers in black and brown coats, and two or three members of the Hunt in pink, they trotted along the amply grassy verges of pleasant lanes and across fertile meadows leading by a line of hand-gates to the Meet, which was reached a quarter of an hour before the appointed time.

A large and well-mounted Field were in attendance, and many were the greetings exchanged, not unmingled with good-humoured "chaff," as friends and acquaintances recognised each other. "Good-morning, Carter," said a dissipated-looking young man riding a well-bred weedy nag ; "got a good entry, eh?" "Thankee, Mr. Buttercup; pretty good— a'most too good to ride over, sir." "Ah! Jem, you'll never forgive that ; but I'll behave better this year." "Good-morning, Mr. Johnson! Glad to see *you* out again this year. The old horse all right, I hope, sir?" "Hullo, Blake!" cried another voice; "why, your reverence has got a new nag!" "True for you, my boy! but I forgot to send you word," was the response of the Reverend Mr. Blake, a hard-riding, sporting parson from the Emerald Isle, commonly known as "Paddy Blake." "Don't like the blaze down his face." "Never mind, old fellow ; sure you'll not see *that* after we get away!" And so on; kindly greetings, alternating with covert sarcasm and open chaff, were bandied good-humouredly from mouth to mouth.

The probable line the fox would take was also warmly discussed, and opinions, as usual, were considerably influenced by the wishes of the speakers. Mr. Bragg,

> "———A gent
> Who rather liked rails, and thought he went,"

was certain the fox would take across Sanderling Common, which stretched away eastward towards the low, newly-enclosed land, called Fenny Flat. Captain Pussyfat, mounted on a rat-tailed, speedy chestnut, with a long tail and weak hocks, opined that Bolsover Common, which led to the endless, fenceless Downs beyond, would be the line; whilst Mr. Weller, on Kingfisher, a noted water-jumper, was "certain sure" he would cross the brook, and make for Thorney Wood, and so by Owl's Coppice to the Forest.

In the meantime the Master, accompanied by half-a-dozen well-mounted men, rode up, and looking at his watch, gave the signal to move on. "Punctuality" (he was in the habit of quoting from his favourite author, Mr. Jorrocks) was "the politeness of Princes;" and at the stroke of eleven, waiting for no man, the hounds invariably moved away from the Meet.

On this occasion they had not far to go; the "Bushes" bounded the farm on one side, and the Gorse, where up to this moment I had lain watchful and motionless, was just below.

A wave of Jem Carter's hand, a half-suppressed cheer, for in truth the eager hounds needed none, and every one was at work in it.

"Hark in! Hark in!" "Drag up to him, Chanticleer! Yoi over, Merriman! Try for him, old hound!" with other sounds of deadly import, greeted my ear, and well knowing their meaning, I at once made up my mind not to wait until my enemies were upon me, but to seek the safety I had found on a former occasion in immediate and rapid flight.

With this view, before even the tender nose of old Pilgrim had detected the stain on the ground, or Purity had sniffed the taint in the air, I made the best of my way to the bottom of the Gorse, fully intending to cross the brook at the same place as before. As I ventured forth, however, I saw, between me and the brook, two figures—a lady and a boy—and at that moment a long-drawn howl, succeeded by a crash of fiendish yells, apprised me that my kennel had been found, and that the fierce hounds were on my track.

A feeling of terror almost overcame me, rendering me incapable of estimating at its true value the assumed danger before me. Turning back I skirted the Gorse, and, keeping still within it, passed into the wood, at the top of which the main body of the Field, with the Master, were assembled. To break here was impossible, and the cry of the hounds, who had dashed over the scent into the open meadow at the spot where I was headed, having for the moment ceased, I lay perfectly still, and endeavoured to regain my wonted courage and coolness with my breath.

"What's up, Dan?" inquired the Master of the young Whip, who, with loose rein, at this moment galloped round the corner.

"Fox has been headed, my Lord, at the bottom of the Gorse, and Mr. Carter sent me up to stop him from breaking at yonder corner; he's afraid he should make for Sandy Spinneys, where the traps are down."

"I wish," muttered his Lordship, "the traps were on their owner's legs. But who the deuce headed him?"

"The lady, my Lord, as belongs to the young gent as kicked Harmony last week." And Danny, cracking his whip, disappeared.

"That's Mrs. Dimity and her precious cub," said my Lord. "The fox will make his point yet, though, if he has the chance. Pussyfat, ride down and tell her if she stops there she'll spoil the sport, as she has done before, confound her!"

Captain Pussyfat was a lady's man, and translating his Lordship's language into phrase more meet for lady's ear, he rode up, and taking off his hat, "with his Lordship's compliments," expressed his great anxiety that she "should not miss the run by getting a bad start, and hoped that she would join him on the hill."

The lady, delighted with the flattering attention, at once rode away with the urbane messenger. "Oh, Captain Pussyfat," said she, "do you know we have seen the fox already; *didn't* we, Johnny? He came just now, and looked at us from underneath the brambles; *didn't* he, Johnny?"

"Oh! yes, mamma; and I cracked my whip at him, or else he'd have run away, *I* know."

By this time I had run the complete round of the covert, and returned to the place at which I had been terrified by the appearance of Mrs. Dimity and her hopeful son.

Finding the coast clear, and the cry of the hounds

coming nearer every moment, I boldly left the covert, and now, stronger and more active than on a former occasion, cleared the brook at a bound. The lower portion of the Gorse and the meadow were not in sight from the upper part, where the Master and the Field were stationed, but as I crossed the meadow which lay below, Ben Brady's cap was held high above the furze, and when, after clearing the brook, I breasted the opposite hill, a repetition of the "view-halloo" which had greeted my entrance into life and exit from the sack was borne shrill and clear upon my ears. It was a sound not to be forgotten and I quickened my pace, so as to place the brow of the hill as speedily as possible betwixt my pursuers and myself.

CHAPTER VI.

THE RUN.

Oh! what a commotion there was on the hill behind me.

"Tally-ho, away! Tally-ho, a-w-a-y!" shouted his Lordship, touching his horse with the spur, and bounding over the gorse in a succession of leaps, like a kangaroo through a pine-swamp.

"'Ark 'oller! 'ark 'oller!" cried Jem Carter, cracking his whip, as turning to the left, he crashed through the rotten fence, and landed from a heavy drop on the soft ploughed field below. He was followed, as he galloped down the hill, by some score or more of horsemen, who had been waiting on that side.

"Gone away! Gone away!"

Crack! crack! crack!

"Forrard, forrard! Get together, hounds! Get together!" yelled Ben Brady, cantering quietly down the opposite side, and setting in motion a still larger part of the field, who, joined by Captain Pussyfat and Mrs. Dimity, had stationed themselves there. Down they all went, some because their horses would go, some because others went, some because they saw the beautiful pack straining up the rising ground before them, carrying a head it was rapture to behold. "You might have covered them with a sheet," as Carter exultingly exclaimed. A big fence intervened between the top of the covert and the brook—there was a gap in it—and towards this there was much struggling and pushing (some strong language was used). Captain Pussyfat and Mrs. Dimity, having been the last to come up, were the first to arrive at it, and passed easily through, but Master Dimity's pony was a methodical animal and timid withal, one that liked to look before he leaped, and planting his fore legs firmly in the ditch, he commenced a deliberate survey of the bottom, before he essayed to climb the opposite bank. This occasioned a stoppage. Mr. Stubbs, who always declared that all the falls were got at gaps, put his young horse at the fence by the side, and cleared it well. Ben Brady, young Buttercup, and the Doctor followed him; while three or four less ambitious horsemen crowded the outlet, which was only wide enough for one at the same time.

"Where *are* you coming, sir?"

"Why didn't *you* pull up, then?"

"Now, sir, if you're not going, let me come."

"You're always in such a —— hurry, *you* are!"

"And *you* ain't; that's just it!"

"Forrard! forrard! forrard!"

In the meantime his Lordship, Jem Carter, Paddy Blake, Squire Haycock, Weller, and some half-dozen more, had approached the brook, and a pretty sight it was to see how gallantly they rode at it. The Master led the way, steadying his horse, while he urged him with the spur—he rode at well-nigh full speed. The good horse scarcely deigned to rise, but covered the fifteen feet of water almost in his stride. Carter's horse, though great at timber, was not a water-jumper; in almost any other hands he would have refused, but with such a rider that was out of the question. Galloping straight at it,

"He spurred the old horse, and he held him tight."

Though, jumping high, he dropped his hind legs, he gained the opposite bank, and rejoined his Lordship, who was by this time galloping some fifty paces behind, and a little to the left of the hounds. The others got over or in, according to chance, or skill, or luck. Some jumped over, and some jumped in; some tried to walk through, and stuck in the muddy bottom, to be recovered at leisure; some horses refused, and some, taking the bit in their mouths, carried their riders over against their wills, who thus found "honour thrust upon them." Mr. Stubbs, who, though a hard rider, was rather nervous about water, followed by some two score horsemen, rode away towards Ivy Bridge, a short half-mile to the right; whilst Captain Pussyfat, who thought it his duty to look after Mrs. Dimity, followed by that lady and her boy, rode for the Bullocks' Ford, the same distance down stream to the left. Ginger, the horse-dealer, who had no notion of a broken back in a fox-hunt, whatever he might risk in a steeple-chase, followed him, with a score or so more; and thus, while the hounds in hot pursuit of luckless me were running due south, three-fourths of my enemies were riding due east or due west.

Leaving Dan to see that no straggling puppy hung

in the gorse, Ben, closely followed by Mr. Muff, put the rat-tailed mare boldly at the brook, and cleared it cleverly. Mr. Muff followed on his line so closely, that one moment's pause, and a bad accident would have been the result. Ben, half-inclined to be saucy, only remarked, "Lucky, sir, you didn't jump atop of me—you might have hurt *yourself*," and, bending towards the left, he galloped on; while Muff, exulting, rode the exact line of the hounds, and catching them as they threw up on the other side of the brow, found himself the object of strong remonstrance on the part of Carter, and animadversion on that of his Lordship.

"*Pray*, sir," said the former, "PRAY don't press the hounds; you've driven them over the scent; you're spoiling your own sport, and ours too."

"Where the —— are you coming to, sir?" shouted his Lordship; "riding over the hounds and making a fool of yourself. I wish to heaven you'd stop at ——"

"Yeo doit! yeo doit! Caroline! Yeo doit! Merriman!" cheered Carter, whose eye at this moment caught the sudden pause of the favourite old hounds, as, feathering, for a moment, they recovered the scent, and, followed by the rest of the pack, dashed away on the track I had taken, whilst his Lordship, leaving Mr. Muff to swallow the few hints he had given him as best he might, with a subdued cheer followed his huntsman.

No sooner had I placed the brow of the hill between myself and my pursuers, than, turning to the left, I skirted the well-known orchard and farm-yard, and passing into the home-close, found myself in the midst of a flock of sheep. The great, woolly, baa-ing idiots all rushed together, as though I were going to eat them, and, galloping with all their might, carried me with them through the open gate-way, and almost to the hedge at the further end of the next field. Here, disengaging myself from my friends, for friends they were (though at the moment I hardly knew their value), I slipped through a meuse, and found myself on the turn-pike road. Following this to where a low stile showed the diverging footpath, I passed through, and leaving Thorney Wood to my right, I set my face straight for Bolsover Forest, where the main earths, if I could but reach them, promised me a safe and welcome refuge.

On then, on! by the narrow footpath, down the sloppy furrow of the rough fallow. On! across the rich pastures, where lazy, white-faced oxen grazed.

who twisted their tails, executed a clumsy caper, and running together, bellowed as I passed them. On! through the closely-cut meadows, where the huddling sheep ran half a circle, and stopping to gaze at me, finished it in the face of the hounds, to their great discomfiture; where the brood mare, looking forth from her comfortable shed in the corner, laid back her ears, and snorted as I passed. On! by the long, high whitethorn hedge, pursued by the chattering magpie. On! across windy commons and rush-grown swamps, where the pewits flapped their wings in my face, and the rooks soaring over my head made ever and anon swoops at me; and so, still on and on, weary and footsore, until the tall pines which towered above the broad beeches and still leafy oaks of Bolsover Forest were at last in sight.

In the meantime the Master, the huntsmen, and their companions, riding somewhat wide of the hounds, but each with a practised eye directed to their movements, followed on. They were in the highest spirits, for there was a burning scent—a good fox before them; they had left the body of the Field behind, and the young hounds were doing wonders.

"Hold hard, my Lord!" said Carter, as crossing

the brow of the hill, the pace suddenly slackened, and the hounds for a few seconds were at fault. Almost instantly, however, Caroline and Merriman hit off the scent to the left, and Carter cheering them to the echo, capped the body of the pack on to the welcome challenge. Crossing the orchard, an awkward fence barred the way; it was a rough, close, oaken paling, with a locked gate, some four feet high, in the middle.

"Take time, my Lord!" said Carter, as the Master rode somewhat hastily at it. "Give him time!" and just in time Jem Carter spoke, for almost in his last stride his Lordship, getting hold of his horse, slackened the dangerous pace, and enabled him to rise, and though he rapped the top bar hard, got safely to the other side. Jem Carter trotted up, pulling the old horse almost on his haunches, he rose steadily, and landed on the other side almost without an effort. Blake and Johnson followed; and it was not till young Buttercup, whose courage was rapidly oozing away with the fumes of the brandy he had primed himself with, rode at it forty miles an hour, and crashing through, fell, horse and man, heavily on the other side, that any accident happened. The rest followed through the hole he had made, and leaving him with a "hope you're not hurt," to pick himself up, galloped after their leaders.

"I thought that would shake 'em together," said old Carter, looking over his shoulder; "push him hard at it, my Lord, there'll be an awful big ditch the other side of this." And so there was; but the good steeds, well handled, carried their bold riders safely over, and again the musical, but to me ominous cheer, was heard, urging the striving pack still "for'ard! for'ard!"

Had it not been for the check occasioned by the stain of the sheep, which gave me two or three minutes' breathing space, I think I could never have stood before them. I heard Carter cry when they came to the road—"Hold hard, gentlemen! pray give them time over the road; hold hard!" but the scent was fearfully good; they ran down the hard road nearly at the pace they did across the grass, and pressed me till at times I almost despaired, and was more than once on the point of lying down to wait for death; but I did not—innate pluck sustained me, and, drooping and exhausted as I was, I still staggered forward.

By this time my appearance was sadly changed for the worse; my fur, so rich and glossy in the morning, now wet and soiled, clung closely to my body; my brush, draggled and foul with mud, swept the ground, and my tongue lolled from my half-open mouth.

Of my pursuers, every man had now settled into his own place; there was no more struggling or striving for precedence, none but the "flyers of the hunt" were there, and each one, however jealously inclined, knew his neighbour's powers, and felt how hopeless, indeed suicidal, would be any attempt to "cut him down." There was little choice of wind, for I had since I turned been running straight down it, and the leading men were about equally divided on either side of the line, each keeping an eager eye on the foremost hounds. Paddy Blake, closely followed by Haycock and the Doctor, took the lead on the left, whilst the Master and Carter, with Johnson and some others, rode on the right; Ben followed, but Dan had not come up. Each man held his horse tight in hand, and, easing him where he could, rode at a swinging, even gallop, taking the fences as they came, but never jumping, if without losing their place it could be avoided; they knew, one and all, how much each leap takes out of a horse, and felt that, hardly yet in condition, theirs would want all that was in them before the day was past. There were some few casualties, but good horsemen rarely fall, and though they do not perpetually fly over gates, rivers, and fences, as on the receptacles for tally-ho sauce, or in the hunting advertisements, still less frequently do they perform acrobatic somersaults over hog-backed stiles and other impracticable fences, as shown in the ordinary run of sporting pictures.

Despite my efforts, the distance between my foes and myself gradually diminished, and at last Truelove, topping a stile, caught a glimpse of me, scarcely a field ahead. Only two enclosures, however, now intervened between me and the Forest fence, and I felt I had still strength to reach it, when suddenly the Captain and Mrs. Dimity, who, having crossed the ford, had ridden best pace along a bridle road leading to the Forest, which the Captain rightly concluded was my point, appeared right in front of me. Fearing to face them, I turned short to the right, and hiding myself under a thick bush in the hedge, exhausted and breathless, gave myself up for lost. Like the sheep, however, my enemies proved my best friends. Maddened with the view, their heads up, and careless for the moment of the scent, the hounds rushed on, and running almost over me, only stopped when they reached the group of horsemen.

At this moment, his Lordship, closely followed by Jem Carter and Ben Brady, appeared on the scene, and was apparently again about to address some remarks the reverse of complimentary to the Captain and the lady, when he was interrupted by the shrill cry which greeted my futile attempt to steal away unobserved. I had, however, managed to place the length of the field between mine enemies and myself, and gaining strength from the confidence inspired by the knowledge that my refuge was at hand, I crept into the covert, and crossing the well-known ride, made for the dell in which the main earths were.

My heart bounded as I reached them, for I was half dead, and felt that my life had been saved more through fortunate accidents than the strength and endurance on which I had prided myself. What was my horror and my dismay at finding the entrance to the hole stopped in such a way that my entrance was impossible! A small faggot, with the points of the sticks towards me, had been firmly fixed in and securely fastened by a stake driven through it. For a moment, more in despair than hope, I seized the sticks with my teeth, and, finding them immovable, wildly endeavoured to tear up the ground around them with my claws. In vain: I felt that my doom was sealed, and, casting a look behind me in the momentary expectation of the arrival of my foes, I determined to sell my life as dearly as I might.

At this moment my eye rested on an old ivy-covered tree, which, having been blown out of the perpendicular long years since, now projected across the entrance to the dell. I had passed it a minute before unnoticed, but the sudden thought now flashed into my mind, that it might afford the means of safety.

Retracing my steps in less time than it takes to tell, I scrambled up the sloping trunk, and lay panting and exhausted, completely hidden amid the green foliage of the friendly ivy. Scarcely had I attained the welcome refuge when, bristling with rage and thirsting for my blood, the hounds rushed up, yelling like demons.*

On they went along the track I had twice followed, and though Bondsman and Blucher, and some of the old hounds who would never go a yard without the scent, threw up their heads at the place where I had

---

* Gentle reader, I am speaking from the Fox's point of view; to my ear, as to yours, hounds "discourse most excellent music."

"I SCRAMBLED UP THE SLOPING TRUNK, AND LAY COMPLETELY HIDDEN."

Page 142.

"Oh! Johnny saw the Fox!"

turned, the young ones rushed on yards beyond it. At that moment a bouncing old hare, which had been disturbed in the fallow, and after running the gauntlet of a dozen horsemen, had almost gone into the mouths of the hounds, was caught sight of by Frantic and Jealousy, who, throwing their tongues, and followed by the whole pack, started in mad pursuit.

"There's the fox," said Master Dimity to his mamma, as the hare popped her stupid old head out of the meuse, and as suddenly retired. "I saw the fox again."

"Oh! Johnny saw the fox," exclaimed the delighted Mrs. Dimity.

"Did you see the fox, ma'am?" said the Captain.

"You saw the fox, sir?" said the next man to him.

"Tally-ho! Tally-ho!" shouted the third, and up rushed my Lord, horn in hand, in a state of frantic excitement, and up came a lot of hounds wildly streaming across the ride. Twang, twang, twang, went the horn.

"No, no, no, my Lord," roared Jem Carter, blundering through the underwood and the wattle fence which bounded it. "No, no, no, my Lord; don't you see them's only puppies? That's a *hare* they're

A Fox's Tale.

running. 'Ware hare, puppies! 'Ware hare! Yoi-o-i back! Yoi-o-i back!" and, followed by the young hounds, who seemed heartily ashamed of themselves, Jem Carter vanished amid the thick underwood, blowing his horn, and vainly endeavouring to recover his lost fox.

CHAPTER VII.

THE FROST.

Loud and bitter were the lamentations over the loss of the fox, and various were the opinions and comments hazarded; of course, as in all misfortunes, some one must be blamed.

"Ladies have no business out hunting!" said Stubbs.

"Nor boys neither," said Peter Buttercup, who had left Cambridge about six months.

"Nor old women like Pussy yonder," added Paddy Blake; "it was all his holloaing that lost the fox."

"Pussy didn't holloa," remarked Johnson; "it was Smith here."

"Well, Robinson holloa'd first."

"Not I; but Brown said he saw the fox."

"I didn't! I only said that Mrs. Dimity said that somebody said he had seen him."

"I wish to heaven!" said the Master, riding up, "that you wouldn't take the trouble to holloa at all. There are plenty of servants paid for holloaing, and who do it much better." And turning away, he rode off, discussing with Carter the mysterious loss of the fox, and lamenting that the hounds had missed blood on their first day.

"Well, my Lord," said Stubbs, who with his companions had just ridden up, "I ain't sorry for it a bit. He's a good fox, and will live to run another day; and as for blood, I don't believe it matters whether hounds have blood or not."

"Nor I neither," said Blake. "There are packs that never, so to say, kill a fox, and show good sport too. Hounds will run a bagman just as keenly as a wild fox. In India they run a jackal well, though they never eat *him*. Indeed, I have seen the Phœnix Hounds run a red herring, or an aniseed drag, as keenly as they, or any others, ever hunted a fox."

"And so have I," said Stubbs, "when I was a boy I hunted a pack of beagles, and to my notion they ran a drag more keenly than ever they did a hare; in fact, there was not a hound in the pack would kill a hare; the first one they ever hunted was tame, brought up as a leveret in their company, and they would have as soon thought of worrying their master as their little companion, or any of its kindred."

"I incline to your opinion," said his Lordship, "when the great race between hounds and horses came off, the hounds of necessity ran a drag—and they beat the horses."

"I wish," said Mr. Stubbs, "that masters in general held the same view; the namby-pamby cry about the cruelty of hunting has literally no foundation whatever, if you do away with the practice of 'digging out' and murdering—there is no other word for it—a fox that has fairly gained a place of refuge, on the plea that the hounds must have blood. By all means kill your fox say I, if you can kill him fairly; if not, let him escape, and live to run another day."

"But," said young Buttercup, "you would not save a ringing beggar that has kept you all day in a wood, because he creeps, like a cur, into a rabbit-hole."

"I would;" said Mr. Stubbs, "that 'ringing beggar' would next time you found him, probably go straight away; a fox is not the crafty, cunning animal he is generally supposed to be; he is a bold, high-spirited, and sagacious one; he refuses to quit the covert because from excess of self-confidence he underrates the danger; having once realised it he will, on the next occasion, go straight away and trust to speed and endurance for safety. Besides, though I love sport, I hate cruelty, and, disguise it as you will, there *is* cruelty in digging out and throwing a fox to the hounds. I heard, last season, of a huntsman whose claim to the celebrity he has acquired rests, not so much on the runs he shows, as upon the number of foxes killed, causing a bold fox that had taken refuge on the ridge of an outhouse, after a good run, to be shoved down into the mouths of the baying hounds below; the same man caused another fox that could not be dislodged by fair means from a drain, and put the terrier sent to dislodge him to ignominious flight, to be *smoked out;* there is an admirable illustration of the foul proceeding in one of Mrs. Edwards' (G. Bowers, of *Punch*) life-like sketches, the poor beast is admirably depicted, with terrified aspect, blinded eyes and singed fur, as he crawls forth to meet his doom :—

> ' Wild and wonder-stricken, even as one
> That staggers forth into the air and sun,

> From the dark chamber of a mortal fever,
> Bewildered and incapable ——'

Such acts are, to my mind, wickedly cruel, and reflect infinite disgrace on all who practice or permit them. I heard, however, that the liveliest dissatisfaction was expressed at either act of barbarity, and it was only want of moral courage prevented active interference on the part of more than one member of the hunt."

This point, however, like that of the propriety of ladies hunting, did not appear very likely to be settled; but all agreed that the run had been first-rate, and that the puppies were the finest entry ever known.

For my part, I lay at first stretched at full length, but afterwards coiled up amid the sheltering ivy, and it was not until the evening that, faint, stiff, and wearied, I descended and sought the food I so much required. The half of a dead hare, which had been killed by the hounds, but dropped, under dread of the lash, before they had time to devour it, afforded me an ample meal, which I did not enjoy the less because my deadly enemies had provided it. Returning to the earths, I found the obstacles removed, and that they were now open. At once entering, I coiled myself up, and slept soundly through the whole of the next day.*

It was some days before I recovered from the effects of the run, but I was happily unmolested during the remainder of the month, and towards December a sharp frost set in. Bitter cold it was, and I found some difficulty in providing myself with sufficient food. To dig out rabbits was impossible; the rats had retired to the corn-stacks; the wild ducks had sought the sea-shore; even the moles had followed the blind worms deep down in the earth, beyond the influence of the frost. Had it not been for the shooters I know not how I should have got on, but many a lost or crippled pheasant, or broken-legged hare, fell to my lot as I roamed the coverts ere the keeper had gone round with his retriever the morning after a battue. Many small birds, too, died of hunger and cold, and were picked up on the banks or in the ditches. The hen-roosts were laid under contribution, nor did I hesitate in my extremity to revisit the scene of my earliest marauding exploit, and again obtain a taste of Mrs. Stubbs's white Dorkings. Once, too, I came upon a crew of hard-

* It is the opinion of many good sportsmen that a hunted fox always returns to his kennel the same night.

drinking ducks, who had gabbled over their liquor until the pool froze and hampered their wings with icicles; I killed them all.

At last the frost broke; the snow, losing its crisp purity, melted into slush; the ice cracked, its surface growing first slimy, then moist, and finally melting into blue scum-covered water. The spirits of hunting men revived, guns were laid aside, boots polished up, and, "weather permitting," the Meet was again advertised for 'Deepdene Grange.'

"I wonder," said Jem Carter, as with a light hand he lathered away at his somewhat obstinate beard, speaking half to himself and half to Danny O, who was in attendance; "I wonder will we find our old customer again that gave us the slip so cleverly the first day of the season; I'll dust his jacket for him if we do, or my name's not Carter."

"I hope I shan't get such a precious ducking as I did in the brook that day, if we should find him," remarked his companion.

"Your own fault, Danny," said Carter; "all your own fault! Riding at water as you did with a loose rein, you're bound to come to grief; the horse swerved in course, the bank broke, and you got under him. From all I hear it's a wonder you warn't drowned."

"Well," said the lad, "I know I drove him hard at it, as you told me."

"That's not enough," said his senior; "there are fences you must ride at pretty fast, if you mean to get t'other side of them; and there are fences you must ride at very slow, if you don't mean to break your neck; but there's *no* fence as you should ride at with a loose rein, and it's just the same with water. It's my belief that the horse thinks when you've got a good hold on his head, that it's *you* that carries *him* over; if you let him go, he's 'all abroad!' Now, missus, I'm ready for my breakfast."

CHAPTER VIII.

THE FINISH.

In the same order, by the same route, and almost with the same company as on the previous occasion, the hounds proceeded towards the Meet; but, though still the same, a marked change had taken place in the appearance of all—men, dogs, and horses. The last were lighter in carcase, and though displaying in their condition the effects of high feeding, careful tending, and thorough grooming, had lost the *bloom* which shone on their coats at the commencement of the season. Some showed scars or swellings, the result of accident or hard work; and a shorter step would here and there indicate the consciousness of a "favourite" leg. Hounds, too, might be observed moving somewhat stiffly—if I may be allowed the expression, "stiltily;" some few were in hospital; Mystery had been ridden over, Harmony kicked, Pilgrim and Tragedy (the wise old bitch that never left Carter's side until a hound challenged, and who always endorsed the challenge if true) had succumbed to age, after vainly striving to hold their own; Frantic and Jealousy, Vanity and Volatile, had been condemned for inveterate riot, and some two or three couple had been drafted at either end on the score of pace. Still, the body of the pack was there, and a likely, lashing lot they were as a fox might wish, or fear, to have on his drag.

In the men was little of change to remark; Carter's honest, close-shaven face wore its usual pleasant, somewhat serious expression. His coat and cap, no longer bright and glossy, showed the stains of many a splash from miry lane or black bog, but his cords were spotless, and his white neckerchief neat as ever. Ben was, as usual, smirky and self-satisfied. Danny, his coat somewhat shrunk and his frame somewhat enlarged, looked like Leech's cab-horse—"his heart too big for his body."

The Grange was soon reached, and every one's wants, real or supposed, hospitably ministered to by

Stubbs and his stalwart sons, who brought out crusts and cheese, ale and cherry-brandy, biscuits and wine to such as could not be tempted to dismount and taste the ample cheer provided within.

"Thank ye, Mr. Stubbs!" said Johnson, "but I came here to *hunt*, and not to *eat*. No offence, I hope?"

"None in the least—Liberty Hall this!—eleven o'clock too,—come, let's be moving."

The field was large, and all our old acquaintances were there—Smith, Brown, and Robinson, Ginger the horse-dealer, Squills the doctor, Johnson, Paddy Blake, Mr. Muff, Captain Pussyfat, and some six score more.

The wind was southerly, and Carter decided for reasons of his own to draw down it, that is, in the same direction as that pursued on the former day.

"You see, my Lord," he said to the Master, "if we can make him break at the upper side, there's nothing to speak of betwixt us and the Crags ten miles off, and fit as the hounds now are, it's *un*possible a fox can live before them that distance, and as to finding him in his kennel, he'll break as soon as the hounds are in covert, whichever way we draw."

I was in consequence at once aware of the approach

of my enemies; indeed, I had returned home somewhat late that morning, and the old hounds owned the drag the instant they entered the covert.

Dashing eagerly forward, leaping over the bushes and over one another's backs, they hurried on to the spot at which they had previously unkennelled me; indeed, hounds always bear in mind the precise spot at which they have once found a fox. I did not tarry to receive them, but creeping rapidly and stealthily along, I passed through the wood, and broke at once on the north side, setting my head straight for Mussel Crag, which, as Carter truly said, was a good ten miles off, though I hoped to find a nearer refuge. If I did, I was disappointed.

"Danny!" said Carter in a low voice, as, after beckoning him to his side, they galloped together round the outer edge of the covert, the hounds in full cry to the right hand—"Danny, you remember the drain on Mr. Tyler's farm where we lost our fox last season?"

"I do, sir!"

"He promised to put a grating at the mouth, but I doubt he ain't done it. Clap on, Danny, and wait there till you see if our fox makes for it."

With a quick gesture of intelligence and obedience

Danny set spurs to his horse, and, dashing through the rough bushes that bounded that side of the covert and over the light fence, rode straight as a crow might fly to the point indicated; and there, when some five minutes later I arrived, I found the lad, grinning and out of breath, holding his horse by the bridle, his cap in his hand, blocking up, by sitting over its entrance, the long drain which, as I knew, led directly into Mr. Tyler's homestead, carrying off the water from his well-roofed farmyard. Danny waved his cap triumphantly at me as I turned away disappointed, but, to my surprise, no "Holloa" greeted my departure.

Meantime the hounds were hot upon my track. The scent was good, and, save for a second when they dashed out of covert on to ground which the horsemen had traversed, there was neither pause nor check. Chanticleer and Affable cleared the fence together, and as they feathered on the headland, Madcap and Modesty, Trinket and Truelove, with Purity, Dexterous, and Columbine making a cast forward, hit the scent off down the furrow, and scoring to cry, every hound in the pack owned the scent and struggled for precedence.

"*Pray,* gentlemen!" shouted Carter; "*pray,*

gentlemen, give them room; *pray*, don't press them."

"Tally-ho away! Tally-ho away! Tally-ho! Tally-ho!" screamed a dozen voices, and, in a few seconds, every hound was streaming across the green pasture which lay between the covert and the rich arable wheat and bean land beyond.

A single, stiffish rail at the upper end protected the young quickset hedge; and at this, Ginger, who regardless of Carter's warnings and entreaties, had gone away with the lead, rode at best pace.

The good horse cleared the rail, but lighting in the narrow ditch beyond, made a complete somersault, throwing its rider, whose seat was fortunately none of the closest, fully five yards in advance of him. As, partially stunned, he lay, with strange lights flashing through his eyes, and strange noises swimming in his ears, he had an indistinct vision of his horse, the bridle loose and broken, his head down, vainly striving to catch the hounds, which were disappearing in the distance. No gap, however, had been made, no opening for those who followed, and as no one selected the same spot, he sat and looked about him in comparative safety.

The Master and Carter took the fence quietly and

cleverly; Paddy Blake hit, but did not break the bar; Mr. Stubbs and the Doctor took rail, and fence, and ditch at a mouthful; a few more followed them, and many, despairing of the obstacles being cleared for them, rode away to the right or to the left, seeking for a gap or a gate.

However, no single rail, or double either, can stand a field of horsemen. Harry Robinson, who prided himself on being a "good, quiet rider," and who, in fact, funked awfully, walked his horse up, and with some difficulty got the animal's fore legs over, and, in attempting to bring the hind ones after them, broke down a rod of the fence. The baffled field poured through the opening like water through a mill-dam.

The ground was heavy, and catching hounds with such a scent no easy matter; however, every one did his best, and it is astonishing, if you only keep hammering along the line, how, from some cause or another, in ordinary runs, hounds "come back" to you.

"He'll get into that confounded drain!" said his Lordship; "the hounds are heading straight for it."

"Not he, my Lord; I sent Danny for'ard, and see, there's his cap in the air."

"Yeo doit! yeo doit, Jester! Yeo doit, Playful! Down the hedgerow it is! Yeo doit, Chanticleer, good hound! There he turned! Hoick! Hoick! Chanticleer! Yoicks! For'ard! For'ard!"

In a moment my untiring enemies had recovered the scent, and were straining with murderous eagerness on my track.

"This way, this way, my Lord!" shouted Carter; "'ware bog, 'ware bog." The warning came too late: as he spoke, his Lordship's horse floundered for a moment, then, stumbling onwards and driving before him a stream of inky water, came suddenly to a stop, and lay with outstretched neck and distended nostril, helpless, immersed up to the saddle-flaps in the black tenacious bog-hole. No whit daunted, the rider threw himself well back on his saddle, and touching the curb-rein smartly while he spurred the horse, encouraged him to a mighty and successful effort, which landed him safely on the other side. Little heeding Paddy Blake and two or three other less fortunate followers, who were left floundering hopelessly in the same "Slough of Despond," he joined his huntsman, and with, if possible, greater ardour the chase swept on.

The country now opened; the enclosures were

larger, the fences fewer and weaker. I had reached the foot of that great hill which for a hundred miles marks the boundary of the Down country, and up it I began to climb, slowly and painfully, for, in excellent condition as I was, the pace had told upon me, and I confess that my heart had sunk within me when I sought the refuge of the drain and found it closed.

As I climbed the hill at an easy angle, stopping once and again to consider my position and decide upon my course, I commanded a full view, as well of my pursuers as of the country behind and beyond them. To one less vitally interested in the issue of the chase was presented a beautiful as well as an exciting scene. In the distance I could plainly distinguish the brown oaks and broad beeches that crowned the Deepdene Gorse. Far beyond again, and only distinguishable by a jagged line on the horizon, appeared the tall pines and dark line of Bolsover Forest, between which and the boggy land skirting the heavy clays directly below me were well-known farms and homesteads, holts and spinneys, woods, dells, and brakes, every one of which was familiar to me, and all, or nearly all, connected in my mind with some successful hunting or marauding expedition.

This, however, was no time for retrospection; the cry of the hounds, redoubled by the echoes of the hill, was borne full upon my ear, nearer and nearer still, and though a few couple, beaten by the pace, still straggled within my view, the body of the pack was hidden from my sight directly beneath me, and climbing upwards at a speed equal to, if not greater than, any I was capable of.

At a short distance behind came the Field, the bright scarlet coats showing on the yellow soil like poppies in a corn-field, and approaching with a swinging movement like that of the pendulum of a clock —I mean the body of the horsemen presented this appearance, for some dozen or more were well ahead of the rest, and many far behind, and some were riding the road which ran below and parallel with the hill, east or west, as they thought best, to seek some easier point of ascent than that I had chosen.

Short space of time did I occupy with the observations above recorded, long as it takes to describe them; but, gaining the brow of the hill, I set my head straight for Mussel Crag, where, as I well knew, were cliffs and fissures for the refuge of a dozen foxes, which no stopping could affect, and no whip drive me from. Again I was disappointed; a few horsemen, rightly guessing my point, had left the hounds some time before, and there I found them directly in my intended course. Turning to the right, I ran perforce the edge of the hill, its smooth, green, springy turf affording a welcome relief to my hot, tired feet, after the wet, rough soil I had traversed below. But if the change were in one respect good for me, it was bad in another and a more vital one. The scent, before good, seemed doubly so on the green turf. Scarcely pausing to work out the few yards I had run in the direction of the cliffs, the pack swung round, and as the leading horseman appeared, with a whimper and a scarce repeated challenge, absolutely raced after me.

"Yoick for'ard!" screeched the Master. Twang, twang, twang, went Carter's horn. "Good hit, little hound! Yeo-o-ick! Madcap and Modesty. Yeo-o-ick! Let's see who'll ride over them *now!*" chuckled the old man as, taking his horse by the head, he settled down into the best pace the somewhat jaded animal could muster. "Let's see who'll ride over them *now!*" And little fear was there of undue pressing. The young hounds took the lead—Madcap and Merriman, Playful and Purity, Bondsman and Butterfly. Age will not be denied; and where there was no stooping for scent, no picking it up by patient effort, the young ones had it all their own way. Not a note was heard; the pace was too good to waste breath, and save where an old hound would give vent occasionally to a short, disappointed whimper, they ran mute.

"Beautiful! Beautiful!" exclaimed his Lordship, as after nearly two miles at best pace, the leading hounds threw their heads up, and circling round, like swallows on the wing, joined their accustomed leaders, who, though overmatched in speed, had carried the scent every yard they ran, and now followed my sudden enforced turn downwards, as though they had been tied to my brush.

It was not on me alone that the pace had told. The two miles passed over showed a tail extended over at least one. In truth, it had been a sort of flat-race, each man going the best pace his horse was capable of, or the best he knew how to get out of him. Had I not turned suddenly as I did, I should have been run into in view; and as it was, I felt that my doom was but delayed a few minutes, and my chances of escape absolutely none. Where could I seek for a refuge? How could I hope, on this bare hill-side, to baffle my pursuers? Still, "Never despair" was, and always has been my motto, and I trundled down the hill in full view of the Field as boldly as though I had been that moment unkennelled, and the boundless forest before me.

"Tally-ho! Tally-ho! Tally-ho!" again burst from a hundred voices. "Tally-ho!" shouted Carter, as, cap in hand, he skimmed along the steep side of the hill carelessly, as though he were riding on the level ground above. Crack, crack, went Ben's whip, as he cantered round and behind the hounds with the same total disregard of the precipitous nature of the ground; while Danny turned his horse's head down the side of a cliff that no one unaccustomed to such a country would have credited aught save a goat or a cat with descending; his object being clearly to head me "*by accident*," and so prevent the possibility of escape.

What shall I do? Where shall I go? Where shall I hide?—I have it. The cottage by the roadside,—the door is open. Giles Jolter, the occupier, is washing potatoes at the entrance. I dash by him, and touching lightly the baby's cradle as I leap over it, dash at once into the family chest in the corner, the lid of which, fortunately for me, stands open. Mrs. Jolter with a scream rushes to take up baby;

the girl who was rocking the cradle recoils in mortal fright; but Giles, whose nerves are not easily shaken, passes in, and shutting down the lid, turns the key in the clumsy lock, and deposits it in his breeches-pocket just in time to meet two or three frantic horsemen, who, having in vain cast round the house without hitting off the scent, had in consequence concluded that I must be within.

"Come, old fellow! where's our fox? We saw him come in."

Your fox!" responded Giles. "What makes him *your* fox, I wonder? He's *my* fox, and I have locked him into yon kish, along with my Sunday clothes."

True enough; I was sitting on them, and beside me lay the worthy fellow's Bible, his wife's best bonnet, the "marriage lines," and a bunch of blue ribbon which he had received by way of prize, "for bringing up twelve children (on wages averaging eleven shillings a week) without parish relief."

"YOUR fox!" repeated Giles.

"Why, we've been running him this hour or more."

"Pity you could'nt cotch him, then,' said Giles, who was somewhat of a wag in his way. "He might have been your'n then; now he's mine."

"You mean, you won't give him up, then?"

"Come, old fellow, where's our Fox?"

The Finish.

"No, I wonnot!"—fine, honest, independent fellow, thought I—"leastways not unless you give me half-a-crown;"—venal, clodhopping brute, was my second reflection.

At this juncture Mr. Stubbs entered. "Servant! Mr. Stubbs, be that thou? I'll give up t'ould fox to *thee*, sir. You be a good measter and a koind friend to the poor."

"Thank ye, Giles; and there's half-a-crown for you.—But, my Lord, we musn't kill him; he's too good to be killed! I'll take him home, and chain him up to the old barrel under the lime-tree at my place, and loose him when the season comes round again; he'll show us another good run yet."

PART III.

BOLSOVER FOREST.

BOLSOVER FOREST.

CHAPTER I.

MASTER B.'S YOUTHFUL REMINISCENCES.

"MASTER B.! Master B.! where *can* Master B. be?" Where indeed? Chin-deep in the hogs-wash, standing tip-toe on the inverted bucket which had happily been left floating in the greasy liquid, my dirty, chubby, tear-furrowed cheeks and streaming eyes just visible above the rim of the tub, into the depths of which my innate love of natural history had plunged me. To watch the movements of the rats in the pigsty, I had crept along the rotten, treacherous boards forming the cover, which breaking had well-nigh committed me to a direr fate than that of "maudlin Clarence in his Malmsey butt!" Out of this delicious bath I was rescued, sobbing and half-choked, by my much-enduring nurse. Mrs. Bedwyn, scolded, shaken, soothed, kissed, and put to bed, from which I rose the next morning neither a sadder nor a wiser child.

I think that during my infancy and boyhood I went through every species of danger and met with every mishap that child or boy could be exposed to. I was tossed by the cow, kicked by the donkey, scratched by the cat, and bitten by the dog (strangers all, for the home creatures knew and loved me); I tumbled off the haystack, and into the pond, and down the well, and out of the cart, and off the apple-tree, and into the bee-hive. I was run away with by the pony, and blew my eyebrows off with gunpowder. I was lost, and found and strayed away, and sent home again, and went through as many adventures before I was twelve years old as many a quiet individual might experience through a long lifetime. All and each however had some reference to my favourite pursuit of natural history, and though, as in the case of the rats in the pigsty, my attempts to watch wild animals and learn their works and ways occasionally ended in discomfiture, I was ever ready to renew the essay, and neither time nor trouble, labour nor pain, was taken into account if in my own mind I could add but one page to the science of which as yet I knew not even the name, Natural History—

> "I could watch from morn till gloom
> The lake-reflected sun illume
> The yellow bee in the ivy bloom."

Yes! and the rats, though not so poetical and not so proverbially industrious or ostensibly useful, were worth watching in their way. When the rotten old boards which had played me such a scurvy trick had been removed and the strong new lid fixed in their place, I would lie at full length upon it, and peeping stealthily over the mud coping of the wall, observe how warily, when the gluttonous hogs had finished their repast and could stuff no longer, the old rats would send the young ones forward like doves from their ark of refuge, and watching them as they stuffed their little skins out, assure themselves of their own safety by the immunity of the baby marauders. Then the half-grown rats, wiser in their generation than the infant brood, would issue forth, rush to the trough, snatch a mouthful, and—find themselves robbed of it by their despotic seniors as they sought to regain their homes. Finally, when assured that there was no immediate danger, the grey-whiskered, yellow-toothed, bright-eyed patriarchs of the horde would run silently and swiftly forth, and having snatched a hasty meal, perform their careful after-dinner toilette before my delighted eyes. In truth there is no animal so cleanly as the despised rat. Whether he live in pigsty, farmyard, drain, or sewer, his face and his whiskers and his pretty paws will be kept clean and white and pure as, nay more so than, any lady's pet, be it of what race it may.

Master B.!—but I have not given the reader the etymology of my curt name. B. is short for Benjamin. My mother's younger brother, who rejoiced in that name, a wild and wayward youth, had gone off some years since to what my nurse called generally "the Injies." He had left the country under a slight cloud and at variance with both my father and mother, but the later cherishing a secret hope that "Uncle Benjamin" would one day return laden with gold and make his namesake, if he found one, his heir, or possibly go through the latter part of the programme without troubling himself about the former, had insisted on christening one of her sons Benjamin. My father, who hated the name, generally abbreviated it by the use of the initial, and commonly referred to me as "little B." The servants and the villagers took it up, and I was universally called Master B.

Master B.'s chosen playmate was little Bill Belt, the cowboy; and deep was the grief that swelled the gentle bosom of his somewhat exclusive nurse at witnessing this, as she considered, degrading intimacy. What would she have said had she been aware that at the moment she was anxiously seeking Master B., that young gentleman was engaged behind the barn in a pugilistic encounter with Bill in defence of the two surviving children of tortoiseshell Tip?

> "The cat's kittened in Charlie's wig,
> There's twa of them living, there's four of them dead;
> T'ane's a son, t'ither's a darter,
> The four dreed their weird in a bucket of water."

Bill, to whose tender mercies Tib's progeny had been confided, was minded to drown the "whole biling," as he called it. I resisted successfully, and at the expense of a black eye rescued the unconscious innocents and restored them to the embraces of their fond mother.

Perhaps in these early days my notions of morality and the strict obligations of truth were undeveloped; at any rate the account I rendered to Nurse Bedwyn of the cause of the disfiguration of my ruddy countenance bore no relation whatever to the real facts of the case. However, the story, whatever it was, was taken as fact; and Old Nathaniel, or Nat Belt, the game-keeper, Bill's father, a man of strict probity and strong religious feelings, was so pleased with my pluck in not splitting on Bill, that he became thenceforth my fast friend: and many a pleasant hour I spent in his cottage, and many a wrinkle on the subject of dogs, game, and wild animals in general, I got from the good, observant old man, and treasured in my memory.

The kittens, I may here state, throve and grew into cathood; and though Sandy, the son, went the way of all cats in early life, and contributed his mite of utility to the scale of creation in the shape of a keeper's cap, young Tibbie, the daughter, lived to a good old age, and was famous among cats for many good and for some bad qualities. She was a splendid mouser and extraordinary bird-catcher, but I am bound to own, a terrible thief and poacher. Nat Belt, out of gratitude, however, condoned her offences in that line; and though she was more than once caught in his traps, he always, after some practical admonitions, set her free. Eventually

Tibbie became thoroughly up to trap, and gins and snares were in vain set for her in the neighbouring woods and coverts, to which, for a great distance round, she paid frequent visits. Indeed, Tib's powers of locomotion were wonderful. She loved me with an intense and enduring love, such as I have never seen exhibited by any other cat; she would follow me long distances across country wherever I went, running up half the trees we passed in our wanderings in search of birds' nests, and then go off poaching at night as if she had only purred on the hearth all day. Tibb's principal employment on my behalf was the bringing up the stray or supernumerary young animals, scions of my prolific and diverse happy family. The "storgè," or natural love of offspring, was deeply implanted in Tib's breast, but it was not of an exclusive kind. Her own young ones, of which she produced a litter about every six months, being destroyed, she would nurse *à discrétion* young rabbits, young squirrels, young ferrets, and, I verily believe, if I had tried her, young rats. She made no coquettish scruples on the subject, affected no natural reluctance, but on the blind helpless young of any of these animals being presented to her, she at once took them up in her mouth, and retiring to her favourite corner, performed the maternal office with as much apparent satisfaction as she would have done in the case of her own murdered innocents. The young ferrets were the most valued by me. They came as do the oysters—but once a year ;* and the old doe had the knack of producing, like an Irish peasant, more than she could possibly maintain. Tib was the America to which the redundant population was carried for support, and very proud she was of the charge, and well she sustained it. Her foster-children in after life repaid her care by bolting the rats from their holes, which Tib—who alone among cats had learnt the art and mystery of ferreting—would catch and kill like a terrier. Very few, if any cats will *face* a rat (I am not sure that Tib would); but, sitting motionless near the mouth of a hole while the ferret was working within, she would seize at a bound the terrified fugitive as he fled from his hole, and run off with him to devour or torment at leisure.

Rat-catching is a noble pursuit. Mr. Buckland has declared there are two descriptious of fishing—salmon fishing and gudgeon fishing; I say there are

* I refer to the pole-cat ferret. The common white ferret breeds twice in the year.

two kinds of hunting—fox hunting and rat hunting. Of the first we have treated elsewhere; of the second no trustworthy record or elementary treatise exists.

"Caret vate sacro."

Would it were otherwise! The rat is the wariest, craftiest, and boldest of beasts. Skill, and caution, and experience, and good ferrets, and well-trained dogs, are essential to the successful pursuit of this noble though as yet unhonoured phase of sporting, and not less hunting strategy than in the chase of bold Reynard. We may in a future chapter give an account of a rat hunt on scientific principles; for the present we proceed with our own, to us, more interesting memoirs.

CHAPTER II.

PUPIL AND PRECEPTOR.

NAT BELT had two children besides my friend Bill—Sam, the eldest, a fine young man, who acted as aide-de-camp (I mean under keeper), and, as his father asserted, "knew a'most as much of game and dogs and vermin as he did himself;" the other, Barbara or Baby Belt, a rosy-cheeked, bright-eyed lass of eighteen, the bosom friend of Patty the nurserymaid, who, under Mrs. Bedwyn's superintendence, had the charge of Master B. Baby was not idle; she kept the lodge clean and tidy, waited on her mother, who was an invalid, fed the fowls, reared the pheasants, taught in the Sunday school, and led the choir in the parish church, besides coming in to work at the Great

House, as ours was called, whenever a county ball or some home festival brought with it more work than my sisters' maid could possibly get through. She was one of the prettiest girls I ever saw, and as good as she was pretty. Indeed, the whole family were good in their way, well bred, well brought up, and well conducted; it was evidently considered that I should take no harm from a rather unusual degree of intimacy with them; and my visits to the keeper's lodge were rather encouraged by my excellent mother, who did not share in Mrs. Bedwyn's class prejudices. I generally had tea at the lodge about once a week; and a present of a pound or two of souchong now and then may have been intended as an equivalent for the inordinate quantity of hot bread and butter which I consumed on such occasions. Tea was eight shillings a pound in those days.

"Can you read, Mr. Belt?" said I one afternoon, sitting over the fire after tea, while Baby was washing up the cups and saucers, and Sam had gone out on his rounds. "Can you read, Mr. Belt?"

"Well, Master B., I can read *my* Bible."

"Or any other person's Bible, I suppose?"

"No, I won't say that, Master B. I was taught to read in *this* Bible here, reaching down an old, red-covered, brazen-clasped book from the shelf beside him. "It was given me by master's brother, the parson, I mean, when I was a boy at his school, more than fifty years ago, and I don't know as I could read out of any other."

I took the book in my hand, and found that though the Gospels were well thumbed and somewhat dirty, the rest of the book was perfectly clean, and the leaves slightly adhered to each other, as if they had been rarely, if ever, opened. Young as I was, I concluded at once that Mr. Belt's powers of reading were limited to the chapters he had thumbed over in the Sunday school fifty years before.

"Then, Mr. Belt," said I, "you can read no book but the Bible?"

"No book but the Bible, Master B."

"I read," said I, "beautiful books about natural history, every day; and if you like I'll teach you."

"Let's know what natural history's all about first, Master B."

"All about birds, and beasts, and trees, and volcanoes, and flying fish," said I.

The suggestion appearing to find favour in Mr. Belt's eyes, I immediately ran home, bringing back with me a beautifully-bound book with coloured prints of British birds, and descriptions of their manners and habits, "for the instruction of children." Opening the book, and pointing to the picture of a bright blue-backed kingfisher, Nat begged me to read what was said about a bird he was in the constant habit of watching by the little river forming on one side the boundary of the manor. Accordingly, perched on a three-legged stool by the chimney-corner, Baby, who had finished washing up the tea-things, sitting opposite, old Belt smoking his pipe with a somewhat critical expression on his countenance, I commenced:

"'The kingfisher, *Alcedo hispida*—'"

"What's that, Master B.?"

"That's the Latin name of the kingfisher, Mr. Belt."

"And what's the use of a Latin name, Master B., when we're talking English?"

"Yes; but we might talk to a foreigner, you know, and then he'd know what bird we meant."

"All right, Master B.; and when I talk to a furriner I'll call it 'Hispider'—only I don't want to. I hate them furrineering papishers."

—"'is one of the most beautiful of the British aquatic birds.'"

"What's 'a quatic,' Master B.?"

"A bird that lives in the water, I think, Mr. Belt."

"But the kingfisher don't live in the water. But go on, sir. I beg pardon for interrupting."

"'Its usual habitat'"—I saw old Belt's mouth twitch, but innate good manners restrained him, and he said nothing—"'is the bank of some meandering stream or silent lake. Its principal food consists of small fish, which the bird catches with singular dexterity. For the purpose of attracting its prey within reach of its unerring aim, Nature, which does nothing in vain, has clothed the kingfisher with brightest feathers of cerulean hue—'"

"I wonder, then," muttered Belt, "that Nature didn't put the blue on the bird's breast, where the fish could see it, instead of on its back where they can't."

"'The kingfisher's nest is composed of fish-bones and similar substances, cemented together by a sort of glue with which the bird is furnished. She takes possession, for the purpose of nidification, of some deserted rat's or sand-martin's hole, always in the close vicinity of water. She lays three or four pinky-coloured eggs, on which she sits alternately with her mate until they are hatched. If taken from the nest it is difficult, not to say impossible, to bring up the young birds.'"

"And you believe all that, Master B.?"

"Why, yes; it's here in print, you see."

Mr. Belt's face wore an expression that made me ask whether he found anything wrong in the account I had read of the kingfisher and its habits.

"Anything wrong, Master B.? Why it's all wrong altogether—leastways all I can understand of it, as I know who have watched them for these forty years. Kingfisher!—why she makes her own hole; I've seen her at it year after year. She lays *seven* eggs, no more, no less; they are white eggs, they are, and the shell so thin you can see the yolk shining through them; she hatches them all, too—there are seven young kingfishers in the nest as sure as there are seven days in the week. Made of fish-bones!—she don't build no nest at all, but as she sits on her eggs she throws up the bits of bones around her, and the young ones afterwards they do so too, and that makes a sort of wall round them, and a very bad smell it has. I've found a nest a mile from the water or more, and brought up the young ones, too! But go on, Master B., and read about something else, please!"

"Shall I read about pigeons, Mr. Belt?" and taking up another book, I commenced: "We have now arrived at the third order of birds, the *Rasores*—'"

"What's they, Master B.?"

"I'm sure I don't know. Oh yes, I see, they are *scratching* birds; the same as cocks and hens, and pheasants, and partridges, you know."

"Well, they *are* scratching birds, they are, and running birds, too. Pigeons neither scratch nor run, their legs ain't made for it."

"'The nest consists of a few sticks laid across, so thin in substance that the eggs or young may sometimes be distinguished through them from below. This structure is usually sixteen or twenty feet above the ground,'"—("I have seen it five, and I have seen it fifty," muttered Belt)—"'and sufficiently broad to afford room for both parents and their young.'"—("There's room for one old bird at a time, and hardly that.")—"'Two eggs are laid,'" —("That's true!")—"'which are hatched in sixteen or seventeen days.'"—("Depends on which they count from.")—"'The young are supplied with food reproduced from the crops of the parent birds, who, inserting their own beak between the mandibles of the young bird, thus feed them with a soft and pulpy mass.'"*

"Read that again, Master B., will you?" I did so. "Well, I thought I understood it right; and now don't read any more. Why, every one who has ever seen a young pigeon feed knows that it shoves its bill into that of the old one, cock or hen, and sucks away, just as a young calf does at his mother. I have seen two young ones with their heads half down their mother's throat, pressing down till they a'most choked her. That's one of the many differences between pigeons and all other birds that ever I knew; and what's the use of your books, that teach such nonsense as you've been reading to me, Master B.? Better come out on the rounds with me or Sam—Sam knows a thing or two, he does!—and see for yourself, than to go wasting your time in reading books full of ignorance, like them."

Slightly nettled at Mr. Belt's contemptuous rejection of the knowledge I had been so anxious to impart to him, I asked in what respect pigeons differed from other birds, especially birds of their own class.

"Well," said Belt, "look at a pheasant or a barn-

* Yarrell; vol. ii. p. 107.

door fowl, Master B. He has strong legs for running, and strong claws for scratching, but weak wings for flying. Look at a pigeon; he has weak legs for running and weak claws for scratching, but strong wings for flying. Then pigeons pair, fowls don't; pigeons build on trees, fowls on the ground; pigeons lay two eggs *always*, fowls a lot of eggs never alike in number. The cock pigeon sits and helps to feed its young, the cock pheasant don't do either. Chickens can pick and feed themselves as soon as they are born; young pigeons—I have told you how they are fed—are as helpless as any birds I know. Pigeons *drink* like a horse, the others are forced to lift up their heads and let the water trickle down their throats. Pigeons have no gall, fowls have. But I've told you enough of differences, haven't I Master B.?"

I confessed he had considerably enlarged my views on the subject, and began in my heart rather to despise my books.

"And now I'll tell you, Master B., how the young pigeons you eat in pies are fed! and you won't find that in your books, I'll be bound. They are brought up by hand, or by mouth rather. They are taken as squabs from the nest, packed by dozens in a large shallow box or basket, and fed by a dirty, ragged boy, who chews boiled peas and bread and stuff in his mouth, and when it is full of pulp he takes them up two at a time, and lets them routle with their bills one at each corner of his mouth, till they have sucked their little crops as full as they will hold. Then he takes up two more, till his mouth is emptied and their crops filled. That's the way pigeon-pies are made, Master B.!"

CHAPTER III.

DOG-BREAKING.

Mr. BELT had hardly done talking when Sam entered the room, accompanied by a young man of about his own age, who was cordially greeted by Mr. Belt as "Charlie," and by Baby as "Mr. Bond;" the greeting of the young lady being accompanied by an arch, not to say meaning, smile. We had just seated ourselves round the crackling hearth when Baby's especial friend Patty made her appearance, in search, as she said, of Master B., who was sure to be in mischief when he was out of her sight. Patty was evidently quite taken by surprise at the presence of the stranger, whom, however, she appeared to know, and greeted very demurely, blushing at the same time more than the occasion seemed to require. Baby giggled, and a somewhat awkward pause ensued, which was broken by Sam's novel remark, that it was a cold night for the time of year; which proposition being assented to, the conversation became general.

Mr. Charles, or, as Belt called him, Charlie Bond, was the subject of no little gossip and speculation in our little world. Whether Mr. Belt or his son knew who or what he was was uncertain, but assuredly no one else did. He was a good-looking young man, with light hair and whiskers, and his hands showed no signs of hard work; indeed, their complexion and that of his face were those of one who is not much in the open air. He lived at Slowton, our market town, about five miles distant, and that was all that was known of him. Some said that he was a brewer's clerk, some a sign painter; others, again, that he was a "literary gent." He seldom came among us, but was always welcome when he did come. Charlie was a proficient in all athletic sports; when in the mood he would perform the most extraordinary gymnastic tricks, which enthralled my youthful imagination. He could bend himself backwards, and pick up a sixpence off the floor; he could touch the back of his head with his toe, place a glass brimful of water on his head, and stooping down, take a pin from the ground in his mouth without spilling a drop; he could twist himself backwards round the balusters like a snake, or, tying himself as it were in a knot, peep at you from between his legs. I never saw his equal on or off the stage. He was quiet and reserved, and rarely spoke of himself; but I once overheard him tell Mr. Belt that he had a permanent position, a guinea a week, and a good house over his head.

It was, as I afterwards understood, pretty well known that Charlie Bond "kept company" with Patty, who, though she seemed to me to be as old as the patriarchs (for what child's nurse or mother is not old in its eyes?), was a particularly nice-looking young woman. An hour had been passed very pleasantly, when Patty declared it was time for me to go to bed. Charlie offered to see us safe home, and Patty acceded to the proposition, on condition that Baby accompanied us; the result of which arrangement was, that the short path being very narrow, Baby and I walked first by ourselves, and Patty, my natural protector, with Charlie Bond, followed at some little distance. There was a little scuffling and confusion at parting, and Patty for the rest of the evening seemed unusually thoughtful and pensive.

I took my accustomed walk to the keeper's lodge immediately after breakfast next morning, and found Mr. Belt engaged with two of his latest pupils, Shot and Grouse, a brace of promising pointer puppies, well bred and handsome. Shot at my entrance was cowering in a corner, evidently in disgrace and suffering under a consciousness of it; his head, nay his whole body, seemed pressed against the sanded floor, as though he would hide himself, and his beseeching eyes, which alone showed signs of life, appeared to ask piteously for some token of forgiveness. Grouse, on the other hand, sat upright on his haunches, with a self-satisfied expression of countenance which seemed to exult over his humiliated brother, and, with little Jack Horner, to cry, "What a good boy am I!"

"What's the matter with Shot, Mr. Belt?"

"He's misbehaved himself, and I've punished him. That's all."

"Did you flog him, Mr. Belt?"

"Flog him! No; I'd never train a dog that wanted flogging. I ain't like that brute Jerry Cant, that flogs his dogs before he goes into the field to make them mind what they're about, he says. I've got a dog-whip up there, as you see, Master B., and I touches 'em with it at times, just that they may know what the whip is; but I'll have no dogs about me as wants flogging, and I won't flog dogs as don't want it."

"But how do you break your dogs in the field, Mr. Belt?"

"Break's a bad word, Master B.; I *train* my dogs, and I train 'em in this very room"—the room was about twelve feet square. "Look'ee, sir, a dog only wishes to know one thing, and that is what you want him to do; and he only wants to learn one thing, and that is how to do it. Come here, Shot."

Shot, twisting his body into impossible contortions, came wriggling towards his master, his hazel eyes full of moisture, and his thin tail vibrating with a rapidity of motion that made you dread it would break into pieces like a stricken slowworm. Having received the seal of pardon in the shape of a slight caress from Belt's horny hand, the dog at once recovered his natural bearing, and giving a yelp of delight, which was echoed by his now sympathising brother Grouse, sat intently watching his master's eye. Surely man is the dog's god!

"Hold up, good dogs!" said Belt; and the creatures at once bounded about the room. "To-ho!" holding up his hand, and at the word both dropped motionless on the sanded floor. As they lay, Belt took up a gun capped, but not loaded, and snapped both barrels over their heads. Grouse pricked up his ears, but on receipt of a reproving "Down charge, sir!" lay perfectly motionless, until the old man had gone through the form of loading his gun, when another "Hold up, good dogs!" set them on their legs again. I was much interested in the lesson, and begged Mr. Belt to repeat it, but he declined, saying it was quite possible to have too much of a good thing, and it was always unwise to weary a puppy by the repetition of a lesson he had already learnt.

"I shall take them pups into the field to-morrow, Master B., and you'll see how they behave."

"But how do you teach them to point?" I asked.

"Nature teaches them that, Master B. I expect that at first a point was only a pause that a dog made to be sure where the game lay before he sprung upon it; but the pause has been lengthened out, first into a stop and then into a point; and the habit has descended from one generation to another till a well-bred puppy points on coming on the scent of the game just as naturally as he curls himself up to sleep, or shakes himself when he awakes."

"But if he point on the scent of game, why should he not on the scent of anything else—a lark or a sparrow, a cat or a mouse?"

"Why, so he will, Master B.; but he soon learns to take no notice of 'em when he sees you don't. He'll do so all the sooner if he's well treated, mind ye; for where's the use of beating a dog for ignorance, like Jerry Cant does? A dog, like a child, must learn what he is to do, and what he isn't, and flogging only confuses and cows him and keeps him looking at the whip, and thinking of it instead of what you want him to think of. When a puppy points at a lark, or a sparrow, or a mouse, or a snake, just take no notice of him, turn away, or, what he feels most of all, just laugh at him quietly—sneer like: neither dog nor horse can abide being laughed at. There are only three things I *teach* my dogs, and every one knows they're the best in the country: to keep to heel till they're told to hunt; to hunt when they *are* told; and to drop to hand. All the rest comes by nature. And now, Master B., if you'll take my old single barrel, I'll show you a bit how to use it, and give you a lesson indoors first, just as I do the puppies. Lay hold of the gun, sir, and cock it—you know how. Very good; only don't cock it another time until the muzzle has got well away from my line, over my head or down on the ground. You can't have a gun in a better position for cocking than when it's nearly upright; and now, Master B., let's see you put it on half-cock." Touching the trigger with my finger, and holding the hammer with my thumb, I let it gradually down until it caught at the half-cock. "That's a dangerous plan, Master B.; always let the hammer down pretty close upon the cap, and then draw it back till you hear the click. Look here, sir," said he, pointing to a detached lock he was cleaning; "this is the tumbler; and the trigger, you see, catches in one or other of those fine nicks, which make the whole or the half-cock. Letting it down as you did is just like shutting a door by turning the handle: it very often catches without going into the groove, and a shake or a jar will make the lock fly open, or set the gun off. Let the *spring* act, and whether it is door-lock or gun-lock it will hold fast. And now, Master B., go to the other end of the room, and for this once take aim at my eye; and mind, you're never to take aim at any living thing again unless you mean to kill it. But this is a lesson, you know, so put your ramrod down to make sure there is nothing in the barrel, and take your place."

I did so, and the clear ringing sound of the ramrod striking upon the breeching showed that, as he well knew, the barrel was empty.

"Now, sir! turn the muzzle away; cock your gun; place your left hand close to the guard, your right forefinger on it. Look straight at my right eye (no! keep both yours open), and bring your gun up to your shoulder. Very good! and now shut one eye and squint down the barrel, and you'll see that it bears straight upon mine. Now! do the same again, and when you have brought the gun up to the shoulder pull the trigger." I followed my instructions, and had the pleasure of hearing the old man say, "Well done, Master B.! you've a true eye, and if your gun had been loaded I should never have heard the report. And now, never let me see the inside of your barrel again as long as I live, except when I'm cleaning of it. How should you carry your gun? some say up, some down, some on the hollow of your arm, some on the shoulder; they are all right at times, but the real safe way of carrying a gun is *never*, even for a moment, to have the muzzle pointed towards man or beast. And now, Master B., to treat you as I do the puppies, I won't give you too much lesson at once."

Early in the ensuing morning Mr. Belt, the puppies, and myself, were on our way to the trial ground, a large field off which a crop of barley had been taken, the short stubble now hidden by a crop of young clover.

"No, no, Shot! softly, Grouse! go to heel, good dogs," said Belt as we approached the gap. "'Ware fence, 'ware fence," and the puppies, who were coupled together, slunk behind their master as he passed into the barley ash. "And now, puppies," taking off the couples as he spoke, "let's see what you're made of." At a wave of the hand the high-bred dogs bounded forth, and it was both a beautiful and an interesting sight to watch the development of what I must consider the reasoning power as apart from, or in addition to, instinct. At the signal they dashed forward, as I have said, seeking with their noses up-wind for something, they knew not what, —but still, in obedience to their master's signals, quartering the ground and seeking on in blind but undoubting confidence of finding it. Grouse took the lead, Shot following closely, the two running, stopping, turning together, as though animated by one spirit. "Shot is shy and modest, you see, sir, but he'll soon take to hunting on his own account; he has the finer nose of the two, Shot has. So-oftly, puppies! so-oftly!" as with a bewildered, anxious air Shot came to a half stop, and Grouse, who was a few yards ahead, turned towards him. A moment of indecision, and then both dogs stood erect, stiff, rigid, and immovable. Excepting that the muscles of the nose quivered they might have been carved out of stone. How beautiful they looked—every muscle at its full tension, living, but apparently spell-bound. "There, sir," whispered Belt, "that's nature, that's breeding. All the breaking in the world couldn't teach that. They'd stand like that for an hour." Then making a considerable circuit we passed round so as to have the birds between us and the dogs. When within ten yards my companion stopped and pointed out to me a brace of partridges which lay crouched close to the ground within six feet of the dogs' noses, their bright eyes fixed upon us. As my eye met the birds, they rose with whirring wing. Grouse plunged forward, but instantly dropped, as Shot had instinctively done at Belt's warning, "To ho! To ho! Down charge!"

A minute elapsed, and they were allowed to hunt again, their first impulse being to rush frantically about the spot, drinking in as it were the lingering scent: but, without rating, they were gradually removed from the spot, and commenced hunting if possible more systematically than before, with a like result.

In accordance with Nat's practice, this lesson did not last too long, and I found myself at home again before half the family were out of bed.

Were it not that I fear to tire the reader with honest Nat Belt, I could recount many excellent lessons I received from him on every point connected with shooting and dog-breaking, from the loading of my gun to the management of my pointers and the carrying home of the game. The first mainly regarded the safety of myself as well as of others, the second the development of the instincts of the dogs and keeping them in subjection without cowing them. To come up to call or whistle, to keep to heel, to drop to hand or shot, were the essentials. All the rest, Mr. Belt affirmed, came from observation, encouragement, and experience. Certainly I never saw dogs that excelled those broken by Nat Belt, in the ordinary or extraordinary qualities of a pointer. They took the wind, they quartered the ground, they backed, they stood, they dropped to shot, and sometimes a very old and wise one was allowed to retrieve, a young one never.

Nat Belt's dogs were not to be excelled.

CHAPTER IV.

BOYHOOD'S PLEASURES.

I FORGET what the story is in which a little boy, his face ruddy from sliding, his hands red-hot from snowballing, rushes in and proclaims to his mamma his simple wish that it might always be winter; he writes down his wish, and again in the spring, after a butterfly chase, and the manufacture of a cowslip ball, he writes down, "Would it were always spring!" He does the same in summer, and the same in autumn; and the beautiful and truthful moral is, that all seasons have their especial pleasures, and, properly enjoyed, are equally delightful. It is the same with life; that season on which retrospection is fixed for the time appears to have been the most delightful, and it is then that we seem to have truly enjoyed life. Certainly this was a happy time in mine; I had got beyond the age of childhood, and my mind was sufficiently open to enjoy, if not to appreciate, the beauties and wonders of nature.

When my brothers were at home from school, our daily pastimes and pursuits were of a rough, boisterous character, as befitted healthy lads of our age—

> "Turning to mirth all things on earth,
> As only boyhood can."

We flew kites and drove hoops, and played leapfrog, and foot-ball, and quoits, and cricket, according to the seasons. We jumped with poles and without poles, we ran races and performed many pedestrian feats, we scampered over the country on rough ponies, and made life as far as possible one long holiday. A favourite pastime, I remember, was to burrow through the huge heaps of straw which, in those days of indifferent farming, were piled up in the yard after harvest. There was a sense of mysterious loneliness and concealment when we arrived at the centre, and formed a sort of nest, wherein we held high council, and matured deep-laid plan of fun or mischief. Hither, too, we conveyed sundry unconsidered trifles of an esculent nature, and enjoyed our feast beyond any measure which the subject-matter could justify. Stolen waters are sweet; but I think that a bottle of unsugared green gooseberries I once got hold of fairly beat us.

Dragging the pond was one of our greatest delights. We always knew when that event was coming off by the presence of a large tub filled with water at the brink; this was to keep those fish alive which had the good fortune to be returned to their native element. The drag was a source of infinite enjoyment. Mr. Belt superintended, and Sam and Bill, and the gardener and the grooms, and George, the good-natured footman, sometimes even Mr. Stokes, the butler himself, assisted. Then there were such splashings at the sides to drive the great fish to the middle of the pond; such hauling to get the net through the weeds; such anxious pauses to allow it to work; and such intense excitement when, as it approached the shore at the remotest corner, the fish appeared floundering, splashing, and gasping amid the black liquid mud which filled the bag. Hauled ashore, each boy seized by hand, or net, or pot, or pan, such fish as he could appropriate: great sulky pike, gasping carp, slimy tench, slippery eels, one and all, were conveyed, amid shouts of laughter, to the big tub; and the best being selected for food or presents, the rest were returned to be dragged forth on some future festive occasion. Bathing was another of our boyish delights. I think the clay-bottomed pond in which I learned to swim must have been of most modest dimensions, but it was a lake in my eyes, and the first half-crown I ever earned was given me by my father for swimming across it. That half-crown, by the way, I presented in the fulness of my delight to the itinerant proprietor of a Punch and Judy exhibition at Slowton. I occupied the dress circle, that is, I sat on the churchyard wall, and witnessed this, the first theatrical exhibition I had ever seen. The manager, who had received my liberal donation in his hat, voted me a young brick, a word just then coined, and after spitting upon it, pocketed the money with great glee. It appeared at the time—and I am not sure even now that my impression was incorrect—that a horrible act of tyranny was performed when my grandfather, a J.P. for the county, happening to pass by, peremptorily ordered the grumbling vagrant to return the money, under a threat of instant incarceration as a rogue and a vagabond.

Our swimming in the pond excited the curiosity of

those strange, harmless creatures, the water-rats, sole representatives of the ancient family of beavers, a colony of whom—rats, I mean, not beavers—had settled in the banks. They would come out of their holes, and, their light bodies half out of water, glide among us, apparently actuated by simple wonder at our appearance and proceedings. Their reception was not such as their simple confidence deserved; but we were generally too eager and excited to hurt them, and the stupid beasts, after diving once or twice among us, would regain their holes in safety.

Bird-catching, by means of brick traps and wicker baskets, snares and springs, was among our favourite pursuits, and many a score of sparrows, larks, and thrushes were caught by these means, or by the bat-folding nets held against the eaves of the stacks, or the dense evergreens which crowded the house. The gardener generally held the net, one boy carried a lighted lantern suspended on a stick behind it, whilst the others beat the bushes or poked under the eaves in front. The barns and cow-houses, nay, the church tower itself, was visited, and some lighted candles being fixed on the beams on which we were perched, the scared birds, naturally seeking the light were struck down by sticks, or caught in the hand.

Hedge-hopping, too, was a favourite pursuit: we would separate on each side of a hedge, and finding a small bird, chase and pelt and drive him till he was fairly beaten into a corner, and fell a quaking victim into our hands. We would wake an old white owl from her dreamy slumber in some lone field barn, and as she flew forth blinded by the sun and frightened by our shouts, pursue with little less than her own speed, until we had captured or destroyed her. Cruel, all this, I know, but boys think little of the pain they inflict; they are cruel because they are thoughtless, and their thoughtlessness seems to increase in precise proportion to their numerical force. I question whether any boy would alone, under any circumstances, take the life of bird or beast.

I know that for myself, the moment that my brothers and their wild companions had left me, I relapsed into a silent, loving contemplation of Nature, and would sit for hours quiet and motionless on the branch of an old pear-tree—a favourite resort of mine—and mark the humble bee as he went buzzing by, or the sharp, sudden turn of the swallow snapping the winged insect I had disturbed, or watch the pretty, lady-like tree-creeper as it ran like a mouse up the tree against which I leaned; or the beautiful nuthatch fixing within a cleft of the bark, the nut of which, making a fulcrum of his tail and using his sharp bill as a hammer, he would break, and devour the kernel. I took pleasant walks with Belt as he visited his traps, and learnt the habits of the wild creatures stigmatized as vermin—then, as now, the objects of a war of extermination. I learnt to distinguish the track of every four-footed beast, the song, or note, or flight of every bird—and there were many birds then common which, alas! are now extinct or passing rare. The fork-tailed kite sailed gracefully with outstretched, motionless wings aloft in the blue air; the kestrel hovered over the field, the sparrowhawk sat wakeful and watching on the dry branch of the oak at the end of the hedgerow, the hen-harrier beat the low ground with the skill and patience of a setter, and the graceful merlins hunted in pairs. Wild notes of the woodpecker, the jay, and the magpie were heard at every corner; and the presence of a dead horse or beast—not then as now sent to market for human food—was attested within a few hours by the deep croak of the raven, whose mission, with the carrion-crow, the buzzard, and birds of their kind is, like that of the vultures in the East, to remove from the face of the earth decaying animal matter, which might otherwise pollute the wholesome air.

My "joy of youthful sports" was birds'-nesting. Cruel again! I hear some excellent old lady of either sex exclaim. I deny it; there is no cruelty in birds'-nesting, though, as in every other pursuit of boy or man, where he is brought into relation with birds or beasts, it may be made the instrument of cruelty. A vast quantity of mawkish rubbish is talked about the agonies of the bereaved mother, the vain flutterings around the desolate home, and twaddle of that sort. Surely such persons should abstain from eating eggs for breakfast, and eschew batter puddings. Do they suppose that an old hen *likes* to have her newly-laid egg abstracted from the nest? Surely not; she *dislikes* it. She protests against it, she pecks the hand or flies at the face of the hen-wife who removes it, she looks disconsolate when it is removed—for a minute or two, and then—forgets all about it, and prepares to lay another. Why, the Bible itself expressly forbids the Hebrew to stretch forth his hand against the sitting bird, and as expressly permits the taking of the eggs or the capture of the young. Birds'-nesting, I venture to say, brings out more good qualities, mental and physical, in boys than any other pursuit to which they addict themselves. Patience, observation, and endurance are brought into play; a keen eye, a cool head, strong muscles, and well-strung nerves are essential to the pursuit. What system of gymnastics comes up to tree-climbing? It is like a paper-chase to a fox-hunt, a sponging-bath to a free swim in the sea.

But we are not writing an essay, but a history. I repeat, my "joy of youthful sports" was birds'-nesting; and the woods and well-timbered hedgerows which abounded in our neighbourhood afforded ample scope to my favourite pursuit. Scarce a copse but held at least one magpie's or crow's nest, frequently both; and Thorney Wood was never known to be without a buzzard's. In the distant forest of Bolsover, a birds'-nesting paradise in my eyes, all wild birds had their eyries and all wild beasts their lairs. There the kites bred, and the raven and the heron, hawks of all kinds, jays, magpies, and woodpeckers. The bald-headed coot, the merry little grebe, and the graceful moorhen tenanted the lone pools which nestled in its depth; and even woodcocks, snipes, and sandpipers were reported at times to breed within its precincts. Foxes, badgers, hedgehogs, stoats, weasels, and their congeners were safely nurtured within its deep recesses, and from thence spread themselves over the country. My notion of the happy hunting-grounds was a dream of Bolsover Forest.

Mr. Belt entered fully into my enthusiasm on this subject, and besides assisting me to feed and bring up the young birds I brought home—generally of the order *Raptores*, kites, hawks, or buzzards—gave me most useful hints as to the whereabouts and the construction of their nests.

"You talked, Master B., the other day about 'classing,' as you call it, the pigeons along with the cocks and hens. If you had thought of their nests, you would never have made that mistake."

"Why, Mr. Belt," said I, " would you class birds by their nests?"

"And why not, if they are to be classed at all? There is no one thing that birds are so constant and regular in as the making of their nests, more especially in their lining. Whoever saw a wren's or a tit's nest that was not full of feathers, or a warbler's with a feather in it? Did you ever know a blackbird line its nest with aught but fibrous roots, or a songthrush collect any soft lining at all? Did you ever see a finch's nest that was not finished to a hair, or a missel-thrush that had not left a lock of wool hanging over the side? Many a missel's nest has escaped taking from the belief that it had been taken already. The lining of a rook's nest is always slovenly, of twitch and fibrous roots mostly; a carrion crow's is round and smooth as a basin, moss and cow and horsehair. Then look at the little grebe—the didopper, as you call her—she dives down to the bottom of the pool for every morsel of weed with which she lines her nest, though lots of the same sort is floating on the surface; the coot and the moor-hen fetch theirs from a distance; while the swan sits on her nest and catches the floating pieces as they pass."

I acknowledged the uniformity of birds in this matter, and remarked that birds were very clever in the art of concealing their nests; but the old man would not admit this.

"I don't believe, Master B., that they ever think of hiding their nests at all, at least not until they have been taken once or twice; and then, as in everything else, they profit by experience. Why should a bird think that you and I want to take its nest? If they did, they would never come, as they do, near houses and homesteads to build. Nine-tenths of the blackbirds' and the thrushes' nests in a wood are within ten feet of the ride. Nature provides for the protection of the eggs by colouring them like the substances near which they are laid. Eggs on the ground are dark; eggs in the bush are green or blue; white eggs are always hid in holes of trees or banks. There are such like differences in the eggs of different birds; but the same birds line their nests the same way, just as they lay the same eggs."

This axiom I verified in numberless instances in after years. I remember an especial one in a wild part of Ireland called Ballycroy, where I lived for some years. There is not a tree in the barony, not one, I think, within four miles of where I was located. I had observed that the water-ouzel invariably places four or five dried oak leaves beneath the first lining of her nest. On examining one taken close to my house, I found the five leaves oak leaves, as usual. Where did they come from?

CHAPTER V.

BIRDS'-NESTING.

ONE morning in the early spring I had obtained permission to spend a long day in the forest birds'-nesting. Bill was to accompany me, as well to "look after" me as to carry a basket of provisions for our al-fresco dinner, consisting of cold fowl, hard-boiled eggs, and plenty of bread and butter.

Light were my slumbers the night before, and at the first rattle of the gravel against the panes I started from my bed, and throwing the casement open, inhaled the sweet, cool air of the morning, and viewed on the horizon the first streaks of the dawn. Short were our orisons, limited our ablutions; hastily swallowing the cup of still hot tea, placed providently by kind hands on the hob, and taking semicircular bites out of a thick piece of bread and butter, I had within five minutes joined my companion on the lawn; and full of gleeful anticipation, we turned our faces in the direction of the distant forest. Our road lay through the Dene, as the beautifully-wooded narrow valley which stretches away to Thorney Wood was called, and passed close to the Grange, an ancient stone-built house surrounded by a moat now partially filled up. It had been a place of note in its time: a pair of massive pieces of masonry showed where a heavy gate once stood, and local antiquaries could trace the remains of fosse and wall, and other defences. The Grange was now nothing more than an excellent farmhouse, and Mr. Stubbs, with whom I was an especial favourite, its owner and occupant.

As we approached the Grange by the southern entrance, the labourer earliest at his work saluted me with a kindly "Good-morning, Master B.! Up betimes, sir!" and looking over the low wall, I recognized the burly form of Mr. Stubbs himself, standing with his hands in his pockets in the only corner of the yard as yet touched by the early sunbeams, contemplating, apparently with much satisfaction, a cluster of two-year old Devon beasts, some of which were lazily stretching themselves, the majority lying asleep, but still chewing the cud, among the thick, dry straw. A greyhound sat on its haunches, nestling his long nose against the flap of Mr. Stubbs's pocket, in search of the hidden hand; and a little rough terrier at his feet, aware of my approach, growled wickedly. Some well-bred, short-faced, fine-coated breeding sows poked their heads out of the litter as they heard the gate-latch rattle, anticipating breakfast; a long line of white Dorking fowls were stepping, in apparently endless succession, in single file, jerkingly out of the hen-house; and a multitude of pigeons overhead emerged from their cote, in little clusters of threes and fours, and commenced ruccattuctooing and bowing to each other in most absurd fashion. A picture of peace and plenty and animal comfort was that farmyard, and dearly did Mr. Stubbs, its presiding genius, love it. I was received with a warm grasp of the hand; and a hearty invitation to breakfast having been declined on the ground of my recent meal, we proceeded together to the house, where my refusal was condoned by the acceptance of a tumbler of rum and milk. We found Mrs. Stubbs and her daughter

Susan in the large hall which served for the general sitting-room of the family; and Mrs. Stubbs, who prided herself on being a farmer's wife, as she was a farmer's daughter, proceeded to the dairy to bring the milk with her own hands. Susan, whose delight it had been to play at nursing me as a baby some ten years before, gave me a hearty kiss, at which Mr. Stubbs laughed, and made some allusion to somebody being jealous. Susan Stubbs was about twenty, a good-tempered, fresh-coloured, smiling girl, with the brightest of eyes and the softest of hair, her nose slightly turned up and her mouth rather too wide for perfect beauty; but as the only daughter and heiress of Mr. Stubbs of the Grange, generally recognised as such. It was understood that amongst her numerous admirers Susan had but to pick and choose. For my own part, I may confess that, next to Baby Belt, I adored Susan Stubbs.

Her mother soon returned with the milk, sweet, warm, and frothing from the pail; a bottle of rum and a sweet cake being produced from a corner cupboard, I, for the first time in my life, tasted that delectable compound, rum and milk. It was possible I might have liked the milk pure and simple better, but there was a charm in the novelty, and rum and milk sounded so manly. I swallowed my tumbler at a draught; Bill, to whom, sitting by the kitchen fire, Mrs. Stubbs had kindly taken a similar jorum, sat prolonging the enjoyment by sipping it slowly, and with intense delight.

"How's the fox, Mr. Stubbs?" said I; "how's Charlie?"

"Oh! he's right enough, Master B. Crafty vagabond! Come and see him."

Truth to tell, a visit to Mr. Stubbs's fox had been almost as much in my mind as the visit to himself and his charming family. "Charlie," the only fox I had ever seen, was an object of unceasing interest to me. His kennel was under the old moss-grown stone steps, constructed long ago to aid the heavily-attired horseman to climb to his bulky steed; they stood beneath a huge elm-tree which grew on the north side of the house. Charlie, a collar round his neck, with chain attached to a strong post, was seen as we approached stretched on the topmost step, his nose hidden between his forepaws, his ears laid flat to his head, his bushy tail at full length in a line with his body. As we came nearer he retained his position, but seemed to press himself closer and closer to the stone, and remained motionless.

"Charlie, you rascal!" said Mr. Stubbs, "what mischief have you been up to now? Eh, Charlie?"

The creature seemed to realise the fact that no compliment was expressed or intended; he opened his mouth to the utmost stretch of which it was capable, displaying a formidable array of sharp teeth, and made a very peculiar noise, which came from his throat, and gave the idea of his having a bone stuck in it.

"Look at him, Master B. Look at him now! The cunning of that crittur beats all I've ever seen or heard of. Would you believe it, he has made two runs round his kennel, so as to cheat the chickens?"

There certainly were two—an inner and an outer, whatever might have been Charlie's intention in making them.

"You see, the fowls soon learnt by experience how far Master Charlie could spring, and always kept outside the ring he had made by running round and round at the full stretch of his chain; so what does he do but make an inner ring, and when the chickens come to pick a bone or any bit of food he may have left (I believe the villain leaves it on purpose), he is down upon them in no time. He killed two last week and buried them. Eh, Charlie? You rogue, you!"

Charlie hawked up another snarl from the pit of his stomach.

"Buried them! Where!"

"Why, under those two stones he has managed to loosen in the pavement; and he will take them up and replace them, too, in less time than it takes me to tell you. I one day laid a pheasant and a rabbit down just here, and turned away but for a moment to speak to a labourer; the pheasant had vanished, and it was only one of his tail feathers sticking out from under the stone that saved me from thinking I was bewitched."

"That looks as if foxes liked pheasants better than rabbits, Mr. Stubbs?"

"So my lord's keeper said; but it's no such thing. The pheasant lay the handiest, so he took it and buried it, as I told you; he had no time for choice. There's nothing, excepting a rat, that a fox likes so much as a rabbit."

We were soon on our road again, our spirits, mine especially, buoyant, boiling over. Perhaps the unaccustomed stimulant had something to do with it; but there was enough to make me joyous without that. Healthy and strong, without fear or care, engaged in the pursuit I loved best, why should I not be happy?

It was a lovely morning, the newly-risen sun made the dewdrops glisten like diamonds on the twigs, the birds sang around and above us, the air was fresh and wholesome, and all Nature seemed to rejoice with us; why should we not be happy?

"Can you sing, Bill?" said I. Bill thought he could, but didn't know any words except those of the Morning Hymn, which he had learnt at Sunday school, and which he believed was only sung "to the praise and glory of God." I proposed that he should sing to the praise and glory of God then and there, which Bill did; and I still think that the hymn was neither out of season nor out of place. After that I sang "How doth the little busy bee," to the same tune, and so we went rejoicing on our way. "Arcades ambo et cantando pares," as I afterwards learnt to quote.

Bolsover Forest was reached at last, and we lost no time in plunging into its deepest recesses—down long natural avenues, beneath oldest moss-grown oaks, crooked thorns, and ancient nuts with trunks like forest trees, and so on by copse and thicket, dell and dingle, wild waste, and swampy rush-grown pasture. Our search had been most successful with regard to the number of eggs, but those which we

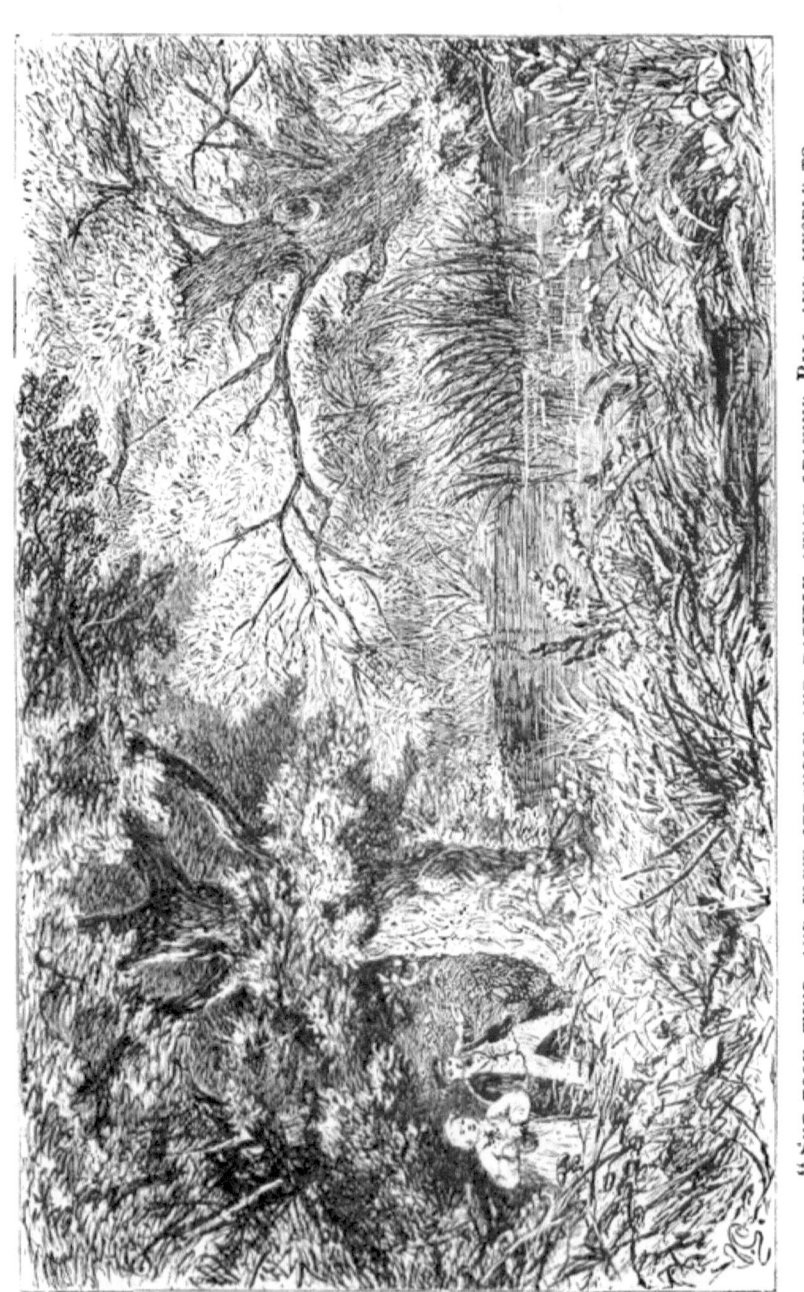

"SHE TOOK WING, AND FLEW STRONGLY AND RAPIDLY AWAY, LEAVING BILL AND MYSELF TO STARE AT EACH OTHER." *Page* 223.

had found were generally the more common ones. The summer birds indeed, although they had arrived, had not as yet built their nests. Our collection comprised nothing beyond blackbirds' and thrushes', hedge-sparrows', chaffinches', and robins', of the smaller birds; a few rooks', magpies', and a single kestrel's of the larger. As we passed along the dank, sedgy outskirts of a deep black pool which, fringed with alders and tussocks of grass, covered many acres of ground, a wounded duck started at my feet; the poor thing could scarcely fly, and with difficulty fluttered along just out of reach of my hand. What I meant to do with it I cannot tell; but a boy, like a puppy, runs after every living thing that runs away from him. In a moment, shouting to Bill to keep near the edge and cut her off from the water, I was in hot pursuit, dashing over the stumps, tumbling over the tussocks, splashing through the pools, ever on the point of catching the wretched bird, which, with terrified cries, still managed to keep just out of reach. I came to a place where the pool, stretching into a sort of bay, intercepted my further progress, when, to my surprise, after fluttering for a few yards along the water, she took wing, and flew strongly and rapidly away, leaving Bill and myself to stare at each other in mute amazement. We had had just the same kind of chase after a lapwing while crossing the bleak common which lay between Thorney Wood and the forest as we approached it in the morning, and we agreed that it was a singular coincidence. As we walked round the bay, our attention was attracted by two or three nests, not unlike rooks' nests, but larger, built in a little clump of picturesque Scotch firs. At our approach, some herons, their long legs stretched behind them, and forming a counterpoise to their prominent necks, took wing, and with wild cries of alarm flew far away. How my heart beat! This must be the heronry which I had heard and dreamt of, but never hoped to see. A heron's egg was the grand desideratum for my collection, and now the great prize seemed within my grasp! On our examining the trees, however, one, and one only, appeared possible to be climbed, but on this was a nest from which we had seen the old bird depart, so we knew for a certainty there were eggs in it. The tree grew on the bank overhanging the tarn, and leaned over the water at a very considerable angle, the great roots which held it being twisted into the bank like the shrouds of a raking schooner-rigged vessel. There were no boughs until near the top, and the nest was at the extremity of one of the lowest of them, but after the first twelve or fifteen feet there were broken spikes sticking out, the remnants of former branches which had been broken by the tempest or by the weight of the snow. Bill wished to venture, but I would not allow it; the honour of taking a heron's nest was too great to be surrendered. In three seconds my jacket was off, and Bill pushing behind, I had commenced swarming towards the coveted prize. The girth of the tree was considerable, but, as I said, it leant over the water at a great angle; the bark too was rough, affording finger-hold betwixt its interstices, and the sugar-loaf buttons on my waistcoat, of which, as was the fashion in those days, there was a favourable eruption, rather assisted me. The spikes, though dead, were not rotten, and eventually I found myself at the base of the branch on which, at the distance of a few feet, the great flat nest was placed. The branch, either naturally, or from the weight placed upon it, bent rather downwards, and I could see its contents, three green eggs, larger than a crows', and much longer, indeed, so long in proportion to their breadth as to be unlike any other bird's I had ever seen. I suppose a heron requires a long egg wherein to pack its long legs.

Pausing for a moment to recover my breath and to steady my nerve, I commenced the dangerous process of climbing along the nearly horizontal bough towards the nest. This, as every bird's-nester knows, is a very ticklish and difficult operation. As you look downwards there is nothing betwixt you and the ground to break your fall should an accident happen, and the ground looks such a terrible depth below you! In this case it was doubly terrifying, for I was immediately over the deep silent pool I have described; and as I involuntarily cast my eyes downwards for a second, it seemed as though a fathomless abyss were beneath me, a new sky somewhere in the remotest depths, and a chubby-faced boy suspended in mid-air gazing upwards at me. Closing my eyes for a second, and repressing with some difficulty a feeling of giddiness, I scrambled onwards, fixing them steadily on the goal of my hopes, and striving, though not with entire success, to close them upon all beside. I reached the nest at last; it was a large, flat structure, composed, like a rook's, externally of sticks, and lined almost entirely with wool. It contained, as I have said, three eggs, two of which I managed to transfer—wrapped up in my little blue pocket-handkerchief—to that general receptacle of a boy's treasures, my cap, and replaced it carefully on my head, tying the strings beneath my chin. How to carry the other was the question. It was too large for my mouth, and, after some reflection, I put it into my trousers pocket, and prepared to descend from my perilous position. Alas! this was no easy matter; the "facilis descensus" is all very well under certain circumstances, but under existing ones the "descensus" was exactly the reverse, and "revocare gradum" was indeed the work. Lying full-length flat upon the bough, and carefully dragging myself backwards, I had got safely over some four or five feet, and was hoping to feel the trunk of the tree I dared not turn my head to look for, when, from the tightness of my trousers, I felt the egg in my pocket break with a crunch. An involuntary start threw me off my balance, and in an instant I had swung round beneath the bough, and, unable to retain my hold, found myself traversing the air towards that mock heaven I had contemplated a few seconds before.

When consciousness returned, I found myself stretched at length on the sunny bank to which the devoted Bill, having rescued me from the pool at the imminent risk of his own life, had dragged me. He was leaning over me, uttering ejaculations of grief and despair, for the lad loved me well, and he thought me dead. Possibly some dread of personal consequences might obtrude itself, and add intensity to his grief, for human motives are never absolutely pure, but his grief was genuine and extreme. "What'll missus say? Oh dear! oh dear? What'll missus say? Master B., Master B.! Pray look up, sir! Oh dear, oh dear!" and then "da capo." Gradually I found strength to comply with his request, and Bill's joy was unbounded when at last I opened my eyes, and gazing dreamingly upon him, asked, "Are the eggs broken?" The answer that they were all right did more to revive me than any ordinary restoratives, had they been at hand, could have done, and I was soon able, with Bill's assistance, and wrapped in his dry coat—for he had fortunately carried that garment in his hand—to reach the edge of the forest, where he left me to proceed at my leisure, and running on to the Grange, speedily returned with Mr. Stubbs in the dog-cart, who brought Susan with him, and wraps and shawls, and much condolence and kind words, and I was taken home and put to bed, from which—for some sort of fever ensued—I did not rise for a month, and then I learnt that, in recognition of the spirited act by which he had saved my life, my father had promised to bind Bill apprentice to any trade he might select. Bill was delighted, for he had always had a soul above cow-boying; Mr. Belt and his wife were grateful, Baby charmed, and I was reconciled to the loss of my playmate by the pleasing intelligence that I was to be sent at once to school.

Bill, at his own request, was bound 'prentice to Mr. Allonby, the well-known white- and black-smith at Slowton, a master of his craft, whose fame extended many miles beyond the town he lived in. Mr. Allonby was especially great as a lock-smith; and Bill, who was a handy lad, and had a natural turn for practical mechanics, could hardly, I think, have chosen better for himself. Some years elapsed before we met again.

CHAPTER VI.

SCHOOL DAYS.

My first school, Ashwell, was kept by a Mr. Payne, and well did he deserve the name, if the infliction of pain on others could justify the nomenclature.

> "Severe by rule nor yet by nature mild,
> He never spared the rod and spoiled the child,
> But spoiled the rod and never spared the child,
> And so with holy rule deemed he was reconciled."

I was flogged continually; I remember the first time was for jumping out of the window of the schoolroom, wherein I had been accidentally locked. I broke a fall of full sixteen feet by catching at a projecting course of bricks, and alighted uninjured on my feet. Nowadays I should have been much praised as a promising athlete, but old Payne, who, looking out of his window, chanced to see me, saw the matter in a different light, and incontinently flogged me. It was a painful process at first, but I soon got use to it. I was flogged for breaking bounds, flogged because my books were stolen, flogged because my cap was lost, or my clothes torn, flogged for not learning lessons beyond my powers, flogged for charging Mother Hardy with stealing my money—a whey-faced old cat! I say that she appropriated three-and-sixpence out of the five shillings I had so confidently intrusted to her keeping. Mother Hardy may be dead now, or she may be alive, but dead or alive, she stole my three-and-six-pence, though I were to be flogged again for it to-morrow! I was starved too; starvation was common enough in those days, even in schools of high character and good repute. Schoolboys of the present day have little notion what their fathers endured before them. True, we had beef and mutton, mutton and beef, boiled rice puddings, and suet dumplings; but the meat which was not boiled to a rag was half raw; and that which was neither raw nor overboiled was baked in a close, dirty oven, and had an unpleasant smell and taste. I could not eat it, and I was flogged to mend my appetite, which it entirely failed to do. I volunteered as assistant to

Harry Hase, the pink and white youth who cleaned (?) our knives and forks. Poor lad, he was in a galloping consumption, and his appetite completely gone. My wages were the roll and cheese allowed for his supper, and which he could not eat; I could, and did, but it was found out, and I was flogged, and Harry Hase discharged.

These were not the pleasantest days of my life; still I have pleasant recollections in connection with them. I had a bosom friend, Charles Wilson, a lad of the same age and like tastes with myself. He was the son of a baronet, and on that account rather favoured by the tuft-hunting old Payne, though he loved flogging too well to let him off altogether. We had a joint purse, and, distrustful of the Hardy bank of deposit, we invested our capital in the purchase of a pistol, and when we could muster powder and shot, and had managed to escape through the washhouse window, or over the playground wall, we roamed forth in search of small birds, at which we constantly fired; but, so far as I remember, without inflicting any serious damage. A wild hope of shooting higher game was cherished in our bosoms, and we wandered, despite the keepers, through the well-preserved woods of the Duke of Churchland. In our own eyes we were elevated to all the dignity of poachers; and doubtless the keepers, had they caught us, would have indulged the fancy, and " fooled us to the top of our bent," but we were hard to catch in those days, and kept a sharp look-out. The woods were very beautiful, and abounded in the spring-time with wild snowdrops and lilies of the valley, the latter a flower I have never met with wild elsewhere in England, though in parts of North Wales it is common. There were lakes in the duke's park, with small islands in them, on which the swans and ducks nested, I have swum across in bitter cold spring weather, and robbed either nest. Snakes, slowworms, and adders were very numerous, and we captured them with as much adroitness and absence of fear as any Indian snake-charmer could have shown. The snakes I would seize wherever I saw them, and, regardless of their twisting round my arm, transfer them to the game-bag, and carry them home. A harmless beast the snake, he possesses but one weapon of defence, and very offensive that is; he has the power at pleasure of emitting a fetid and most disgusting odour, which it is almost impossible to wash out or get rid of. Luckily, he only resorts to this as a last extremity, and if properly treated, may be handled with perfect impunity. Slowworms we generally killed; why, I cannot say, except that the fact being ascertained that a blow with a thin stick disintegrated the creature, and having no capacity for being made a pet of, such blow was usually administered for the sake of realising that, to him and to us, interesting fact.

With vipers more caution was used: we recognised the venomous beast by the flat head and wicked eye. A forked stick was cut and thrust suddenly over his neck into the ground; thus secured he was teased into biting a bit of cloth, or flannel, which was snatched away until the poison was exhausted or the fangs extracted. I believe both would have grown again, but they never had the chance. Our comrades tolerated the snakes, but there were weird stories of the effects of viper bites, and they were invariably slain. The snakes, on the other hand, were much petted; they were kept in a white deal box, with plenty of moss, and fed daily with milk.* Sometimes a frog was given, but not often, for the frog must be alive, or the creature would not touch it. On such occasions, a single frog was shut up in a box with a single snake, which speedily swallowed the

* I am by no means certain that they drank it, though at the time I had no doubt about it.

helpless, staring, squeaking, struggling batrachian. The disgusting cruelty practised, more especially on Sundays, at the Zoological Gardens, principally for the amusement of ladies (?) and children, of dropping a frog amongst a colony of snakes, each of which seizes a separate portion of the writhing victim, prolonging its terror and torture for an indefinite time, was abhorrent to our nature.* The snakes, I think, knew us, and would crawl up our jacket-sleeves, and poke their lithe necks out at the collars, twisting round our ears with great apparent satisfaction to themselves.

There was a hornets' nest, I remember, built at an angle formed by the wooden roof of a shed, where it rested on the paling, the boundary of our playground.

* Since writing the above I have been made acquainted with another instance of horrible and useless cruelty constantly practised in these gardens, and which requires only to be known to be put a stop to, by the humane and intelligent managers of that popular institution. Pigeons and sparrows with their quill feathers plucked out, and thereby disabled from flying, are introduced to the dens of the python and other snakes. Frogs may or may not feel acutely. I think they do not; but there is no question about the sensitiveness of these warm-blooded creatures. The stupid rabbit is ignorant or careless of the presence of its deadly enemy, but with the birds it is different; their agony is intense, and the cruel mutilation they have endured renders them incapable even of flight. Morbid

The other boys were somehow afraid of it. One who had carelessly slammed the door and shaken the fabric had been stung on the head. There was a tradition that five hornets could kill a horse, and, with laudable prudence, my companions gave the nest a wide berth. I had no fear of the hornets; in fact, in those days, through ignorance, I suppose, I did not know what fear meant; I feared no creature, bird, beast, or insect, at any rate. My favourite position was on one of the posts which supported the palings, with my head as close to the nest as it well could be, listening to the unintelligible but continuous hum of conversation kept up by the inhabitants within, and watching with deep interest the proceedings of those who went forth on foraging or predatory expeditions. I don't think I learnt much, but I observed a good deal, and some things which I am still unable to

sentimentality is not at all in my line, and I gladly avoid a description of the sufferings of the victims—sufferings which conduce to no end whatsoever, scientific or otherwise, for what is learned by witnessing a boa-constrictor gorge himself with a half-plucked, agonized pigeon? Surely stuffed specimens of foreign snakes would answer every purpose better even than live ones, for they need not be wrapped in blankets, and if by a simple mechanical contrivance their jaws were made to open occasionally not one visitor in ten thousand would ever find out the difference.

account for. How did the nest increase, as it did, from the size of a turnip to that of the largest pumpkin? The loose outside "papier-maché" shell grew like a vegetable daily, but I never saw a hornet at work outside. The combs, no doubt, were added to and enlarged, and the outer covering grew, and was enlarged proportionally; but how? Besides the main entrance there were several external covered ways by which the insects took their departure, but I never saw one that flew straight away either from gate or postern; they invariably walked, not only over the surface of the nest, but along some two feet of boarding, until they came to an especial angle, whence, with a solemn twang, that is now always associated in my mind with the departure of the spirits through the mouths of the dead companions of the Ancient Mariner, they flew away far and fast in a direct and undeviating career.

> "And every soul it passed me by,
> Like the whirr of my cross-bow."

When they returned, they brought with them food, or building materials, or water; the first generally consisting of the trunk of a large fly neatly packed, that is, with legs and wings bitten off close to the body; the second of a pellet of moistened wood;

and the third, a clearest drop of dew or water, retained between the proboscis and mandibles. Thirsty souls, those hornets! for half, at least, brought water. In October I witnessed the operation of that strange instinct, inverse "storgé," which teaches the Indian squaw in purest love to destroy her female offspring, to save the child from the miseries of a squaw life, and the wasp and hornet to drag forth their embryo young, rather than expose them to a lingering death from starvation and cold—their assured fate if permitted at that season of the year to arrive at wasp or hornet estate.

While at Ashwell I had proof of the extraordinary perseverance of that despised animal, the rat. He is in fact one of the most persistent and indefatigable beasts in creation. Whatever he undertakes, be it for good or be it for ill, he goes through with to the end. The one I am now thinking of worked regularly, day by day, for more than a year, at a self-imposed task, and eventually completed it, but little to his own gain.

The hours at second school were from ten to one, and for an hour after that the first class remained "doing" mathematics. Of course there was at this time a great silence, the more observable from the cessation of the previous hum of many voices.

School Days.

In the first quiet hour after Midsummer holidays a rat was heard gnawing at the oaken floor beneath our feet. Crake! crake! In vain I endeavoured to fix my mind on the problem before me: "*From the point A*"—crake! crake! my soul is absorbed in the well-understood sound, and will take in nothing else—"*describe the circle B C D.*" Crake! crake! crake! It is of no use—the first problem of Euclid, the keystone of the arch, is as a thing of nought; the problem working in my mind is, When will the creature appear? How long will it take it to gnaw through the time-hardened oaken boards, three inches thick, that form the floor? A long time, surely; but it proved far longer than I could have imagined. Crake! crake! I attribute my subsequent failure in mathematics at Cambridge to that rat's proceedings. Euclid had no chance against the absorbing interest excited in my mind by the monotonous "crake" of the persevering rodent.

It was not until the end of the second half-year that a portion of the long yellow teeth appeared above the board, shortly followed by the pinky-white tip of a restless inquiring nose; but weeks elapsed before the hole was sufficiently enlarged to admit of the passage of the rest of the body. At last the day came. No doubt *Mus Rattus* prided himself on the successful result of his labours, and uttered some commonplaces on the beneficial results of perseverance. "Now," said he, "I shall have what I have toiled for—a complete run over as well as under this hard solid floor." Alas for the vanity of rattish wishes! By means of a dictionary cover I had long since contrived a sort of sliding door, which worked by a string over the increasing aperture, and the first appearance of the deluded beast was his last on that or any other stage. Scarcely had he set foot on this new territory than the cover closed over the hole, and he found himself a prisoner at large in the long-coveted domain. The hole it had taken months to open was closed in a moment—carefully stopped, and a ferret, the property of the groom-gardener, placed upon the floor.

It is always curious and interesting to observe the workings of instinct in animals naturally antagonistic to each other; in none more so than in the case of the ferret and the rat.

I should say that Rat, after a few vain attempts to regain his home, had taken matters pretty easily. Cantering quietly round the room, seeking meanwhile for some outlet, he had evidently taken in the whole situation, and prepared himself for an emergency by retiring to the darkest corner, where he sat hunching up his back, occasionally washing his whiskers, and moving them as well as his nose rapidly and nervously. Although put down at the furthest end of the room, the rat was evidently aware of the presence of his deadly enemy the instant the ferret touched the floor, and at once altered his tactics, taking up a fresh position with his back to the light, where, availing himself of a slight inequality in the skirting-board, he sat firm and fast.

> "Come one, come all! This rock shall fly
> From its firm base as soon as I!"

The ferret meanwhile had commenced running the scent, inch by inch, foot by foot, turning where the rat had turned, pausing where the rat had paused, but ever, with depressed body and nose close to the boards, approaching the spot where, full in view, though in deep shadow, uneasily watching her movements, sat the doomed intruder.

The ferret approaches, and is now within full view of her quarry, which hitherto she has not seen. The rat, springing on all-fours six inches off the ground, utters a shrill cry of mingled terror and defiance, and makes a feint of attack. Now is the time when, certain of its true position, the ferret should rush in and slay the rat, which, as I have elsewhere said, is no match for her—no, not even for a second; but few, excepting an old dog-ferret, will do a "deed of such derring-do." The pretty doe now on the floor deems discretion the better part of valour; and it is curious to see her affected air of ignorance as to the meaning of the squeak and the whereabouts of the utterer. She looks like a bully who, having chased a small boy with evil intent, finds himself suddenly confronted by his big brother. After a movement or two of indecision she pretends to look round, and snuffs about as though to recover the scent, and then, crossing to the corner at which she had begun to hunt, takes up the old scent again with affected eagerness. Her owner, who feels for her disgrace, catches her up, and an old dog-ferret being, despite my indignant remonstrances, introduced, speedily puts a stop to the poor rat's vapouring.

I stayed at Ashwell some three years, and then having had really a good deal of Greek and Latin for my age flogged into me, and with a thorough knowledge of boot and shoe cleaning, I was transferred to Downham, now one of the largest and best schools in England; then, although richly endowed, a very small one of some forty boys, of whom two or three went to Cambridge annually, and enjoyed the scholarships which fell to their lot without any great exertion on their own parts.

Of course during these three years I had been at home for my holidays. Things and persons remained from half to half very much as I had left them. Mr. Belt had grown somewhat older, and transferred more and more of his duties into Sam's willing hands. Sam himself was the pattern of a keeper, active, steady, sober, but of an unsocial disposition, as a keeper must be; he was not a popular character, and few out of his own family cared for him or knew his good qualities. Sam, in short, was not generally liked, but he was a fine, strapping fellow, and found favour in the eyes of Jemima the cook, to whom he paid a weekly visit, when he generally sat or stood by her side in a dreary attitude in the back kitchen some twenty minutes almost without speaking a word. However, though they spoke little, they understood one another. The rather monotonous proceeding was relieved by an occasional squeeze on the part of the swain and a coy " Don't " on that of the damsel. It was perfectly understood in the village that Jerry Cant, who had aspired to the fair hand of Jemima, had had his nose put out of joint by Sam Belt. Baby was still unmarried, but had many admirers, among others the rejected Jerry. Patty, after many inward misgivings, had married the mysterious Charlie Bond, who, it appeared, was turnkey, or "second officer," as he styled himself, at the county gaol at Slowton. Bill was going on capitally at Mr. Allonby's, and before I went to Downham I took the opportunity of paying him a visit. I found Bill with a black face, and still blacker hands, sitting in a little detached hole opening out of the shop, filing away at a large key of apparently delicate workmanship. He greeted me warmly, and despite the colour of his, our hands met in the closest squeeze. He told me he was working at the key of the condemned cell in Slowton Prison, but he had made a mistake, and was doing it all over again. "You see, Master B.," he said, "I have cut out this little bit which ought to touch the tumbler." "Then it would not act on the lock?" I said. "Oh yes! it would," replied Bill, "but it would be a skeleton key, you see. I wouldn't like to show Mr. Allonby a piece of work like that;" and throwing the key down on a heap of old iron by his side, he selected a new piece, and commenced patiently filing away at it.

CHAPTER VII.

RATCATCHING.

Our school days are generally supposed to have been the happiest of our lives, and that might be truly said of mine at Downham. We were allowed much liberty; in fact, so long as we answered roll-call in the course of the afternoon, we wandered over the country pretty much at our own sweet will. My early acquaintance with the habits of birds and beasts, my skill in the management of dogs and ferrets, acquired under Nat Belt's tuition, and a natural aptitude for such pursuits as boys chiefly affect, placed me at once in a high position among my schoolfellows. I was the leader in all outdoor sports requiring strength and agility, the fox in the paper-chase, and the captain in the snowballing matches. Above all, my taste for birds'-nesting had full scope. I think that I knew the nest of every large bird within four miles of Downham. Then I possessed a wonderful breed of ferrets and a couple of rough-mouthed terriers, mother and daughter, rejoicing in the names of Old Vic and Young Vic. I may mention a singular circumstance relating to the younger Vic, who, from a propensity to seek me out in school, or church, or other forbidden places, was sentenced to banishment. I gave her to a friend at Slowton, fully five miles from our abode. On my way home each half-year I passed through the town, and that was all, and yet during several years that I remained at school, Vic never failed to present herself at the house within twelve hours of my arrival for the holidays. How did she know I was at home? She never, so far as I could learn, came during the half to inquire. I can give no explanation, but such was the fact.

There was a long-legged, weak-eyed, shambling sort of a fellow, called Frank Beading, who kept our dogs, and aided and abetted in our forbidden pursuits, such as ratcatching, rabbit-hunting, and the like. Frank was, I suspect, a poacher, and found it con-

venient to have the dogs, which were as much his as
ours, kept without expense to himself, and no doubt
they were used by night and by day without our
knowledge; at any rate, they were often very stiff
and tired when wanted. They became, though, one
and all, almost supernaturally knowing. Well do I
remember them each one, and their peculiarities:
there was old Busy, an ugly mugger's cur, a cross
between a bulldog and a pointer, tawny in colour,
sulky in temper, but wondrous wise; there was Old
Vic, recorded above, a black and tan terrier with a
grey muzzle, and, excepting that she was too long
in the leg, really handsome; she was rather hasty and
excitable, but a capital ratter, and fast enough to run
a rabbit down. There was Nettle, a white terrier,
with no legs to speak of, showing a stain of the turn-
spit, who had the remarkable faculty of knowing the
footstep of every boy in the school; she boarded at a
saddler's, and, though ready to tear the house down
at the approach of a strange footstep, would jump
from her seat, and hurry to the door to meet any one
of the dozen lads who might chance to be sent for
her, and accompany him to the trysting place. There
was old Pincher and little Pincher, valuable curs, but,
excepting for the fate which befel the former, and

which I may record hereafter, there was little of interest attached to the character of either.

Such was our ratting establishment; but before I left Downham my ideas had become enlarged, and I had set up the prettiest little pack of beagles that ever ran in hopeless pursuit of a hare. Frank Beading was kennel huntsman, feeder, and so on, but I hunted my own hounds in the field; the pack consisted of five, Tippler and Tuneful, Lavish, Lasher, and little Fiddler, a rough nondescript animal, with a hoarse voice like to nothing canine or human that has ever met my ears since. A capital hound, however, was Fiddler, and always led the cry. We hunted rabbits in the hedgerows, and sometimes a hare, when we could find one; but the little hounds having, on one or two occasions, run clean away from us, we obtained a leveret, which was regularly hunted every half-holiday, and when caught replaced in her basket and carried home. The little hounds would hunt her with the greatest eagerness, but coming up to the place where she had lain down, which she generally did after five or ten minutes, they would stretch themselves lazily by her side, and except, perhaps, licking her fur, pay no attention whatever to her, but wait quietly till we came up. I do not think

the hare was the least afraid; she ran away, to be
sure, and crouched down, as " 'tis her nature to," but
when returned to the basket, she instantly began to
feed, and so, on the whole, enjoyed her life as much,
I think, as any other hare. By degrees she grew
bigger and stronger, our runs were longer, and eventually she run us clean out of scent and time, and
escaped. I took the pack home in a hamper, and sold
them to my uncle, one of the best sportsmen in
England, for the first five-pound note it was ever my
lot to possess.

It was little that in those days was thought about
High Church and Low Church. Had the clergyman
preached in a red coat, hardly less astonishment
would have been excited than if he had preached in a
white surplice. The rubrics were, however, diligently
and anxiously consulted by us to find out the saints'
days, on each of which, by ancient prescription, we
claimed a whole holiday. One, I think, St. Matthias,
falls early in the year, February or March, and we
had arranged to celebrate the day by an especial rat-hunt. No little strategic science was brought into
play on such occasions. Dogs and ferrets were
forbidden ware; I hardly think they were even
knowingly connived at by our worthy doctor, a

capital classic and a good mathematician, but as ignorant of boy-nature as he was of that of bird or beast. If he thought at all about a hawk and her egg, it was to wonder whether the one originally came from the other, or the other from the one; whether the hawk produced the egg, or the egg produced the hawk, or which or either; there was a Lord Dundrearyism about the doctor, which prevented his ever running a scent down, or arriving at any conclusion out of Euclid from given premises. He would see the ferrets, for instance, in the bottom study, in which they were kept, and deduced from seeing them nothing beyond the fact that boys loved pets, and selected very strange ones. Dogs would stray into the court, and he would simply wonder what attraction there could be for the dogs there. He would occasionally visit the home-made nests of hawks or crows, and it never occurred to him that they must have come from the preserved woods into which we were warned not to enter. When Colonel L———, master of the hounds, complained of our yelping curs disturbing his best coverts, I suggested to the doctor, who took sweet counsel with me on the occasion, that he must refer to the paper-chases, and the doctor, accepting the explanation, looked upon the colonel as a harsh, disagreeable sort of a person, averse to boys' natural and healthful amusements, and answered his letter in a style that effectually precluded further correspondence. I have seen a brace of foxes go away from the Gorse where we had been rabbiting the morning before the hounds met there and drew blank.

On the morning referred to, our arrangements were of the most elaborate kind. Three or four junior boys met us with the dogs at the tollgate, and when my companion and myself joined them with the ferrets in a bag, two trotted on before by way of advance guard. If they came upon the master as they rounded a corner, an agreed signal was to be given, which sent us with our curs scampering across the fields at too great a distance to be recognised; but no such misadventure occurred, and we got over two miles of road within the first twenty minutes. Warley Wood lay between us and the farm for which we were bound, and through this with one companion I made my way, the other boys taking the dogs by the road. Scarcely had we entered when a wild wail was heard overhead, and looking upwards we saw a pair of buzzards flapping their great round wings, and settling ever and again despondingly on an oak a little in advance. Our hearts beat high, for we knew the nature and habit of birds when their nesting-place is approached, and a buzzard's nest were indeed a prize, equal almost to the well-remembered heron's. Following on the track the bird's seemed to lead us we arrived at the very centre of the wood, and there, on the fork of a huge oak bough, about twenty feet above the bole of one of the largest trees, we saw the coveted nest. The poor stupid birds sat with drooping wing and dejected eye on the dead branch of a neighbouring pine, ever and anon making a half circle in the air and again and again repeating their wailing cry of remonstrance. How to reach the nest was the question. The trunk was twenty feet in circumference, and though by the aid of climbing spurs (iron hooks fastened by straps to our feet) we could readily ascend the trunk, to get round the projecting bole was impossible. We were not to be beaten however in that way. A thin sapling ash grew within the circumference of the mighty oak, and starved and stunted in "the cold shade of aristocracy," turned its head as much away from the great oppressor's branches as possible, still almost touching them. Swarming lightly up this, I transferred myself cautiously to the thin but strong oak bough, and creeping carefully along soon arrived at the nest; it contained three eggs of a dirty white colour. more or less blotched with reddish-brown spots; the nest was large, at least twice as big as a crow's, constructed of great sticks and lined principally with wool mingled with moss and hair. The eggs had not yet been sat upon, so there was no larder provided for the hen-bird, as is invariably the case with birds of the order *Raptores*, when she is sitting; no rabbit, no rat, no leveret; indeed it was too early in the year for this last. Lowering the eggs down by means of a string fastened to my cap, I descended myself in a mode which would have astonished a London acrobat; swinging myself in fact from the lowest branch I could find, and dropping harmlessly from a height I am now afraid to think of. Very proud we felt as we rejoined our companions, and speedily found ourselves at the scene of our intended raid upon the rats.

Taking in at a rapid glance the prominent features of the yard, the plan of campaign was instantly formed, and as speedily carried into execution. The stacks stood two or three deep in a corner of an enclosure formed by a rough edge and a ragged bank on two sides, with a large pond from which the cattle drank on the third, the fourth facing the farmyard. Nothing could have been better contrived in the way of a " preserve " for that noble animal the rat. The bank to breed in, the pond to drink from, the wheat stacks to flee to for food and shelter. As I expected, the bank was perforated with holes, and the runs towards the pond were numerous and well-trodden. Rats cannot live without water; thirsty souls, they may be seen in the early morning drinking the dew which hangs upon the barn thatch, or the blades of grass, and when there is no dew they resort to the horsepond, without which no large colony of rats will ever be found in a stack yard. Stamping in some holes, stopping others with straw, and placing bundles of it in the most frequented runs, the boys and dogs were stationed principally betwixt the stack on which the first attack was to be made and the fence I have described. Each boy was armed with a stick, and each dog had his allotted place, from which neither, under any provocation, was permitted to move. A natural dread of the ferret, indeed of every animal of the weasel tribe, is deeply implanted in the breast of the rat; and though one of the boldest and fiercest of quadrupeds, he flees at the sight or even smell of a ferret, reckless of any danger which may lie before him. This dread, like every other feeling implanted by instinct, wears off by degrees. Instinct is only instinct so long as experience is absent; a latent power of reasoning is present in the higher order of animals, and speedily modifies or supersedes its promptings. After a few ferretings, rats learn that in avoiding their natural enemies they rush into more certain destruction at the hands of boys and dogs. They argue that "a rat's a rat for a' that;" that they are many and the ferret one, and eventually philosophising with Hamlet—

> "Rather bear the ills they have,
> Than fly to others that they know not of,"

they stand manfully up against their enemies, and fight "pro aris et focis." From a defensive they soon proceed to wage an offensive war; and I have seen ferrets driven ignominiously from a too-often hunted stack, the triumphant rat following the crestfallen invader a yard out of his hole or more. There was no fear of any such *contretemps* on this occasion; the farmer was too pennywise to pay a ratcatcher, and the wasteful beasts had made sad havoc with the corn. The fewer ferrets that are put into a stack under such circumstances the better; there was a possibility of young rats even at this early time of the year, and if a ferret find herself in a rat nursery, she murders all the innocents, sucks their blood, and then enjoys an indefinite sleep in the soft warm nest they lately occupied. Too many ferrets, moreover, are apt to play at cross purposes, heading the rat occasionally. As a rule, the ferret is not so bold as the rat; it is an understood thing that the rat is to run away and the ferret is to run after it; but when by accident or intention a rat is driven into a corner, few ferrets, as I have before shown, dare face him. Where many ferrets are employed, it frequently happens that a rat escaping from one runs straight into the jaws of another. There is no chance or hope for him then; a rat may fight, a rat may bite, but the tremendous strength of the ferret, especially in the neck and jaw, and his numerous teeth, sharp as needles, give him an instant and undoubted victory; the rat seized close behind the ear appears paralysed. It doubles up in a sulky mass, and dies, almost without a squeak; the ferrets join in a grumbling meal, and as a general rule lie down to sleep as regardless of their waiting owner as is a fashionable lady of her coachman and horses left out in the cold at a ball.

Two ferrets, then, are put into the stack on the opposite side from the bank; all is hushed and still—

"What ails old Vic?"

Page 257.

Old Vic at one corner, Busy at the other, attendant boys immediately behind them; young Vic, not yet thoroughly broken, is held in a string, and little Pincher sits justs behind, and out of sight of a well-used side run; old Pincher, who understands more about it than any other there, biped or quadruped, and has besides a will of his own, takes his station on the bank. A solemn pause ensues. What ails old Vic? A slight tremor passes through her frame, her hackles bristle, and she seems to sit as it were on the tip of her toes, her eyes glisten, her head is turned slightly, and one ear is bent downwards. A half-grown rat rushes out, and in a succession of rapid jumps makes for the bank. Vic moves not till it is well clear of the stack, and then at a bound she seizes it; a snap, a squeak, and all is over; there is no *shaking*—dogs shake rats because they are afraid of their biting. No dog of ours, excepting perhaps little Pincher, whose small size excused him, or young Vic, whose education was not yet complete, would shake a rat; a snap, a crunch, and the rat was dead. Vic could hardly turn round before another and another had bolted; one was killed with a blow of the stick, the other Busy solemnly chopped and dropped, and then half-a-dozen of all ages rushed towards the bank. Pincher was in his glory. A truculent animal, he accompanied us not so much for love of sport as that of killing; he spared the ferrets because they ministered to his slaying propensities, but he killed every other living thing. He scarcely owned us masters, but followed to share in the carnage we provided. Pincher excelled himself that day; he had calculated, as we had, that the rats driven from the stack would seek their summer residences in the bank, and seeing their holes stuffed with straw he knew that the bewildered beasts would pause at the obstructed entrance before seeking a safer place of refuge. Nor was he disappointed; Pincher had the savage luxury of killing at least a dozen rats to his own tooth. Hearing a rustling above my head, I looked up and saw a rat which in its haste had lost its footing, rolling down the steep thatch. The creatures had formed zigzag covered ways just inside the rough straw at the end of the stack, by which they had reached the roof, and one of the ferrets following, was driving them pell-mell from their lofty but untenable citadel.

I know not how many rats we had killed; I think forty, but the day wore on, and now to catch our ferrets, and home before roll-call. Luckily there were no young rats; the season had been miserably cold and backward; our ferrets were singularly tame and well-trained. One rolled down the thatch, and fell unharmed; the other came out, and being presented with a dead rat, seized hold, and allowed itself to be caught at once. Caution must always be used in handling ferrets; the pretty, playful little animal, fed on bread and milk, which will roll and dance like a kitten, take your finger innocently in its mouth when you tickle it, lick your hand and crouch down for a caress, is, when its destroying instinct is awakened, the "amor dapis atque sanguinis" aroused, a different creature altogether, and must, I repeat, be handled carefully, for the bite of a ferret is no joke. Wear no glove, never make a snatch at him, let him get well out of the hole, then seize him quickly, firmly, and tenderly by the neck and shoulder, your forefinger between the head and the right foreleg, your thumb behind the left foreleg, and your other fingers opposite; keep a firm but gentle grasp; if you are not rough, the ferret will not even struggle, but resign herself with apparent indifference to be returned to the bag, or put to another hole, which, if she refuse to enter, you may be quite sure does not contain a rat.

Having received the farmer's grateful acknowledgments, which, I fear, as far as he was personally concerned, we hardly deserved, we started, highly elated with our success, on our return. Our pack melted away by degrees: Pincher, the misanthrope, had trotted home without leave, asked or given, the moment the ferrets were taken up; the others, with more or less courtesy, departed to their several kennels, as they were taught to do on approaching the outskirts of the town. We marched with innocent faces and buoyant hearts to our respective studies, where, the ferrets having been safely stowed away, with two or three young rats for a treat, I sat for at least an hour gloating over my newly-acquired egg-treasures.

CHAPTER VIII.

THE BADGER.

"THERE's a precious game afoot, Master B., down by Warley Wood, some morning early when you can get out," said Frank Beading to me one day.

"What's that, Frank?"

"Why, Master B., there's an old brock has kennelled there, and we're going to dig him out. You shall see him bolted, if you like."

"What is a brock, Frank?"

"A brock! why, a badger, to be sure. You've never seen a badger-bait, I dare say?" I never had; but I have since, and a more disgusting exhibition of brutality I can hardly conceive. The wretched animal, naturally quiet, harmless, and inoffensive, is placed in an artificial box or burrow of some twelve or fifteen feet; at the end the owner of the ill-used beast generally constructs a chamber at right angles, sitting in which the badger has an advantage over the dogs who are sent in to " draw " him, that is, to seize him by the scruff of his neck, and drag him out into the open air. A strong, determined bull-terrier will do this pretty readily, but while the quarry is fresh and strong, by no means with impunity; the badger's teeth are of the sharpest, his power of jaw considerable, the looseness of the skin about the neck enables him to turn his head with the greatest ease and activity, and his usual mode of defence is to tuck his nose between his fore paws, and, when seized by the only projecting part, his neck, to bite right and left at the legs and through the neck of the attacking dog. The badger is a plucky, enduring beast, too, and will sustain the attacks of many dogs before he succumb; but the cruelty and absence of any real sporting feeling amongst his persecutors induces them to run dog after dog at him, until his spirit is cowed, and the veriest cur will draw him, as he might an old sheep, without meeting with anything beyond a passive resistance.

However, I was charmed at the prospect of the

adventure, and agreed to meet Frank at five o'clock the next morning, at the old sand-pits by Warley Wood. Accordingly, at about four I was out of bed and dressed; slipping between the bars of our bedroom window,—I think they were not more than six inches apart,—I dropped fearlessly to the ground, and patting the head of old Don, the pointer watch-dog, on the same principle as that on which fair Margaret caressed

> "the shaggy bloodhound
> Lest his baying should waken the castle round,"

I stepped lightly on his huge kennel, and, springing from it, caught the coping of the wall, to the top of which I had no difficulty in raising myself. A run of two miles brought me to the sand-hills, and there I found Frank Beading and another man, whose name I afterwards learnt was Guy Drake, covered with sand, and working with all their might at a huge hole they had excavated in the bank. "You're just in time, Master B.," said Frank; "we stopped him in last night, and Guy and I have been working hard at it, off and on, since two o'clock this morning. Guy slept over the hole, he did." The man referred to, a sulky-looking fellow, with an unprepossessing countenance, made me a clumsy salute, and proceeded with his work. Pincher lay coiled up on his master's coat, which, with Guy's, and a large sack, lay upon the bank. It was a picturesque spot altogether. Some tall Scotch firs grew on the very edge of the bank into which the men were boring, and which had doubtless been formed years before by the removal of sand for agricultural or other purposes; the ground was in some places sloping, and clothed with brambles; in others, seamed with pits and holes, many full of water, and overhung by alders, sallows, and other trees which rejoice in wet, undrained soil.

"We shall have him directly, Master B.; run a willow stick round the mouth of the sack to keep it open, and we'll try and get him to bolt into it." I had hardly done this, when a mass of sand fell, half burying Guy Drake, and as he floundered out, the object of our pursuit appeared too, rushing at full speed towards the rough bank immediately behind us. Excited beyond measure at the appearance of the beast, and utterly regardless of danger, I rushed at him, and as he was gaining the friendly shelter of the bushes, seized him by the hind-leg. Fortunately for me, he was half through the meuse, and before he could turn Pincher had dashed forward, and seizing the badger by his throat, effectually diverted his attention. The two rolled over, fighting and struggling in deadly hate for some seconds before the men could separate them, but Guy, seizing the badger by his tail, and Frank, at no little risk, pinching the dog's throat, this was effected, and Guy Drake held the clumsy, writhing animal, unable to turn more than his head upwards, at arm's length by his tail.

"Put the sack down in the run, Master B.!" cried Frank, who had enough to do holding the dog,— "put the sack in the run, sir!" and I did so. The other man then putting the badger on the ground, the animal rushed blindly forward into the sack, the mouth of which was instantly closed and securely fastened.

"Well done, Master B.!" said Guy Drake,— "that was about the pluckiest thing I ever saw done. He'd have got away if it hadn't been for you! Nat Belt would have been pleased to see that, sir, he would."

"Why, what do you know about Nat Belt, or me either, if you come to that?"

"Bless you, Master B., I live at Slowton when

I'm at home, and I've been about your father's woods now, and again."

"Did you come to the lodge, then?"

"Not exactly; it might not have been convenient," said my acquaintance, rather dryly. "But I know Nat Belt, and Nat Belt knows me. Good-morning, sir."

"Good-morning; good-bye, Frank. I'll come and see the badger to-morrow."

"By the bye," said Frank, as he was turning away, "there's a kite's nest in Stockbrook Wood. I've seen the old cock bird sailing about for some time past."

"Whereabouts is it, Frank?" said I eagerly.

"Well, I can't say exactly, but it's sure to be pretty near the middle of the wood, and it's not so small but you'll see it without glasses." And so saying, Frank and his companion jumped into a small tax-cart, to which a rough wiry pony was attached, and rattled away with their captive at a good pace. On the back of the cart was painted "Guy Drake, Slowton, Licensed Hawker and Dealer in Game." It occurred to me at once that there might be very sufficient reasons for its owner declining to perform the courtesy of a personal call upon Nat

Belt, and I could not but fancy that his absence from home might have something to do with some irregular proceedings with respect to the purchase or sale of game. However, that was a passing thought, and my mind, as I hurried home, was fully occupied with the thoughts of the late successful capture, the doubt whether I should get home undiscovered, and the prospect of the crowning glory of bird's-nesting—the acquisition of a kite's egg.

Two days afterwards, I may here say, I went with a companion to Stockbrook Wood, discovered the nest in the part indicated, and climbed the tree, an oak, without difficulty. The nest was placed in the main fork, a huge structure, as much larger than the buzzard's as the buzzard's is larger than the crow's. It must have been nearly five feet in diameter. I could have lain down in it safely. It was almost as flat as a table, and I think lined principally with moss and cow-hair, but I am not sure ; it is a long time ago, and I wish I had taken more accurate note. "Non cuivis contingit." It is not one man in a million who has taken a kite's nest, and very few have even seen the bird. The nest contained two young birds, apparently just hatched, and one egg, which I at first thought was addled, but on examination found it cracked from end to end, with a hole as big as my little finger on the lower part. The young bird, in fact, was in the act of liberating itself from the shell. I gently aided its efforts, and, strange as it may appear, I reared this as well as its elder brothers to kite's estate, and for a long time they were to me a source of unceasing interest. The egg was almost white, a dirty white, with round reddish blotches like the buzzard's, but larger. On the side of the nest lay two young rabbits, two rats, and some bird, I forget what, all fresh, but headless. Besides these substantial tokens of his affection, the old cock bird had brought, to gladden the heart of his sitting partner, a long tendril of early woodbine, the soft green leaf of which was just bursting forth under the influence of the early spring sun. Of course, this may have been accidental, but the tendril was there; and in the only other kite's nest I ever had the good fortune to take (two years later) I found the very same thing. The hen-bird was sitting, and beside her were headless rabbits and rats, and a long wreath of the early woodbine.* While I was taking the nest, the old birds flew wildly above

* I cannot but think it was a delicate attention on the part of kite père. He had " found out a gift for his love."

me in great circles, uttering their shrill whistling cry, but never approaching or settling, as the buzzards did, on the neighbouring trees; their cry was one more of remonstrance and indignation than of pitiful, wailing complaint such as the buzzards' under similar circumstances. But I have never seen any bird fight for its eggs or young,* except, perhaps, the little blue-tit, who will sit in his hole, puff himself out, hiss like a snake, and peck at the intrusive finger in the most spirited manner, the hen partridge, and the carrion-crow, a pair of whom once drove me ignominiously from their nursery. Their nest was situate, as the crow's invariably is, on the fork of the bough, but the fork was at the extremity of the bough, and it was a long dangerous climb to reach it. Four half-fledged younglings were in it. They had just arrived at an age to be interesting and very dear to their parents; and the bold birds determined not to lose them without a struggle. As I crawled along the horizontal bough at a giddy height, the sharp-billed creatures continually dashed

* Yarrell says, "The nest (of the kite) is vigorously defended. A boy who climbed to one had a hole pecked in his hat, and his hand severely wounded before he could drive the old bird away." Yarrell never took a kite's nest—moreover, kites don't "peck."

at me, uttering, as their wings almost touched my cheek, a hoarse, ominous croak, then settling on a branch a few feet distant, reiterated the tale of their wrongs, and encouraged each other to renewed resistance. So fierce were they, and so precarious my hold on the unsteady bough, that my humane feelings came out unusually strong, and, like the public with the cabmen, when the latter had given evidence of their power of annoyance, I determined that the birds' remonstrances were reasonable, and that it would be unfair and useless to take their young. "I think," said I to Fred Haylock, who waited below, "it would be a pity to take them; they're not worth having, and we've plenty of birds." Caroke! caroke! said the old birds, approvingly. "Never mind, throw 'em down," said Fred. "I think I won't," said I, looking at the old crows, and half turning round; "it would be so cruel." And the old birds again unanimously expressed their approval of the sentiment. Finally, I descended the tree, leaving the old birds to rejoice with their rescued little ones, and to exult over the great moral victory they had obtained. But I am forgetting my kites. I took them home, kept them warm, and fed them with pieces of such young birds and young quadrupeds as I could obtain. There are no birds, as I think I have said, so easily reared as kites and hawks. The food presented to them is, in fact, identically the same with that which would be supplied by the parent birds; they require but a sufficiency of it and warmth.: with those requisites, and luck, success is certain. While young, they are covered all over with white down, but have not a feather; the beak and eyes are of disproportionate size, and the thigh bone elevated above the back. They are unable to stand on their feet for at least six weeks, but squat upon their haunches, and altogether present a singular and most uncouth appearance. Their natural instincts are developed at the earliest stage of their existence. The bird I had liberated from the egg the very next day would open its beak to receive a morsel of flesh, but take no notice of a proffered piece of bread, and, what is more strange, while a dog might smell at it, and in fact touch it with his nose without causing the least alarm, the presence, even at some distance, of a cat or a ferret would excite the strongest manifestations of terror and hatred. The little creature, unable to stand, would throw itself on its side, clutch with its impotent claws, and open its soft beak, as though it required only the power to tear its acknowledged enemy to pieces. Why this instinctive hatred should exist between the cat and weasel tribes on the one side, and the hawk tribe on the other, I cannot say, but I have repeatedly witnessed it.

On visiting Frank Beading the morning after the badger hunt, I found him smoking his pipe with a very lugubrious expression of countenance; his little pug nose worked convulsively, and his watery eyes were unusually suffused. "Pincher's dead!" said he, mournfully, in reply to my inquiring look. "Poor old Pincher's dead!" "Bless me, Frank!" cried I, "how did that happen?" "Well, sir! he was killed, murdered outright by that owdacious badger out yonder," pointing to a large tub in the corner of of the yard. "What!" said I, "did the badger get out of his tub and worry poor Pincher?" "No, sir, not that exactly, but Pincher, you see, wasn't altogether a nice-tempered dog." I admitted that sweet temper was not Pincher's weak point.

"He wasn't a forgiving sort of dog, you see, Master B., and he was badly punished down in the sand-pits yonder. Well, he couldn't forget it all day. He was oneasy like, going in and out, growling to hisself. I couldn't tell what was up with the old dog; but at night, after he was chained up, he managed to slip the collar over his ears, jumped atop of the barrel, and scratched and bit away the covering, and jumped down, as I suppose, to have it out with the badger." "That looks like Pincher's murdering the badger, doesn't it, Frank?"

"Yes, sir; but the badger murdered him. I found him in the morning terribly bitten about the head and legs, quite dead in the barrel, and that nasty varmint curled up asleep or shamming. Drat him; I shall never see Pincher's like again!"

"He was a sulky, bad-tempered dog, though, Frank," said I. "Ah! Master B., you only saw him out of doors, on business like. Bless you, when we went out a poa—ferreting, I mean, he wouldn't follow me nearer than a hundred yards, and if I turned back, he wouldn't let on to know me. He ran home by hisself, too; but at night, when he was left indoors, you should just have seed how he jumped about, and on to my lap, or Betsy's there, and be just as kind-like as a lap-dog." Betsy, Frank's black-eyed sister, confirmed this account of poor Pincher's domestic qualities, and I was bound to throw no discredit on their statements; but I could not concur in Frank's notion that the badger had murdered Pincher.

T

I could run on for pages with old recollections of my Downham pursuits and adventures, but, interesting as they might be to myself or an old schoolfellow my readers might weary of them.

"With our school days we part."

I was to return home and have a year's private coaching before entering the university; and in due time, taking with me a menagerie of dogs, ferrets, kites, hawks, and owls, I arrived at the paternal mansion, and was warmly greeted by every soul in it, from the old squire to the cowboy, who filled the place of my early friend, Bill Belt.

CHAPTER IX.

FEN-SHOOTING.

There is no shooting which to my mind equals fen-shooting, and that sport we, under Belt's able guidance, enjoyed to perfection in the holidays. Our home lay on the slope of the long ridge of hills which, running through the middle of England, bounds the vast swamp that under the name of fenland stretches from the ocean westward for well-nigh a hundred miles. The fens in those day presented a very different appearance from that which they present now; and the passenger by a Great Northern train traversing fertile fields and green pastures at the rate of forty miles an hour can hardly picture to his imagination the black, boundless flat, houseless and treeless, which then presented itself to view. Except a few dilapidated windmills—I mean mills moved by the wind for the purpose of raising the accumulated water from one dead level to another scarcely more elevated—and a few scattered turf-stacks, no object higher than a bulrush rose between the eye and the horizon. In the centre of this dreary expanse lay a stagnant lake or mere, as it was called, well stocked with coarse fish, the haunt of unnumbered wild-fowl.

Of the real extent of these fens I have no conception; in my boyish imagination they were boundless. They must have extended over very many thousand acres; but except on the outskirts there were literally no inhabitants. A few hard-working, self-denying men, fever-stricken one-half the year, and palsied with ague the other half, waged war with Nature under the name of fen-farmers. Gangs of labourers in black boots and red shirts, called "bankers," the originals of that great institution the "navvies," worked in them by day, but retreated at night to sleep in the villages and towns nearest to their work. Like the backwoodsmen of America, the fen-farmers were the precursors of civilised agriculturists. Instead of fences their lands were divided by dikes, eight, twelve, or sixteen feet in width, cut at right angles to each other, and for the most part full to the brim of stagnant water. The rents were low, and it is difficult to understand how any could be paid; here and there a field—if the term can in any way be applied to the swampy, ditch-divided parallelogram—was pared, and during the hot weather burned, manured, and planted with potatoes; the scanty crop was followed by one of rape, after which came oats; a slow and unremunerative process, and the ultimate result always doubtful. Animal life, as distinguished from human, and vegetable life distinct from cereals, flourished luxuriantly; wild birds of rarest types, strange caterpillars, gorgeous butterflies, beetles of many colours, especially that pest of farmers, the wireworm. Sedge, rush and reed, and sweet-smelling aromatic shrubs abounded. After three years' work the crop was constantly destroyed by the insects above named, or when just ready for the sickle carried away bodily, torn up by a hurricane from the light, dry, spongy soil, on which its hold was so insecure. The burning had a singular effect; for months after it had been lighted the fire would creep along the ground, leaving a white impalpable ash like snow some inches deep on the surface; a red coal beneath that burned the soles from your boots if incautiously you trod upon it—it was dangerous work traversing those white fields,

> "Per ignes
> Suppositos cineri doloso."

The track of the smallest bird or beast was plainly visible; it was comparatively safe to follow the latter.

We were four miles from these fens, and there was no road. Our expeditions thither were necessarily made on horseback. The stud, though neither extensive nor valuable, was generally sufficient for the purpose, at least during the holidays, when the butcher's spare pony and the innkeeper's rest post-horse were pressed into the service. Besides, we were not proud, and if, as generally happened, there were more riders than horses, the long-backed ones among the latter were accommodated with two of the former—an arrangement to which the unreasonable brutes generally offered a most determined resistance

Great was the excitement of starting. When two men ride on one horse one must ride behind, and as the foremost horseman had the advantage of a saddle, while his companion sat on the hard bare backbone of the horse, the seat of honour was warmly contested.

That point settled between the bipeds, the quadrupeds took up their share of the controversy, and by a series of violent kicks frequently deposited the occupier of the saddle on the earth, and seated his companion in his place, which he of course retained. Kicking with a double load is not a game to be carried on for any length of time, and a few minutes generally sufficed to start the whole party, with guns, gamebags, commissariat, and munitions, fairly on their way. We were not first-class horsemen in those days, but I still think there are many crack riders in the shires whose nerves would have been shaken had they sat, gun in hand, on a raw-boned, bare-backed steed, driven at best pace through, if not over, some ugly bullfinch, with perhaps a yawning ditch on the other side.

Arrived at the fens, a friendly farmer, one Dale, put up our reeking steeds in his ample barn and supplied them liberally with the dried sedge and rushes which his farm horses were fain to consume as hay. Our better-fed brutes turned up their noses at such fare, but were glad enough of it before the long day was done.

Passing through the little oasis which constitutes our friend Mr. Dale's farmyard, we find ourselves at once on the border—the brink I should say—of the deep fen, "the world before us," a moist, eerie, unfinished-looking world, such as Professor Buckland imaged forth in the frontispiece to his pre-Adamite treatise.

A narrow plank laid across a twelve-foot drain is cautiously traversed in single file.

As we touch the opposite bank a jack-snipe, rising at our feet, is hastily fired at by two of our party, and being neither injured nor apparently alarmed, drops behind a bunch of rushes some fifty paces distant. A second "more advised aim" is successful, and picking up the puny delicate bird, we proceed on our way rejoicing.

I should have said that our leaping-pole, without the aid of which the most active of fen-shooters, and we were of them, could not have proceeded a quarter of a mile, had been sent forward on the back of an ancient donkey, under the charge of George Kilderkin, a lank, active youth, born with an intense love of sport and bred a turf-cutter.

We proceed in line; Search, a steady old waterproof setter, a capital retriever, trotting slowly ahead, staunch, steady, and impassive, seldom hunting, never hurrying, but rarely missing a bird.

Game, properly so termed, is scarce, but we find plenty to shoot or shoot at, and the uncertainty of what may be the next object of our aim, with the wild and almost dangerous character of the ground traversed, gives additional excitement to the sport. There is water everywhere, and the form of a hare which splashes up at our feet is instantly filled, as though she had sat in a slipper-bath. The black liquid mud churned up from her feet is spurned yards behind her as she runs, and she presents the spectacle of "a moist, unpleasant body" as George Kilderkin, rushing forward, picks her out of the puddle into which I have rolled her. A brace of blue rock-pigeons, which may have travelled forty miles that morning to feed in the fens, offer a capital right-and-left shot. A hen-harrier, beating his hunting ground with the regularity of a well-trained setter, is fired at and missed.

We are now stopped by one of the larger drains, cut originally sixteen feet wide, requiring, with its rotten banks, a clear jump of at least eighteen; it is full to the brim, "a sluggish water, black as ink." My gun is handed to Kilderkin, who places the pole in my hands. Sounding with the shoe at its foot, I find something like a firm bottom about three feet from the bank, and advancing my right hand to within a few inches from the top, my left firmly grasping the pole below, with a bounding spring I pass lightly through the air, experiencing as I do so the delightful feeling which may be supposed to accompany the act of flying, and settle like a bird on the opposite bank. Thrusting the pole back, I am ready to catch the gun, which George holds poised in readiness, the butt resting on his right hand, the barrel midway on his left. It is deftly thrown and lightly caught; that of my companion follows, and then comes his turn to jump. He is rather a young hand and nervous; his spring is insufficient, and for a moment the pole poises at the perpendicular; it rights, however, and narrowly escaping a complete ducking he lands with a splash in two feet of water, out of which he is instantly dragged.

We are now in the true snipe ground; the fens are in capital order, wet—not too wet—and there has been a bright moon for some nights past. We are full of hope and anticipation. The wind, which is tolerably high, is in our back, and our old dog, though it gives him extra trouble, does not object, for he knows that snipe will lie better, and, always rising up wind, present after the first twist a fairer mark. We have hardly proceeded twenty yards when a harsh squeak with a whirr of wings disproportioned to the size of the bird is heard, and waiting until his first eccentric and rapid movements are over, we drop him cleverly. My companion does the same by a second—a third, a fourth rises as we proceed; some are missed, some killed, but we have bagged three couple before we leave that splash, and face another ditch of greater width and still more impracticable character than the last. We get safely to the other side at the expense of a slight wetting, and find ourselves in the neighbourhood of Fowl Mere, a noted resort of wild birds of all kinds. It is too wet for snipe, for that bird, though it loves moist ground, must have dry places to rest on and bog to bore in, not too saturated to contain the worms which constitute its favourite food.

A brace of wild ducks which have been put up by a turf-barge on the mere, at this moment pass rapidly at a great height over our heads; we watch their flight with longing eyes, and are rewarded by seeing them curl round and drop with a splash on to a little tarn ahead. Meantime Search is poking after something at the bottom of the ditch—he has long held himself absolved from all conventionalities—squattering through the liquid mud and water, and at times dipping his sagacious old nose actually into it. We think he smells a rat, maybe a moorhen, or possibly a jack-snipe, at any rate we know that the wise dog will wait for us if there is anything worth waiting for, and leaving him to settle to his point we proceed with rapid but stealthy steps to stalk the ducks.

Wild ducks are by no means difficult of approach if you keep out of their sight ; once mark ducks under a bank, and it is your own fault if you do not get a shot. The mallard rises at an easy distance, and falls to my companion's gun. In the excitement of the moment (for a duck is a much-coveted prize), I miss his companion with both barrels, but she is not destined to escape. At this moment a rush of wings is heard overhead, and a falcon, probably a gos-hawk, dashes at her, and within a distance of some two hundred yards, regardless of our presence, strikes his quarry, which falls amid a shower of feathers lifeless to the ground. The hawk, like a skater who has passed the ball at hockey, wheels round as speedily as his rapid course admits of, but too late to intercept the dead duck before it touches the earth, and rushing in with wild shouts, we secure the prey the bold bird had so gallantly struck down. We find a streak down the back of the duck where the hinder talons had scraped it in the falcon's swoop, showing at once the cause of death and of the cloud of feathers which accompanied the fall. As we turn away a shrill plaintive squeak is heard, and looking into the ditch a snake is seen making his repast in the horrible cruel manner peculiar to those creatures—gradually sucking down his capacious throat a large live frog, seized by one of its hind legs. Pausing for a second to rescue the wretched creature, we return to our friend Search, and find him squatting under the bank, half in, half out of the water. A dark brown bird which had been lying close under his nose creeps a yard or two in advance as we approach, and flies slowly and clumsily along the line of the ditch. It is shot, of course, for all birds are game in the fens, but it is a useless addition to the bag—the water-rail, a distant cousin of the delicate land-rail, well-shaped, with pretty feathers, but bad to eat and offensive to smell.

The day is wearing away, and we turn our faces resolutely towards the blue hill in the distant horizon. The bag is heavy, and we are fain to relieve its bearer by putting some of its contents into our capacious pockets. A shooting-coat was not then what it is now; it was made for use, not ornament, of strongest material, and amply provided with pockets. I could put anything smaller than a calf into the inner one of mine.

We pass over fresh ground as we return, and our bag increases in number if not in respectability. A white owl flopping out of a ruined mill is thoughtlessly shot, to the great dismay of Kilderkin, who reluctantly picks up the ill-omened bird. He has been in high spirits all day, but he appears at once to have lost all heart, and strides along in silence with a most dejected air. The owl is a mystic bird in his eyes, and her death bodes disaster. "You shouldn't have fired, Master B.; the other gentleman would have missed her. There's very few as can shoot a howl. I remember last year Muster Willum, he shot at a howl; she sat on a dead bough of the wild pear-tree in Long Lane. I never see a *real* howl sit on a dead bough. Muster Willum, he ups with his gun, and I says, 'For any sake, Muster Willum,' says I, 'don't fire, sir. *You don't know what it may be.*' But he did, and down come the bough, and away flew the howl. But bless you, Master B.," he

"You should not have fired, master."

added solemnly, "*I knowed it were no howl.*" Kilderkin afterwards told me confidentially that it was said, though he did not believe it, that Mother Flaunders, who was, as we all knew, a witch, commonly assumed the shape and feathers of an owl.

Whether in consequence I am in doubt, but certainly before we reached Dale's lonely dwelling, our pole broke, and we were forced to face some half-dozen cold ditches, twelve and sixteen feet wide, as best we might; but the spirit of the slaughtered bird having been appeased by this slight contretemps, we reached Dale's in safety, and eventually arrived at home, very wet, very tired, but in highest spirits, and well satisfied with our bag, which when turned out exhibited a goodly show of varied game; snipe and partridge, duck and teal, peewits, hare, the water-rail before mentioned, a hoodie-crow, a barn-owl, a magpie, and, strange inmate of a game-bag, a pike of about two pounds weight. I have been many times a sharer in battues where pheasants were killed by the score and hares by the dozen, and not enjoyed myself one tenth part so much as I did on one of these wild days on the fens.

By the way, I must give the history of the pike I have just referred to, and I entreat my readers to believe it on my testimony. When the surface of the fens is covered with water these fish frequently come in with the flood into certain narrow pits or dykes out of which the turf has been cut, and are left as it recedes without the possibility of escape. It is no unusual thing to see a solitary jack in one of these watery graves; but in a particular pit a brace had been left as nearly as possible of the same size and weight, between one and two pounds each. The water, though stained, is clear as wine, and I had watched these fish for a long time previously. We always shot fish when they were big enough, but these hardly appeared worth powder; besides, they lay in capital ground, and it is not pleasant to see a full snipe rise just within shot as you slay a worthless pike. On this day, however, only *one* of its accustomed occupants was visible in the pit, and that presented a singular appearance, floating uneasily near the surface. Aiming well beneath the fish, at least double his apparent distance below the surface, I fired, and on getting him out with the pole, found that so far as in him lay he had *swallowed his companion;* the head and shoulders with the greater part of the body were actually digested, whilst the tail stuck out at one corner of its wicked mouth.

As they lay in the water on former occasions I could not have said which was the bigger of the two, so nearly were they of a size; but as the *majus continet in se* the *minus*, we may assume that it was the larger of the twain that I shot.

CHAPTER X.

WILD AND TAME ANIMALS.

QUAIK! quaik! quaik! "Ay, there you go No manners. Mallards first. A cock-pheasant now, always waits for the ladies." Quack! quack! quack! "Four, five, six brace—there's a pretty sight, Master B.!" And so it was. Rising in two or three lots— the mallards, as Belt observed, taking the lead— a small flock of wild ducks took wing from the old reed-fringed moat near the lodge, and cleaving the air with their powerful wings, after circling round the pond, flew away in a long string towards the forest.

"Your ducks don't seem very tame yet, Mr. Belt," said I.

"Pretty well for that, Master B. They'll come to my whistle to feed, if there's nothing to fright 'em; and they generally stay about the moat here all day. This is flight time, you see, sir."

"But they'll get quite tame by degrees, I suppose, like the others?"

"Not they, Master B.; they'll no more grow into tame ducks than they will into tame pigeons."

"But surely the tame ducks were all wild once?"

"I'd like you to tell me *when* and who tamed them, and how. I've tried it, I know, for well-nigh twenty year, hatching the wild bird's egg, pinioning the young, hatching *their* eggs, and so on; and except just in the way of knowing me like, and coming to my whistle when I throw the food down, the last brood is just every bit as wild as the first, takes its flight at flight time, as you see them do now, pair off in the spring—you never see tame ducks pair—and bring their young uns out into the world together, like the father and mother of a family."*

"But still," said I, "they must have been tamed *some time*."

---

* "Smiles she to see the stately *drake*
   Lead forth his brood upon the lake."
                                                SCOTT.

"Perhaps so, Master B., but it was before your time or my time, or anybody's time in this world, for that matter. Who changed their nature, Master B.? I say nothing of their shape. Who taught 'em to waddle instead of walk? Who made them swim after their food instead of diving for it? Who made them sleep at night instead of in the day? Who taught them to drop their evening flight, and give up their separate mates, like Yankee Mormons? Who——"

"I quite agree with Mr. Belt," said my tutor, Mr. Bedford, a gentleman under whose care I had recently been placed by my father, in order to be prepared for the university, to which I was to go in the following October. Mr. Bedford deserves a more special introduction, but this is not the place for it. He was a gentleman of great learning, an ardent lover of natural history, if not an eminent naturalist, and a good observer, so that, besides engaging me in deeper studies, he confirmed my taste for the delightful pursuit of natural history; and many a pleasant walk we had together, and many a pleasant lecture upon common objects and common birds and beasts and insects did he bestow upon me, with some of which I may venture, at some future time, to trouble my indulgent readers.

"I agree with our friend Mr. Belt in the opinion that tame ducks, like other tame—I mean domesticated—birds and animals, derive their origin from a type entirely differing from that of their wild congeners. The reasons adduced by him are to my mind conclusive, and I would add that the colour of the wild duck is uniform. No generation, so long as the wild strain is adhered to, ever varies a feather. Nay, though crossed, and in consequence particoloured, they will recur to that original colour after generations. As in the octoroon, the black blood asserts itself:

'Naturam expellas furcâ, tamen usque recurret.'

You never see this in the tame duck."

"But surely, sir, some tame birds derive their origin directly from the wild—the goose, for instance? There is scarcely a feather to choose in appearance between the wild and the tame bird."

"In appearance, no, but in character and habit, and in all essential points, yes: indeed, I know of no kind of birds that differ more. In none is the domestic principle, the tendency to seek man's society and man's government and protection, more unequivocally developed than in the tame goose; in none are the opposite qualities more manifestly innate than in the wild. Did you ever hear of a *tame* wild goose? Zoological Gardens? Bah! The birds are pinioned or plucked. Let their pen-feathers grow, and what in the early spring becomes of your tamed wild goose? 'She's away to the forest to hear a love-tale;' and the goslings bred in the cold swamps of Canada, or on

> 'the gloomy shore
> Of stern and pitiless Labrador,'

will show no more token of their mother's enforced submission to the rule of man—man, the abhorred of all truly wild animals—than they would have done had she never left those dreary swamps. Has a wild goose in confinement ever laid, or hatched her eggs, if she laid any? I think never.

> 'The prisoned eagle will not pair.'

nor will the wild goose, as wild a bird, as noble a bird, and better eating too. No, the wild goose was born wild, and wild he must ever remain. The tame goose was framed by Nature solely for the use and food of man. Heavy in body, clumsy in gait, dependent in character, Hamlet's uncle did not furnish a stronger contrast to his 'wholesome brother,' than he does to the wild, independent, untamable 'Anas ferus.' His one virtue is domesticity—ineradicable domesticity. I remember the sad days of the Irish famine, when men lay dead, starved to death by the sides of roads or mountains, and by streams where they had crawled to devour some succulent, unwholesome weed; I have watched them by scores as they tottered or crept along the road-side, gathering for pot-herbs a crisp mealy-leaved weed—I do not know its name—always found there, and I have closed my eyes in horror as I passed, to shut out a spectacle of misery it was out of my power to relieve, and then, when such a thing as a potato-paring or a cabbage-stalk, or a dry crust—the usual perquisites of the pigs and poultry—would have been fought for by ravenous men, I have seen great flocks of geese sheltering themselves, night after night, under the lee of some miserable cabin on the edge of a sloppy bog stretching forth and ending in a vast lake, whence they drew their daily food, and where, had they so listed, they might have abided free from the control and interference of the wretched peasants that owned them. Did they take advantage of their position? Did they desert man that had reared, but never fed them? No! they and their ancestors were, and from the beginning had been *tame geese*, domesticated birds, tamed by the hand of their Maker and given to man for his use; so, though they received neither food, nor shelter, nor protection, they abode with him, clung to him, and in, return were caught up, as they are to this day twice a year, and deliberately *plucked alive*, every feather ruthlessly torn out from the bleeding body—in Ireland considered in the light of a hot-bed on which to grow feathers for sale."

"But the cats? Surely the domestic cat, the purring, treacherous, mouse-and-bird-killing cat, has its origin directly from the wild species which still, in reduced numbers, tenant the wilds of Cumberland and the mountains of Scotland?"

"I think not: indeed, I feel sure not. A wild cat, like a wild ass, a wild duck, a wild sheep, a wild pigeon, a wild goose, is incapable of tameness—I mean domestication. A more irreclaimably savage beast does not exist. Physically, there are great and important differences; the colour of the wild species is uniform, sandy or grey; of the tame, indefinitely varied; the shape of the body, especially of the tail, differs essentially; the intestines of the wild cat are those of a wild beast, short, straight, and simple, totally dissimilar to those of the tame species, which are far longer and more complicated. But I take my stand on the *moral* attributes, a wild cat cannot be tamed — a tame cat never becomes wild."

"But Nat Belt often catches wild cats in the woods."

"Not wild cats, but tame cats that, from neglect, desertion, or innate love of independence, have renounced their allegiance to man, and, like the gipsies, adopted a wild life, free from the restraints and exempted from the responsibilities of civilization. Such creatures, though not properly classed as wild, cannot be permanently reclaimed; the same is asserted of men who from some cause or other have lived a savage or solitary life for a length of time; they never return to civilization, but the offspring of either, taken young, would be as tractable and docile as were their parents before they lapsed into wild habits."

"I beg pardon," said old Belt," "but *I* think it was just the Deluge that done it. I think that the tame animals were bred from them that Noah brought out of the ark with him, and the wild ones from them that were left on parts of the earth as parson says the flood never reached."

"A fanciful theory, perhaps," remarked my tutor; "but there may be truth in it. That the whole world, as *we* understand the term, was not covered by water is now admitted on all hands; and the comprehensive description of the creatures that went up with Noah into the ark may also bear a restricted interpretation, and be confined to such as were intended for the absolute use of man. Remember the command given to Noah was that he should replenish the earth and *subdue* it. The latter could only be carried out upon animals *feræ naturæ*, and so it was. We read that Nimrod was 'a mighty hunter.' The antiquity of domesticated animals is proved by references to them in the most ancient writings. Job, for instance, possessed asses, and camels, and flocks, and herds; so did Abraham and Lot.* When and how were their assumed progenitors tamed? We cannot do it now with all our means and appliances; it has been tried by men of skill and science, with wealth, and time, and skilled assistance to their aid, and they have utterly

---

* Abel was a "Keeper of Sheep."

failed. No bird or beast has ever been tamed — again I mean domesticated — within the time to which the records of civilized man run. How could the ignorant savage, without a cord or a strap to fasten, without a paddock to confine, without a notion of any power save that of brute force, effect what we, with all the aids of civilization, failed to do? Van Amburgh* *tamed* lions and tigers, gorged with food and cowed by an iron rod, but he never *domesticated* them. Rarey* subdued Cruiser, but utterly failed when he tried his hand on an old zebra that had been twenty years in the Zoological Gardens. Look at yon 'foal of an oppressed race.' What affinity is there betwixt him and the wild, untameable quagga or onager of the desert, his assumed progenitor, the swiftest of beasts, bold, crafty, savage in his wildness? What primitive Rarey broke the noble beast? What acclimatisation society domesticated him? As I said, we cannot do it now; our fathers could not do it; neither could they who

---

* Of course these are anachronisms; but in illustrating an axiom *four thousand years old* an ante-dating of thirty may be excused. Mr. Bedford, though, might have quoted "The Irish Whisperer" and the slave Androcles, who lived— least the former—long before his time.

lived in the days of old. The domestic ass, the humble, ill-used 'moke,' was given to be the drudge and slave and treasure of man; of the rich in the days of Abraham and the prophets, of the poor in the days of Disraeli and the costermongers. The wild ass was neither more nor less wild in the days of Job than he is now."

"But surely the raven is recorded to have been a denizen of the ark?"

"Perhaps he is the exception that proves the rule. But the raven renounced his allegiance. He went into the ark with Noah, but deserted it voluntarily; the dove, on the contrary, returned, and doubtless became the ancestor of our numberless breeds of tame pigeons. We know that dovecots of enormous size existed in the days of the Pharaohs; and that reminds me that you will rarely find an Egyptian hieroglyphic without a cat or a dog, the former exactly resembling the tame Egyptian cat of the present day. True, these ancient paintings are not very accurate, but in such simple drawings peculiarities are *exaggerated*, not ignored. Had the wild animal sat for its picture, the thick neck, the large head, and the bushy tail—the characteristics of the wild breed—would surely have been depicted. The dogs are very peculiar, long-legged, long-tailed, thin-flanked, high in the quarters, not unlike a badly-shaped greyhound. The late John Keast Lord,* one of the best practical naturalists and most scientific men of the day, assures me that the identical animal is common in Syria at the present time. What then becomes of the wolf or the hyena ancestor now given to the dog? Surely between the Deluge and the building of the Pyramids there was not time to change so completely the form and nature of the animal; and why, if such was not the case, has not the change been progressive? The lanky, prick-eared, long-sided, Eastern cur is not, as we know, the perfection of his race. Yes; on the whole I am inclined to believe, with Belt, that domesticated birds and beasts originated from ancestors the companions of Noah in the ark."

* See note on preceding page.

CHAPTER XI.

A QUARREL AND ITS RESULT.

THE following day was the day of the village feast—a great event in the eyes of the simple-minded folk among whom we lived. The sports and pastimes were of the rudest kind; but they were types and symbols of mirth and good-fellowship, and they answered the purpose for which they were intended as well as or better than more refined amusements might have done. After all, it is not the paper on which it is written that gives value to the bank-note. Our country lads and lasses were as well pleased throwing balls over garlands, playing skittles and ninepins, or competing for the prize in sack-jumping, pole-climbing, or holding a pig with a greased tail, as they could have been knocking snuff-boxes off a stick, or a pipe out of Aunt Sally's mouth on the most aristocratic of racecourses.

It was the squire's custom to walk through the fair in the afternoon; and warm and respectful were the greetings he received as he passed. I accompanied him, and was greatly pleased and interested by the objects of marvel or luxury devised to lure the hard-earned pence out of the rustic pocket. Two " Cheap Johns," ostensibly rivals — really partners — with much pretended abuse of each other, and bandying time-worn jokes as each led up to the other's hand, offered unheard-of bargains in the shape of knives, combs, diamond rings, gold watchkeys, resplendent jewellery of every description, to the gaping rustics. The pig-faced lady, the huge live boa-constrictor (in a small deal box), the stuffed mermaid, and the calf with six legs (in a bottle), in turn claimed my notice. All was mirth and jollity, when our attention was attracted by a considerable crowd assembled near the 'Three Horse-shoes,' the only public-house in the village. The clamour of many tongues, some in an angry tone, the expostulating cry of women, and the surging to and fro of the spectators, showed that a fight — unusual occurrence — was going on. The hubbub ceased as the squire elbowed his burly form into the ring, and the combatants shrunk away abashed, but muttering threats of future vengeance on each other, as angry men under such circumstances will. They vanished quickly, but not until I had recognised, with pain, the well-remembered faces of Sam Belt and his supplanted rival, Jerry Cant. My father, with true tact, accepted this practical proof of his just influence, made neither comment nor inquiry, but passed on, speaking kindly to those who met and greeted him.

That night the village wore its accustomed aspect of joyous, careless happiness incident to the festival; there was little drunkenness—none, I may say—and no recurrence of the afternoon's unwonted quarrel; the lads and lasses danced till a late hour—say nine o'clock — and refreshed themselves with copious draughts of heavy beer, and Humphrey gallantly saw Dorothy home to her cottage door, returning to dream, if his intellect was capable of such exertion, of "the ball's fair partner;" while she exercised her imagination in calculating how long it would be before another feast-day came round. All at night was peace and goodwill and simple enjoyment. In the morning, a frightful rumour rose,

"A horrid whisper fell o'er us as we lay,"

and ripening into reality, ran through the village. A man had been found murdered in an old pit in Bryerly Wood, dead and cold; a dreadful gash upon his forehead disclosed the cause of death, and that was all; his pockets, with a few shillings in them, were unrifled, his silver watch still going in his fob; the murdered man was Jerry Cant. Who was his murderer?

* * * * * *

Who indeed? In a few short hours, first incredulously, then hesitatingly, then doubtfully, lastly authoritatively, popular rumour laid the horrid crime to the charge of SAM BELT.

Could it be? Sam Belt! old Nat's son, Baby's brother, *a murderer!* It must be a dream; it was impossible! and yet three days later Sam had been apprehended under the coroner's warrant, and stood charged with the dreadful crime.

* * * * * *

I hastened to my father. "You don't think Sam guilty, sir?" said I. "You *can't* think Sam guilty?"

"No, Ben," he said thoughtfully (I had risen of late to the first syllable of my name)—"No, Ben, not of murder certainly; but I think there is little doubt that he killed Jerry Cant, either in self-defence or under provocation. I would gladly think him innocent if I could. 'Crowner's 'Quest Law' is not the perfection of reason, and the jurors on an inquest are not always conjurers; but that he killed Jerry Cant I think is clear."

"May I visit him in prison?"

"Yes, I think you may. It is possible he may make a clean breast of it to you: and the crime, if I read it rightly, is far removed from that of deliberate murder. If Sam should tell you how the matter happened, get his permission and go and tell Mr. Lovell, who has kindly taken up his case, all you know. Mind, *I* don't want to hear anything about it."

Availing myself of my father's permission, I rode over to Slowton, and made my way to the gaol, where I was at once admitted. The turnkey, Charles Bond, had known me formerly; his wife had been my nurse and besides I was supported by my father's authority. I found poor Sam in a small room on the ground-floor sitting on his bed—almost the only article of furniture it contained—with a very dejected expression of countenance. He rose at my entrance, half putting forward his hand, but immediately withdrawing it. I saw the action, and held mine out, which he grasped warmly.

"You don't think me guilty, then, Master B. I was sure *you* wouldn't."

"No, Sam! that I never did for a moment; but I thought perhaps you might have met in the wood—and gone on again with your quarrel—and perhaps——"

"No, sir! We never met again. I have never set eyes on Jerry since the fight at the feast."

"What did you fight about, Sam?"

"Well, sir, you know Jerry and I were both courting Jemima, and she took up with me, and Jerry didn't like that, and then he wanted to make up to Baby; and as he wasn't a bad-looking chap and had a good business down yonder, mayhap Baby might have come round to him, but father and I knew him for a poacher and a bad lot in more ways than one, and so we stopped that, and turned him out of the house, and that's what's set him agin me; and when we met at the feast he had been drinking, and picked a quarrel, and at last struck me, and so we fought."

"But is it true that you threatened him when you separated?"

"I don't know about threatening; but he said he'd

have killed me if we hadn't been parted, and I told him to mind that I didn't kill him, or something of that sort."

Our conversation lasted some time, and I left the prison thoroughly convinced that Sam was innocent. I hastened to Mr. Lovell to apprise him of the fact, thinking that it would be a relief to his mind; but he did not seem to adopt my conclusions, as I anticipated that he would. During the recital he once or twice muttered, "Better have made a clean breast of it! Better have made a clean breast! We could have got it reduced to manslaughter." And to my earnest asseveration of Sam's undoubted innocency, the lawyer, nursing his left leg on his right knee, simply replied with a long-drawn whistle.

"Well, Mr. Benjamin" (it was the first time in my life I had ever been called by my full name), "we shall see, we shall see. Your excellent father is an old friend and a valued client of mine, and takes great interest in this young man. I have retained counsel; and the best that can be done for him shall be done, but"—again sinking his voice—" I wish he had made a clean breast of it! I wish he had made a clean breast of it!"

Sadly and wearily—for poor Sam at least—the

A Quarrel and its Result.

time passed on. The day of the assizes approached, the lodgings for the judges were secured, the high-sheriff's old family coach rubbed up, two of his best cart-horses promoted to the carriage for the nonce, and the pair that ordinarily dragged that aristocratic vehicle converted into leaders; a score of ploughboys and other retainers of the family, clothed in long great coats and liveried hats, acting as javelin men; the jury is sworn, and Samuel Belt stands before the country to be tried for the murder of Jeremiah Cant.

I confess that, with all my confidence in Sam's innocence, I was staggered at the array of proof which was adduced against him, and which, although my instinct rebelled against it, my reason acknowledged to be very cogent.

It was proved, without question, that great personal animosity existed between the two; the prisoner had not only been the successful rival of the murdered man, but had interfered with his addresses when transferred to his sister; there had also been misunderstandings between them on the subject of poaching, the fight before recorded was described as of a particularly savage character, and threats of future vengeance were proved to have been uttered by the prisoner. He was shown to have been absent from home the night of the murder, and footsteps corresponding with the shoes he wore were traced close to the old pit where the body was found. He had been seen early in the same morning to hide himself at the approach of one of the witnesses for the prosecution, a policeman, in a culvert which ran under the Slowton Road, and to leave it after looking circumspectly round in the direction of his home, carrying in his hand something which the witness believed to have been a hatchet. In an outhouse adjoining old Belt's cottage, to which Sam had access, was found, behind some faggots, a light butcher's cleaver, answering this description; on it were blood stains and morsels of dark hair, which, when examined under a microscope, were alleged to be human, dark in colour, and identical with that of the murdered man. On applying the weapon to what the surgeon described as "an incised wound on the pericranium," the immediate cause of death, it was found to fit exactly. Sam's clothes, moreover, were spotted with blood in many places. Poor fellow! his demeanour at the trial was not much in his favour. Accustomed to a life of comparative seclusion, he was frightened and confused; he had few friends (a good keeper, as before remarked, never has many), and close confinement had told more upon him physically and mentally than it would have done upon one less accustomed to a free life in the open air. In truth, he presented a sorry appearance in the dock—as many an innocent man has before him.

Mr. Lovell had kept his word, and done all that could be done for him; able counsel were retained on his behalf, and all they could—and that was little —they did. That wonderful rule which even where a human life is at stake prescribes the exact routine under which a man may or may not prove his innocence was even stronger in those days than it is now. A witness could not even be called to character, without giving the right of reply to the counsel on the opposite side; and the last word had a considerable effect upon the dozen intelligent men, who, if they had not made up their minds before they came into the box, generally found their verdict " for Counsellor A." or " for Serjeant B.," as the case might be. It was urged in the prisoner's defence that the alleged threats had been at least mutual, that the prisoner's general habits were quiet and inoffensive, that his avocation constantly led him through the wood in question, and that a keeper's clothes must necessarily be spotted with blood. It was suggested, though of course it could not be proved, that he had crept into the culvert to take up one of his traps, and it was that which, in the dim light of the morning, the policeman mistook for a hatchet. That a keeper should look round before he left a place of concealment was natural enough; and, though the door of the outhouse was locked, the window was admitted to have been open and facing the high-road.

After a short deliberation the jury returned a verdict of "Guilty" against poor Sam, and the sense of the numerous spectators was evidently in favour of the verdict. Sentence of death in the usual impressive manner was passed by the presiding judge; and Samuel Belt, my boyish companion, instructor, and in some sort my friend, was left for execution.

I may here say that, though great influence was used, and a recommendation to mercy urged at the Home Office, no favourable effect was produced. The sentence on an atrocious murderer had with ill-judged lenity been recently commuted, greatly to the disgust of the public. It was necessary that an example should be made; and ten days after the trial it was understood that no hope of reprieve or commutation remained.

CHAPTER XII.

THE CONDEMNED CELL.

"May I pay poor Sam another visit?" said I to my father one morning after breakfast.

"Well, Ben, I think you had better not; it would be very painful to both, and no possible good could come of it."

"I think, sir, that Belt and his wife would wish it very much: and I shouldn't like Sam to think I had deserted him."

"Ah! poor old Nat!" said my father, "we must think of him in his sorrow. Yes! you may go, my boy; here's an order," writing one as he spoke; "they'll be more particular now, I suppose. And Ben," added he, as I was leaving the room, "if there is anything that we could send that would make him more comfortable in any way, you may offer it, but it shouldn't come exactly from *me*, you know. Poor Sam!"

Armed with the order, I mounted my horse and rode to Slowton. Bond, who received me at first, declared that it was impossible that I could be admitted; but my father was one of the visiting justices, and his authority was considered sufficient justification for a breach of the general orders. I found Sam the solitary inmate of the condemned cell, to which he had been removed—a dreary den at the end of a passage, into which it opened by a massive iron door. There was no chimney in the room, and the window, which revealed the thickness of the outer wall, was far too narrow, even were the bars that intersected it removed, to admit of the passage of a human body. I felt, as the iron door clashed behind me, as Sam had doubtless felt before, that hope had been left behind. It was little I could say, for my heart was full, and I could find no topic either of hope or comfort; besides we were not alone: a prisoner condemned to death is never left by himself, and it was only for a few seconds, as the turnkey who was called away by other duties exchanged his guard for that of the governor of the gaol, that a few whispered words passed between us; but those few words caused Sam's face to brighten considerably. I was leaving the cell as the governor entered. "God bless you Sam! good-bye," said I, wringing his hand once more.

"Good-bye, sir! and God bless you! we shall never meet again in this world."

"Sam," said I, turning at the door, "my father bade me say that if there was any little comfort you fancied from the house, I might send it—if the captain here would allow me."

Poor Sam's eyes glistened, and so did the governor's for that matter.

"Thank ye, sir! the squire was always kind. Do you think, sir, he'd allow Jemima to make me a rabbit pie?"

"I am sure he will, Sam, if the captain will take it in."

"Why, Mr. Benjamin," said the governor, "it is against rules to allow a condemned prisoner anything to eat but what's cooked in the prison."

"Well," said I, "then I'll send the pie, and you can bake it here, you know."

"That'll do," said the captain, opening the door for me.

From the gaol I proceeded to Mr. Allonby's shop in the High Street. Bill, who had grown into a tall young man, and was reckoned a first-class workman, had risen to the rank of foreman; I thought it but kind to call and bestow a few words of comfort upon him. I found him seated on the identical stool in the same dirty little corner where I had last seen him; neither his face nor his hands were cleaner, excepting where the former was furrowed with recent tears. Though grown, he was little changed; and as I looked at him I could not but recall the doleful face that greeted my returning consciousness after the fall in Bolsover Forest. Bill was working away as he had been before with file and oil and steel saw: and the heap of old keys and rusty iron, though somewhat larger, appeared the same as when I had visited him five years before.

I spent a quarter of an hour with Bill; and when I returned home I at once communicated Sam's wishes to Jemima, who, like several whom I had met that day, I found in tears. She, however, as if glad to distract her thoughts by some occupation, set diligently to work, and in an hour the pie was made; I superintended the operation, and made an addition to its contents little dreamed of by the sorrowful young woman; then availing myself of my father's permission, I sent the coachman off with the pie, who delivered it safely into the governor's own hands.

This was Friday; the execution was to take place on the following Monday.

On Saturday night I could not sleep for thinking of the impending tragedy, and at dawn on the following morning I had risen, and was looking out of my bedroom window. Still, I had some grounds for hope, my addition to the pie having been the castaway key, Bill's early work. A slight noise attracted my attention, and peering through the gloom I saw Sam, half hidden by the laurels, pale, wan, and haggard, but Sam himself, before me. In an instant I had dropped from the window, and was by his side. "Thank heaven! you have escaped then; but why did you come here? They will surely seek you."

"Well, Master B., I couldn't help coming to the old folk at the lodge, you know, and besides, they'll never think I would be such a fool as to run home; they won't look for me here."

"Did you come straight here, Sam?"

"Yes, sir, excepting that I turned up Raveley Lane, to look at a box trap I had left there, and to see there was no poor crittur of a varmint pining in it. I know what imprisonment is, Master B."

"Kind-hearted fellow," thought I; "and this is the man they would have hanged for murder." But time was precious. It was Sunday morning, fortunately, and no labourers were about. Sam was hastily hidden in a hole scooped out of the straw-stack, the mouth of which I concealed by an armful carelessly thrown over; and obliterating the marks of my own footsteps, I regained my room unobserved.

The particulars of Sam's escape I learned subsequently. He had opened the door of his cell by means of the key, and by the connivance of his old friend Charlie Bond, who pretended he had been attacked and nearly murdered, gained the outer gate the key of which he had taken from Bond. The following statement appeared in the *Slowton Gazette* of the ensuing week, and was never contradicted in any material feature by the result of the careful investigation which followed. It was headed:

"EXTRAORDINARY ESCAPE OF THE CONVICT BELT, AND ATTEMPT AT DOUBLE MURDER.

"It is with amazement and regret we inform our readers that the blood-stained murderer, Samuel

The Escape.

Belt, whose crime was by a righteous judgment to have been expiated on the scaffold last Monday morning, has—we trust for a time only—evaded the doom he so richly merited. The exact mode of his escape is still shrouded in mystery; but from the evidence taken before the magistrates, it would seem that by some inexplicable means the prisoner had drawn back the massive bolts it was thought impossible to move except by the key which fitted the lock of the condemned cell, and which was in the governor's custody day and night; this, however, was by some means effected, and the evidence of the turnkey, Charles Bond, and his wife Margaret, sufficiently explain the rest. Unconscious of the vicinity of the self-liberated captive, Bond had opened the door which leads to the condemned cell at the moment that his wife, who acts as housemaid, was approaching to sweep out the passage. Rushing by him, the sanguinary wretch seized his wife, and dashed her violently to the ground. But that her head came in contact with the thick door-mat, she must have added another to the grim list of the murderer's victims. As it was, she lay stunned and helpless, unable even to cry out for help. Her condition is still precarious. Bond, it appears, closed at once with the murderer in mortal conflict. He was, however, no match for the convict—a man of great physical power—who appears to have throttled him, bent him backwards over the iron balusters, and then, with fiendish malice, twisted his head between the rails so as to bring it almost in contact with his heels, in which position he was found shortly afterwards, his back apparently broken, and almost dead; but little hope of his recovery is entertained. The murderer, taking the keys that had been thrown down in the scuffle, let himself out at the great gates, and locking them behind him proceeded, unnoticed at that early hour in the morning, towards Bryerly Wood, the scene of his first (known) murder. He was seen to enter the wood, and hot pursuit at once set on foot. The ground being moist from recent rain, his footsteps were traced through the wood by the very scene of the murder, until they turned eastward towards the village of Raveley, on the hard road towards which place they were lost. It is probable that the felon at first intended to seek the shelter of his former home, but altered his plan, from a natural expectation of being sought for there."

Thus then, thought I, as I read the account, poor Sam's kindness of heart put his enemies on a false scent, for it was at the point mentioned he had turned away to liberate the supposed prisoner from his box trap.

A later paragraph stated that Margaret Bond, the wife of the turnkey, was gradually recovering, though still suffering from the effects of the blow; and, strange to say, her husband, whose back was supposed to have been broken, though not out of danger, was certainly better, and some hopes were entertained of his recovery. Neither, however, was capable of giving evidence or supporting a lengthened examination.

After breakfast I proceeded to the lodge, where I found old Nat and his wife just recovering from the wonderment and delight occasioned by the reappearance of their dearly-beloved son. They were seated side by side, with Nat's old Bible open before them. At my entrance both arose, and Nat Belt, laying his hand on my shoulder, poured out blessings and thanks, earnest and heartfelt, none the worse that they were but imperfectly expressed. Mrs. Belt, more impulsive, threw her arms round my neck and sobbed over me, as doubtless she had done over her son a short time previously. Baby nestled towards us, and taking my hand between hers as she sat on the floor, covered it with kisses. It was clear that in the minds of these simple people I was somehow connected with Sam's escape.

The scene became altogether too touching. I was always soft-hearted, and my only resource was to rush from the lodge, the " big round tears coursing one another down my innocent nose."

I had not run fifty yards from the door when in the narrow pathway which leads from the lodge to the Hall I encountered Holder, the policeman, one of the witnesses at the trial. I ran, in fact, right into his arms.

" Bless me! Mr. Benjamin," said he, " where *are* you going in such a hurry?" and then, looking into my face he added, good-naturedly, " Ah! I see, sir; well, you needn't take on about old Belt's son down there this turn. He'll not be hung to-morrow, after all."

" What! " said I, recovering my presence of mind; " has he been reprieved?"

" No, sir; but he's *escaped!*"

" Escaped! impossible! How *could* he?"

" How, indeed! It's the most mysterious event that ever I had information of."

" Do tell me all about it."

"I'll tell you, sir, all I know, and that's not much. He must be an oudacious clever fellow, that Sam! He managed not only to get the chains off his legs, but to force back the bolts and pick the best and strongest lock in the county. There are three bolts, and Mr. Allonby, who's just mad about it, swears as nothing but the key *could* have shot 'em. However, he's wrong there, for there's only one key, and that was under the captain's pillow. Mr. Benjamin, that artful dodger opened the lock somehow, and got out at five o'clock this morning, lays wait in the passage, pretty nigh murders Charles Bond and his wife, takes the keys from 'em, and walks out of the main entrance like a gentleman at large—and that's what he is at this minute—but won't be much longer I expect."

"But Bond and his wife—do you say he killed them?"

"I don't say that quite; but he just tied Bond up in a knot like over the balusters, dislocated the vibrating column, the doctor calls it, and left him for dead; and as for Mrs. Bond—I suppose he had not time for much ceremony—he just dashed her down, and left her stunned and helpless. Had it not been for the door-mat she would have been killed too; they are both so bad that they could give no evidence on the case."

"But why do you think he will be taken again?"

"Well, sir, they tracked him through the wood, you see, and towards Raveley, but he couldn't go there; it was too late in the day. So no doubt he's hid in the wood somewhere. They'll find him when the reward's large enough. I've come here on guard like; but, bless you! he'll never come here; he's too wide awake for that." And so the policeman, in whose opinion Sam evidently stood very high, left me much relieved in my mind.

The strictest search was made for many consecutive days. Large rewards were offered, but without effect. I believe there was not a rabbit-hole in Bryerly Wood that was not searched, but without result. Sam had been seen to enter the wood, and it appeared impossible he could have left it unobserved.

> "Had he sunk into earth?
> Had he melted in air?
> They saw not, they knew not,
> But nothing was there."

And so by degrees the nine days' wonder ceased, and Sam's escape was considered one of the unexplained mysteries of the day.

* * * * * *

I am not sure whether or not my father knew or suspected Sam's concealment on the grounds ; I think he did. Contrary to his usual custom, he retired to his own room to read the papers the moment breakfast was over, and was unusually particular about having plenty of cold meat on the side-board at that meal. The servants must have given some one credit for a prodigious appetite. Sam was a bit of a philosopher, and had been by no means overfed of late. When the farm people were away I took him huge hunches of bread and meat; and a bucket of water, daily renewed from the well, with an occasional bottle of beer, sufficed for ablutions and drink. He took his exercise at night in the walled garden, to which he got access through the barn that bounded it, and on the whole found himself much more comfortable than when an inmate of the condemned cell in Slowton Gaol.

* * * * * *

A fortnight afterwards a respectable-looking individual, with neatly-trimmed beard, hair, and whiskers, attired in a not over-new suit of black cloth, a moderately clean neckcloth, Wellington boots, and well-brushed hat, a bundle in his hand, and an excellent butler's character, in the form of an open letter, addressed to "Henry Jones, Esquire, Stock Exchange, Liverpool," in his pocket, took his place outside the Slowton coach, at 5 A.M.

"I'll write if I get safe off, Master B.; and if any good luck turn up, put an advertisement in the *New York Herald.* God bless you, sir."

It was upwards of a year afterwards that the following paragraph appeared in the *Slowton Gazette:*

"CAPTURE OF A POACHER AND RECEIVER OF STOLEN GOODS, AND EXTRAORDINARY CONFESSION OF A MURDER.

" On Thursday last Guy Drake, a person well known to the police as carrying on, under the guise of a pork-butcher and game-dealer, a nefarious traffic in poached game and stolen goods, was brought before the magistrates and committed to Slowton Gaol on a charge of complicity in various recent robberies. It appears that he reached the gaol in the dusk of the evening, and passing through the prisoners' yard, across which, as some of our readers may be aware, a light iron bridge is suspended, his attention was attracted by the tall dark form of a prisoner crossing, who to his distempered imagination appeared to be walking in the air. Believing that he saw a ghost, and urged by remorse, he sent for the chaplain of the gaol, and confessed that it was he, and not Samuel Belt—who so nearly suffered for the crime—who murdered Jeremiah Cant in Bryerly Wood, upwards of a year since. He stated that on the night of the murder he had met Jerry Cant by appointment near the old gravel pits, to settle an outstanding account; that after some dispute, Jerry, whose temper appeared to be much ruffled, and who had been drinking, struck him and seized him by the throat, upon which he snatched out of his cart the cleaver he ordinarily used, and struck him with it across the forehead. The blow was fatal, and the murderer, terrified at what he had done, jumped into his cart and drove off, careless in what direction. It occurred to him in passing an outhouse to get rid of the weapon by hiding it there, and the door being locked, he threw it through the window, whence it fell behind the faggots, where it was subsequently found. The wretched culprit stated that he was not aware to whom the outhouse belonged, nor—having left the country at once—did he hear until after the event of the narrow escape Sam Belt had had of being hanged for his crime. That the main part of this confession is true, we can have no doubt, although the latter portion can scarcely be credited. It is rarely that, even under the influence of remorse, a criminal confesses the whole truth. Our readers will remember that at the time we expressed considerable doubts of the truth of the charge preferred against Sam Belt; and we heartily congratulate that young man's respectable relatives upon the establishment of his undoubted innocence."

I need not describe the joy of the family at the lodge; the whole village rejoiced; and my father, though he seldom referred to the subject, was as much pleased as any one. Her Majesty was graciously pleased to extend her free pardon to poor Sam for a deed he had never done, and an advertisement inserted as he had directed shortly brought him back to this country, looking much more like himself than when he left it.

PART IV.

THE BAGMAN.

THE BAGMAN.

CHAPTER I.

Mr. Thomas Wood, or, as he liked to be styled, Thomas Wood, Esquire, was a person of no small importance in the little town of Slowton. Of his origin little or nothing was known except that he had held a situation from his earliest youth in the family of the Earl of Bagwash, in whose pay and confidential employ he still continued. The Earl had been a good sportsman in his day, and still kept a pack of foxhounds in the neighbourhood of London, but he had become somewhat *blasé*, cared little for a cold ride and a long draw, and preferred the brisk and certain gallop afforded by a bag fox, to the legitimate pleasures of the chase. He kept a capital pack of dwarf foxhounds, which he called harriers, in a distant county, accessible by rail, before whom a fox was turned down once or twice a week. Mr. Wood's principal employment, besides overlooking the kennel establishment, was to provide a hebdomadal relay of foxes for this purpose—and hard enough work he found it.

Mr. Wood was enjoying his glass of hot brandy and water after an early dinner one fine afternoon in January, when the boy in buttons, who officiated as butler, announced "a young man" as wanting to speak with him. On inquiry the young man's name was stated to be "Billy," or, as Buttons was charged to add, "Slender Billy." A thin, tall, hungry-looking man of about thirty followed close upon the heels of Buttons, and holding his fur cap in his left hand, saluted Mr. Wood by a tug at his hair with his right.

"Sarvant, Guv'nor; we've got a real good un this time!"

"Let's look at him," said Mr. Wood.

"Bless you, sir! he's not to be looked at; he's in his kennel. My pardners and me we've been diggin' since last night, and we can just touch him with a stick."

"I'll come and look at the hole then," said Mr.

Wood; "I'm not going to be put off with a Leadenhall fox again."

"All right, master; it's on'y five miles off. Jump into my trap, and you'll be there in no time."

Mr. Wood apparently did not relish this proposition, and, after much bargaining, agreed to purchase the fox for three pounds, one of which Slender Billy insisted upon being paid in advance. Having received a sovereign, Billy appealed successfully for a glass of brandy and unsuccessfully for a shilling to save melting the sov., and departed, pledging himself to return with the fox by five o'clock the following morning.

Billy had probably over-estimated the distance, or else the ragged, spavined pony that was rope-harnessed to the rickety vehicle he styled "the trap" travelled at an unprecedented pace, for within ten minutes from the time he had quitted Mr. Wood's parlour he found himself in the presence of his "pals." True, they were, not digging—indeed, they did not look as if digging would come natural to them —but they were, as Billy had averred, at 'The Fox's Hole.' I allude to the public-house so designated, and which, as our readers know, stands close to Bryerly Wood, and within a mile of the Grange, the residence of John Stubbs, Esq.

Mr. Stubbs had used his personal interest with the noble master of the Deepdene hounds to save the life of a fine fox which had taken refuge in a labourer's cottage after a brilliant run at the end of the last season, and had since kept him chained in a comfortable kennel under some old elm trees, in front of his house, where "Charlie," as Mr. Stubbs called him, had become an object of considerable interest to all the neighbours and visitors who frequented that hospitable mansion. It was the intention of Slender Billy and his accomplices to steal this animal, and palm him off upon Mr. Wood as a wild fox just dug out of his earth. After informing his "pals" that he had made a bargain for two pounds, which, as he showed, would be just "one for them two and one for him too," and expatiating upon the niggardliness of that gentleman who wouldn't so much as stand him a drop to drink or give him a shilling to buy one, the plans were laid and successfully carried out, and by four in the morning the ragged pony and the rickety cart, the three men seated side by side in front, and the fox in a sack behind, were in Mr. Wood's yard.

Under that gentleman's direction the fox was turned into a small paddock closely fenced all round, with a kennel in one corner and a little clump of evergreens on each side. Billy having received his two pounds with some grumbling, which he took care his companions should hear, while he drowned the allusion to the one paid in advance, proceeded to divide them in the equitable manner suggested.

Mr. Wood having examined his purchase was well pleased at finding a really magnificent animal, though perhaps something of the fattest.

"Never mind," said Mr. Wood, "we'll soon get that !" and called to his man John to bring the broom. John appeared, broom in hand, and immediately commenced hustling the unlucky animal round and round the paddock, sometimes allowing him a minute's rest in one or other of the laurel clumps, but keeping him moving at a rattling pace, till the fox was so exhausted he could run no more. This course of treatment was pursued day by day for a month until the animal, although well fed, had attained the highest possible condition, and was as lank as a greyhound.

CHAPTER II.

THE MEET.

"Friday 15th—Lord Bagwash's—Newton Tollbar 12."

Such was the announcement which, under the heading of "Harriers," appeared in the sporting papers of Saturday, February 9th, 186—; and a little before that hour a tolerably large muster of well-mounted men approached the place of meeting from all points of the compass. The meet, however, hardly presented to the practised eye a sportsman-like appearance. There were good men there, it is true, and good horses, two or three hard riders from the neighbouring hunts, some officers from the barracks, and a sprinkling of farmers, but there was a want of spirit about the affair; the men of the different hunts looked suspiciously at each other, like men who meet in town in September, and old Sam Caird, the huntsman, had the appearance of one who was doing a duty he was a little ashamed of. Indeed, several thought it necessary to make excuses for being there at all; one had got a new horse to try; another was sick of blank days and hunting runs, and wanted "a spin;" a third had come out for the first time from curiosity to see a bagman turned out; Mr. Stubbs had come at the especial request of his friend Mr. Wood, and he, too, had a promising young one to try. There was besides a sprinkling of men who, deceived by the advertisement, really believed they had come out to "hunt the sprightly hare."

Three or four hours previously, the fox, deceived by a pane of glass fixed to the end of a box trap, through which he vainly essayed to escape, had been caged, turned upon his back, and as in struggling his feet protruded through the barred bottom of the trap, had been anointed on each with a drop of aniseed. Transferred to a more roomy box, he was then conveyed by Slender Billy to a copse, about a quarter of a mile from the meet, with instructions when he heard the horn to "open the box and turn him down."

z

"There's my lord on his horse looking for the hounds, sir," said Ben, the first whip, to Mr. Caird, "a top of the hill yonder."

"I'll give him a blow," said Caird, and immediately produced two sounding notes upon his horn. Hounds are, or always ought to be, excited by the sound of the horn, but the pack on this occasion appeared almost wild; some careered about, many opened as though in full cry, and it was with great difficulty they were restrained by the voice of the huntsman and the efforts of the whips from breaking away in mad pursuit apparently of they knew not what.

In a few minutes his lordship appeared, accompanied by some members of his hunt, several strangers arriving at the same time.

"Deuced late these hounds meet!" remarked young Charles Sydney, a pink and white youth, fresh from Cambridge and the drag, to his companion, a rough, red-whiskered yokel, attired in an ill-fitting coat and rusty cap, generally known as "Dandy Jones," to distinguish him from "Gentleman Jones," a different person. "Deuced late! the day is half gone."

"Well, it is late," replied his companion. "But they don't lose much time drawing, you see."

The Meet.

" Plenty of hares, eh ? " said Sydney.

" Ya-as, plenty of hares ! "

"Don't much like this sort of thing," muttered our friend Stubbs ; " feel somehow kinder ashamed of myself, but the colt's hot and won't stand that sort of dodging work we so often get with the fox-hounds in this cramped country ; besides, it's only for once ; " and looking with the eye of a sportsman over the hounds, as clustering round Sam Caird's horse they came suddenly round the corner, " a beautiful lot they are, surely. Call them harriers ! Why I never set eyes on a likelier pack of fox-hounds ! "

The noble master had arrived in a brougham by himself; but a light dog-cart bearing his crest and coronet had conveyed to the meet two visitors at the Castle, foreigners apparently. Both were smoking and extensively got up ; one, the younger, evidently in a state of great excitement, all anxiety to witness an English " chase of the fox," and burning to distinguish himself as a horseman. This was the Count Heitansek, a German nobleman ; the other a Yankee officer of high rank in his own country, General Lucius Junius A. Grubb. The General was a heavy, coarse man, with large hands, rather dirty, a husky voice, a small, restless eye, and a damp, unpleasant expression of countenance. He had come to England ostensibly on a diplomatic mission, but in reality to palm off upon gullible John Bull a swindling Californian gold-mining speculation, in which object he had succeeded entirely to his own satisfaction. Possessing, in common with most of his countrymen, unbounded assurance and the highest credentials, he had called personally on her Majesty's principal ministers, of whom Lord Bagwash was one, and, on the strength of a vague and undefined hope of "one day seeing him at the Castle," the General had presented himself on an elastic visit at that hospitable abode a few days previously. His lordship—the most courteous of men—was sorely put out and greatly disgusted, but what could he do? He could *not* turn him out, but he *could* give him a mount, and he did —on one of his splendid carriage horses. The General's steed was a showy beast, and good of his sort, but he was not altogether a hunter; he stood sixteen three, iron grey, with a Roman nose, a ewe neck, and a bang tail down to his hocks, had capital knee action and no more mouth than an ox. His rider, who had mounted at the cross roads, showed already signs of considerable discomfort.

CHAPTER III.

THE RUN.

THE hounds at once moved down the lane, heads and sterns up, and apparently ready to break away at short notice. Ben opening a gate to the right, the pack passed rapidly through, and hardly waiting for the huntsman's accustomed cheer and wave of the hand, swung rapidly round, picking up the scent as they swung, and went off in a southerly direction directly upwind.

There was a tremendous bustle and hustle, of course, every one trying to get a good place at the start. Our friend Mr. Stubbs, touching his horse lightly with the spur, bounded over the low fence to the left, and rattled down at best pace almost in a line with the leading hounds.

"Why! they've got on a fox," said young Sydney.

"Shouldn't wonder," replied his friend; "they often do."

"Not that way, master; ride to the left," said Slender Billy to his patron; "I *seed* him turn under the 'edge. He's gone Bolsover ways."

Billy had *not* seen this, but he was right, nevertheless; the fox had turned, and was now heading straight for the well-remembered forest.

Mr. Wood, availing himself of the hint, turned his horse's head in the direction indicated, and, closely followed by the count, joined Mr. Stubbs at the corner of the field, where an accommodating gate stood wide open.

Meanwhile the General's horse—

> "Right glad to miss
> The lumbering of the wheels,"

had gone off at score, his head down and his great knees showing at every plunge above his ears like the pistons of a steam engine; his rider, with toes turned out, and hands on a level with his eyes, vainly striving

"Truly my lord was avenged."

to guide or stop him. The swamp, however, into which he floundered speedily effected the latter object; and just as the hounds and the leading portion of the field disappeared over the brow of Crowhurst Hill, the gallant General found himself mid-leg deep in the black liquid slime of a bottomless bog, his horse's outstretched neck and head just appearing above the "verdant mud." After a long struggle he emerged, wet, dirty, sore, and sulky: truly my lord was avenged! The German, who did not lack pluck, and was well-mounted, followed close upon Mr. Wood, his elbows out, his coat-tails flying in the wind, in a state of uproarious excitement. Our friend was in considerable danger of being ridden down, but fortunately for him both steeds rose in the air at the same moment at the same gap, and cannoning midway, the lightest—poor Heitausek—was shot into a soft ploughed field, with little damage but much dirt. Stubbs and Wood, and a few of the best mounted of the field kept their place some sixty or seventy yards to the right of the hounds, taking their fences as they came in gallant style, but husbanding their horses for what they felt must be a trying day. The body of the field meanwhile rattled along the high road, or the grass that skirted it, parallel with their course, at no great distance to the left. The hounds literally raced, carrying a capital head, fleet as swallows, mute as mice.

"By all that's beautiful," quoth Stubbs, "if this be not *the* real thing, it's wonderfully like it; but," added he, the exulting gleam fading from his jolly face, "it's *not* the real thing—sheep dogs could run that scent; I could run it myself; it's a sin to waste hounds' noses on it," and, squeezing his hat over his eyes, and taking a pull at the young horse, he drove him at the low wall that bounded the field before him.

"Not there!—not there, Stubbs!" shouted Tom Haylock. "*Not there*, for your life!" but too late; the good horse had already risen at the wall which bounded a deep almost empty pond beyond. Nothing but great presence of mind and admirable horsemanship saved Stubbs from a serious accident. He had ridden at the fence much faster than he ought; his horse was young, and, truth to say, though over sixty, so was his master. Becoming aware of his danger as he rose to the leap, the rider cleverly shifted his whip to his left hand, and throwing his body as far backward as possible, seized the cantle of the saddle with his right. Happily, a foot or two of mud had collected at the bottom of the pond, which, moistened by the recent rains, broke the force of the fall, and the rider's great strength enabled him to keep his seat. Such, however, was the strain that the saddle, firmly held by triple girth, was broken in the middle and doubled up as it were under him. The horse scrambled out snorting and terrified, but unhurt, and Stubbs, muttering something to himself expressive of "wonder whether he would ever grow older," speedily regained his place.

The bounds were still running at a rattling pace, but hardly that at which they had started. The distance had told, and it must be confessed they straggled considerably. Fine noses were of little use, and the old hunting hounds were fain to follow the dashing puppies as best they might. Of the field the majority were fairly beaten, and one by one dropped behind till only about a score were with the hounds, and each of that number inwardly prayed for a check, if but for a minute, to enable their blown horses to catch their wind. This, however, was not to be; a view halloo a short distance ahead told that the fox had entered Bryerly Copse; and in another minute the hounds, no longer mute, were making the old oaks ring again with their cheery music as they ran parallel with the road which bounds it. Leaving the friendly covert and thick underwood, the ferns and tangled briars, many parts of which might well have afforded shelter, and still running right into the eye of the wind, the bold fox headed directly for Thorney Wood. Entering by the beeches at the north side, like one that knew the country from cubhood, he ran right through the covert, through the gorse at the bottom, and swimming the now flooded river below, was viewed just as, about to vanish, he reached the summit of the rising ground on the opposite side.

It was a gallant sight to see the four or five leading men charge the water that day. The recent rains had swelled it into something like a river, narrow, perhaps, but not the less dangerous on that account. Full to the brim, the turbid, brown stream rolled rapidly along; and it required no small amount of pluck in Tom Haylock, who was leading, to drive his horse at it, but he did so, and with more or less assumed eagerness the others followed. It is not a pleasant sensation to find your horse disappearing under you, little but his head and ears visible, snorting with fear, and swimming rapidly but uneasily, whilst the cold water rises well-nigh to your hips, and searches every aperture in boots and breeches. Still the gallant few struggled on, and reaching the opposite shore landed safely, and followed as best they might the dripping pack, which had preceded them by a few moments only, each hound having shaken himself as he landed, showering the drops around him like a trundled mop.

Scarcely had the fox put the brow between himself and his pursuers than a new danger awaited him. A red, rough-coated, tailless, shepherd's dog, viewing the draggled beast as he sped wearily along, rushed at him open-mouthed. Bow, wow, wow! bow, wow! At the insult and unprovoked attack, all the savage instinct of the beast was aroused. Like the wearied, jaded Deloraine when he "marked the crane on the baron's crest," and recognized his feudal enemy, "no whit weary did he seem." With arched back and bloodshot, angry eye, glistening with hate and rage, every hair on his dank body standing on end, the wild animal waited not the attack. With a wicked snarl from the bottom of his throat, he met the dog more than halfway, and as they closed made his sharp fangs meet through the foreleg. *Wough, wough, wough! pen-a-neek; pen-a-neek!* yelped the cur, as he fled limping back to his kennel at the homestead the other side of the field. The fox turned short to the left, and running low down the furrow gained the hedge on that side, whence he pursued his course unobserved. This apparently untoward accident saved him.* At the scene of the conflict the hounds threw up, and while they were yet puzzling over the mixed scent, Count Heitansek, who had gallantly breasted the brook, still thirsting for fame and, notwithstanding various heavy falls, uproarious and jubilant, was in the midst of them. Catching sight of the retreating cur as he jumped the palings, and mistaking him for the fox, he seized the opportunity of immortalizing himself. "*Tailoo! taleo! Get avaa—oldard—hoop—yocks—tailho!*" yelled he, vociferating, as best he might, all the sounds his quick ear had caught during the run, and riding, as he yelled, in the direction of the retreating sheep-dog. The hounds, though his language was a mystery, comprehended his action; their heads were up in a second, and Volatile and Vanity, catching sight of the red back of the dog as it vanished beyond the palings, dashed away, followed

---

* This the reader will observe is the *third* time my life was saved by the intervention of enemies.—*E l.*

The Run.

by half the pack. Old Caird, with Ben, however, now appeared, and taking in the situation at half a glance, lost no time in cursing the German, but blowing his horn recalled the scattered pack, and, aided by his whip, once more put them on the track of the beaten fox, now heading directly for the forest, which, however, he did not enter, holding on as if he had a point beyond, though what that might be no one could guess. As the reader knows, a considerable brook runs at the bottom of Thorney Wood.

Was our friend Mr. Stubbs among the gallant band that crossed the brook? He was not. During the run he might have been heard muttering to himself, or remarking to a neighbour the extraordinary knowledge of the country apparently possessed by a strange fox; but when the forest, the gorse, and the woods were alike left behind, and the draggled, weary beast was seen struggling up the opposite bank of the river, he reined his horse up suddenly, exclaiming, "I thought so! I knew it all along!" and striking him with the spurs he rode off at the best pace he could command in a direct line for the Grange. Crashing through the rotten fence before him he found himself on the high road, and not stopping to pay the toll galloped along the grass at the side till he arrived at his own gate, just in time to see the fox, dead beat, and with scarce strength to surmount the old wall which bounded the premises, creep into the stone kennel, and turning round lie exhausted, his red tongue hanging from his mouth, panting for dear life. Springing with more agility than his figure promised from his reeking steed, he flung the rein to a passing labourer, and planted himself before the kennel, just as Ringlet and Rallywood, Bondsman and Butterfly, followed by five or six couple more, topped the wall, and, thirsting for blood, dashed across the little paddock which lay between it and the kennel beneath the elms. Crack! crack! went the honest yeoman's whip. Crack! crack!! crack!!! "Get away, hounds! Get away! To think that it should come to this; that they should murder my Charlie!" Crack! crack!! Wow! wow! "I wouldn't hurt you, but—" crack, crack! "get away, get away!!! Oh, here you are, Ben; thank goodness! . . . . Well, if ever I go after a bag fox again!—it's lucky I did, though, this time; but *if* ever I go again. It's fast enough, I must allow; but it's not *the* right thing —not for any one who calls himself a sportsman, at all events; and as for Charlie, I'll never tie him up again; he may stay or go as he pleases; and if he ever runs again before a pack of hounds, it shall be after a fair find, and no odds against him but the honest scent he leaves behind him!"

THE END.

PRINTED BY TAYLOR AND CO.,
LITTLE QUEEN STREET, LINCOLN'S INN FIELDS.

BY THE SAME AUTHOR.

Now Ready, price 5s,

TALES AND SKETCHES.

NOTICES OF THE PRESS.

"In the papers called 'The Fox at Home,' 'Buck Shooting,' 'Three Days at Ballynahinch,' and 'The Decoy,' Mr. Rooper writes with all his accustomed spirit, describing a splendid run after the fox, the hero of his earlier story, and other scenes of shooting and fishing, with bits of Irish landscape and of the fen country."—*Athenæum.*

"Mr. Rooper is well known as a lively and accurate writer on field sports and natural history, and the little volume before us will sustain his reputation."—*Pall Mall Gazette.*

"A collection of light, but amusing, breezy, and characteristic articles, creditably free from that peculiar sort of English, supposed—to the detriment of sport in public estimation—to confer a *timbre* upon the literature of the turf and the hunting field. There is an excellent variety, too, in Mr. Rooper's sketches, which do ample justice to the special open air pursuits of all our three kingdoms."—*Daily Telegraph.*

"'Tales and Sketches' treat of sporting matters in a familiar and instructive style, well calculated to render them popular with sportsmen."—*Standard.*

"A spirited description of sport, by a sportsman, observant and experienced."—*Globe.*

"The two opening pieces, 'The Fox at Home,' and 'Buck Shooting,' are as good as anything that Mr. Rooper has done, and the rest of the volume is capital light reading. . . . Mr. Rooper possesses an inexhaustible fund of humour."—*Echo.*

"Mr. Rooper knows what he is writing about. Let us hope he will extend the scene of his operations, and give us a few more of these charming sketches, drawn a little further from home. . . . 'The Decoy' is perhaps the best sketch in a volume that will interest all lovers of moorland, stream, and forest."—*Court Circular.*

"The production of a man who knows what he is writing about, and enjoys the sports he describes."—*Scotsman.*

THAMES AND TWEED.

Second Edition. Price 3s. 6d.

W. ISBISTER AND CO., 56, LUDGATE HILL, LONDON.

DALDY, ISBISTER, & CO.'S BOOK LIST.

ABLE TO SAVE; or Encouragement to Patient Waiting. By the Author of "The Pathway of Promise." Cloth antique, 2s. 6d.

ABOUT'S (EDMOND) Handbook of Social Economy; or the Worker's A B C. Crown 8vo, 5s.

ACKWORTH VOCABULARY, or English Spelling Book; with the Meaning attached to each Word. Compiled for the use of Ackworth School. New Edition. 18mo, 1s. 6d.

ADAMS' (W. H. DAVENPORT) Famous Ships of the British Navy; or Stories of the Enterprise and Daring of British Seamen. With Illustrations. Crown 8vo, cloth gilt extra, 3s. 6d.

ÆSOP'S FABLES. With 100 Illustrations, by Wolf, Zwecke, and Dalziel. Square 32mo, cloth gilt extra, 2s. 6d.; next cloth, 1s. 6d.

AIDS TO PRAYER. Cloth Antique, 1s. 6d.

AGAINST THE STREAM. The Story of an Heroic Age in England. By the Author of "The Schonberg-Cotta Family." With Illustrations. Post 8vo, 6s. 6d.

ALFORD'S (DEAN) The Book of Genesis and Part of the Book of Exodus. A Revised Version, with Marginal References and an Explanatory Commentary. Demy 8vo, 12s.

Daldy, Isbister, and Co.'s

ALFORD'S (DEAN) The New Testament. Authorised Version Revised. Long Primer, crown 8vo, 6s.; Brevier, fcap. 8vo, 3s. 6d.; Nonpariel, small 8vo, 1s. 6d., or in calf extra, 4s. 6d.

————— Essays and Addresses, chiefly on Church Subjects. Demy 8vo, 7s. 6d.

————— The Year of Prayer; being Family Prayers for the Christian Year. Crown 8vo, 3s. 6d.; small 8vo, 1s. 6d.

————— The Week of Prayer. An Abridgment of "The Year of Prayer;" intended for use in Schools. Neat cloth, 9d.

————— The Year of Praise; being Hymns with Tunes, for the Sundays and Holidays of the Year. Large type, with music, 3s. 6d.; without music, 1s. Small type, with music, 1s. 6d; without music, 6d. Tonic Sol-fa Edition, crown 8vo, 1s. 6d.

————— How to Study the New Testament, Part I. The Gospels and the Acts.—II. The Epistles (first section).—III. The Epistles (second section) and the Revelation. Small 8vo, 3s. 6d. each.

————— Eastertide Sermons. Small 8vo, 3s. 6d.

————— The Queen's English. A Manual of Idiom and Usage. Enlarged Edition. Small 8vo, 5s.

————— Meditations: Advent, Creation, and Providence. Small 8vo, 3s. 6d.

————— Letters from Abroad. Crown 8vo, 7s. 6d.

————— Poetical Works. New and Enlarged Edition. Crown 8vo, 5s.

————— Biblical Revision: Its Duties and Conditions. A Sermon preached in St. Paul's. Sewed, 1s.

AMOS'S (PROFESSOR SHELDON) An English Code; its Difficulties and the Modes of Overcoming Them; a Practical Application of the Science of Jurisprudence. Demy 8vo, 12s.

ANDERSEN'S (HANS CHRISTIAN) The Will-o'-the-Wisps are in Town; and other New Tales. With Illustrations. Square 32mo, 1s. 6d.

Book List.

ANDREWS' (Rev. S. J.) The Bible-Student's Life of Our Lord. Crown 8vo, 3s. 6d.

ARGYLL'S (The Duke of) The Reign of Law. Crown 8vo, 6s. People's Edition, limp cloth, 2s. 6d.

———— Primeval Man. An Examination of some Recent Speculations. Crown 8vo, 4s. 6d.

———— Iona. With Illustrations. Crown 8vo, Crown 8vo, 3s. 6d.

BARTLETT'S (W. H.) Walks about the City and Environs of Jerusalem. With 25 Steel Engravings and numerous Woodcut Illustrations. 4to, cloth gilt extra, 10s. 6d.

ATCHERLEY'S (R. J., Ph.D.) Adulterations of Food, with short Processes for their Detection. With Illustrations. Small 8vo, 2s. 6d.

AUGUST STORIES (The). By Jacob Abbott. Four Crown 8vo volumes, with Illustrations, 3s. 6d. each.
August and Elvie.   Schooner Mary Ann.
Hunter and Tom.   Granville Valley.

BAUR'S (William) Religious Life in Germany during the Wars of Independence, in a series of Historical and Biographical Sketches. Crown 8vo, 7s. 6d.

BAYNE'S (Peter) Life and Letters of Hugh Miller. Two Vols., demy 8vo, 32s.

———— The Days of Jezebel. An Historical Drama. Crown 8vo, 6s.

BEACH'S (Charles) Now or Never; or, the Trials and Perilous Adventures of Frederick Lonsdale. Crown 8vo, cloth gilt extra, 3s. 6d.

BEECHER'S (Henry Ward, D.D.) Prayers in the Congregation. Crown 8vo, 3s. 6d.

———— Life Thoughts. Small 8vo, 2s. 6d.

———— Royal Truths. Crown 8vo, 3s. 6d.

———— Pleasant Talk about Fruits, Flowers, and Farming. Small 8vo, 2s. 6d.

BENNOCH'S (Francis, F.S.A.) Sir Ralph de Rayne and Lilian Grey. Small 8vo, 1s. 6d. Sewed, 1s.

BENONI BLAKE, M.D. By the Author of "Peasant Life in the North." Two Vols., crown 8vo, 21s.

BERRIDGE'S (John) The Christian World Unmasked. With Life of the Author by the late Dr. Guthrie. Small 8vo, 2s. 6d.

BEVERLEY'S (May) Romantic Tales from English History. New Edition, with 21 Illustrations. Crown 8vo, cloth gilt extra, 3s. 6d.

BJÖRNSON'S (Björnstjerne) Arne; a Sketch of Norwegian Peasant Life. Translated by Augusta Plesner and Susan Rugeley-Powers. Crown 8vo, 5s.

BLACKIE'S (J. S.) Lays of the Highlands and Islands. Small 8vo, 6s.

BLAIKIE'S (W. G., D.D.) For the Work of the Ministry. A Manual of Homiletical and Pastoral Theology. Crown 8vo, 7s. 6d.

——— Better Days for Working People. Crown 8vo, boards, 1s. 6d.

——— Counsel and Cheer for the Battle of Life. Crown 8vo, boards, 1s. 6d.

——— Heads and Hands in the World of Labour. Crown 8vo, 3s. 6d.

BOARDMAN'S (Rev. W. E.) Faith Work; or, the Labours of Dr. Cullis in Boston. Crown 8vo, 3s. 6d.

——— The Higher Christian Life. Small 8vo, 1s.

BRADY'S (W. Maziere, D.D.) Essays on the English State Church in Ireland. Demy 8vo, 12s.

BRAMSTON'S (Mary) Cecy's Recollections. A Story of Obscure Lives. Crown 8vo, cloth gilt extra, 5s.

BRITISH SPORTS AND PASTIMES. Edited by Anthony Trollope. Post 8vo, 10s. 6d.

BROWN'S (John, M.D.) Plain Words on Health. Lay Sermons to Working People. Sewed, 6d.

BROWN'S (J. E. A.) Lights Through a Lattice. Small 8vo, 3s. 6d.

——— Palm Leaves. From the German of Karl Gerok. Cloth antique, 6s.

BROWN'S (J. E. A.) Thoughts through the Year. Sonnets suggested by the Collects. Small 8vo, 2s. 6d.

BROWNE'S (MATTHEW) Views and Opinions. Crown 8vo, 6s.

BUCHANAN'S (ROBERT) Idyls and Legends of Inverburn. Crown 8vo, 6s.

——————— London Poems. Crown 8vo, 6s.

——————— Undertones. Small 8vo, 6s.

——————— The Book of Orm. Crown 8vo, 6s.

——————— Napoleon Fallen. A Lyrical Drama. Crown 8vo, 3s. 6d.

——————— The Drama of Kings. Post 8vo, 12s.

——————— The Fleshly School of Poetry. Crown 8vo, sewed, 2s. 6d.

BUCHSEL'S (REV. DR.) My Ministerial Experiences. Crown 8vo, 3s. 6d.

BULLOCK'S (REV. CHARLES) The Way Home; or the Gospel in the Parable. Small 8vo, 1s. 6d.

BUSHNELL'S (HORACE, D.D.) Moral Uses of Dark Things. Crown 8vo, 6s.

——————— Christ and His Salvation, in Sermons variously related thereto. Crown 8vo, 4s. 6d.

——————— Christian Nurture; or the Godly Upbringing of Children. Crown 8vo, 3s. 6d.

——————— Nature and the Supernatural, as Together constituting the One System of God. Crown 8vo, 3s. 6d.

——————— The Character of Jesus. Limp cloth, 6d.

——————— The New Life. Crown 8vo, 3s. 6d.

——————— The Vicarious Sacrifice, grounded on Principles of Universal Obligation. Crown 8vo, 7s. 6d.

——————— Work and Play. Crown 8vo, 3s. 6d.

CAIRNS' (JOHN, D.D.) Romanism and Rationalism, as opposed to Pure Christianity. Sewed, 1s.

CAMDEN'S (CHARLES) When I was Young. A Book for Boys. With Illustrations. Crown 8vo, cloth extra, 2s. 6d.

———— The Boys of Axleford. With Illustrations. Crown 8vo, cloth gilt extra, 5s.

CAPES' (REV. J. M.) Reasons for Returning to the Church of England. Crown 8vo, 5s.

CARLYLE'S (REV. GAVIN) The Light of all Ages. Crown 8vo, 5s.

CARTWRIGHT (PETER, the Backwoods Preacher), Autobiography of. Edited by W. P. Strickland. Crown 8vo, 2s.

CHILD WORLD. By the Authors of "Poems written for a Child." With Illustrations. Square 32mo, cloth gilt extra, 3s. 6d.

CHILD NATURE. By one of the Authors of "Child World." With Illustrations. Square 32mo, cloth gilt extra, 3s. 6d.

CHILDREN'S JOURNEY (THE), &c. By the Author of "Voyage en Zigzag." With Illustrations. Square 8vo, cloth extra, 10s. 6d.

CHRISTIAN COMPANIONSHIP FOR RETIRED HOURS. Crown 8vo, cloth gilt extra, 3s. 6d.

CHURCH LIFE: Its Grounds and Obligations. By the Author of "Ecclesia Dei." Crown 8vo, 2s. 6d.

CONDER'S (E. R.) Sleepy Forest and other Stories for Children, with Illustrations. Crown 8vo, cloth gilt extra, 3s. 6d.

CONDER'S (F. R.) The Child's History of Jerusalem. With Illustrations by Whymper. Crown 8vo, cloth gilt extra, 5s.

CONTRASTS. Dedicated to the Ratepayers of London. Crown 8vo, 5s.

COOLIE (THE): His Rights and Wrongs. Notes of a Journey to British Guiana, with a Review of the System, and the Recent Commission of Inquiry. By the Author of "Ginx's Baby." Post 8vo, 16s.

COX'S (REV. SAMUEL) The Resurrection. Crown 8vo, 5s.

COX'S (Rev. Samuel) The Private Letters of St. Paul and St. John. Crown 8vo, 3s.

————— The Quest of the Chief Good. Expository Lectures on the Book of Ecclesiastes, with a new Translation. Small 4to, 7s. 6d.

CRAIG'S (Isa) Duchess Agnes, and other Poems. Small 8vo, 5s.

CRITICAL ENGLISH TESTAMENT (The); Being an Adaptation of Bengel's Gnomon, with numerous Notes, showing the Precise Results of Modern Criticism and Exegesis. Edited by Rev. W. L. Blackley, M.A., and Rev. James Hawes, M.A. Complete in Three Volumes, averaging 750 pages. Crown 8vo, 6s. each.

CUPPLES' (Mrs. George) Tappy's Chicks, and other Links between Nature and Human Nature. With Illustrations. Crown 8vo, cloth gilt extra, 5s.

DAILY DEVOTIONS FOR CHILDREN. 32mo, 1s. 6d.

DAILY MEDITATIONS FOR CHILDREN. 32mo, 1s. 6d.

DALE'S (R. W.) Week-Day Sermons. Crown 8vo, 3s. 6d.

DALTON'S (Wm.) Adventures in the Wilds of Abyssinia; or, The Tiger Prince. With Illustrations. Crown 8vo, cloth gilt extra, 3s. 6d.

DAVIES' (Emily) The Higher Education of Women. Small 8vo, 3s. 6d.

DE GASPARIN'S (Countess) Human Sadness. Small 8vo, 5s.

————————— The Near and the Heavenly Horizons. Crown 8vo, 3s. 6d.

DE GUERIN'S (Eugenie) Journal. Crown 8vo, 5s.

————————— Letters. Crown 8vo, 5s.

DE LIEFDE'S (John) The Charities of Europe. With Illustrations. Crown 8vo, 5s.

DE LIEFDE'S (John) The Postman's Bag. A Story
Book for Boys and Girls. With Illustrations. Crown 8vo,
cloth gilt extra, 3s. 6d.

———————— Days of Grace. With Illustrations.
Crown 8vo, cloth extra, 5s.

———————— The Pastor of Gegenburg, and other
Stories. With Illustrations. Crown 8vo, cloth extra, 5s.

DE WITT'S (Madame, née Guizot) A French
Country Family. Translated by the Author of "John
Halifax." With Illustrations. Crown 8vo, cloth gilt
extra, 5s.

DENISON'S (E. B., LL.B., Q.C., F.R.A.S., &c.)
Life of Bishop Lonsdale. Crown 8vo, 2s. 6d.

DICKSEE'S (J. R.) School Perspective. A Progressive Course of Instruction in Linear Perspective.
Post 8vo, 5s.

DOBNEY'S (Rev. H. H.) Free Churches. Post 8vo.
4s. 6d.

———————— A Vision of Redemption. Sewed, 4d.

DODD'S (G.) Dictionary of Manufactures. Post 8vo,
5s.

DRESSER'S (C.) Unity in Variety, as deduced from
the Vegetable Kingdom. With Illustrations. 8vo,
10s. 6d.

———————— Rudiments of Botany, Structural and
Physiological; being an Introduction to the Study of
the Vegetable Kingdom. With Illustrations. 8vo, 15s.

DU LYS' (Count Vetter) Irma. A Tale of Hungarian Life. Two Vols., post 8vo, 18s.

DUPANLOUP'S (Mgr., Bp. of Orleans) Studious
Women. Translated by R. M. Phillimore. Crown 8vo,
4s.

ECCLESIA DEI: The Place and Function of the
Church in the Divine Order of the Universe, and its
Relations with the World. Demy 8vo, 7s. 6d.

EDWARDS' (M. Betham) Holiday Letters. Crown
8vo, 7s. 6d.

EIGHT MONTHS ON DUTY. The Diary of a Young Officer in Chanzy's Army. With a Preface by C. J. Vaughan, D.D., Master of the Temple. Crown 8vo, 5s.

ENGLAND'S DAY. A War Saga. Commended to Gortschakoff, Grant, and Bismarck, and Dedicated to the British Navy. Sewed, 6d.

EPISODES IN AN OBSCURE LIFE. Crown 8vo, 6s.

EVENINGS AT THE TEA TABLE. With Illustrations. Uniform with "Stories told to a Child." Square 32mo, cloth gilt extra, 3s. 6d.

EWING'S (BISHOP) Revelation considered as Light. Post 8vo, 7s. 6d.

FABER'S HYMNS. Selected by R. Pearsall Smith. Crown 8vo, cloth gilt extra, 5s. Small 8vo, sewed, 1s. 6d.

FAIRHOLT'S (F. W.) Dictionary of Terms in Art. With numerous Illustrations. Post 8vo, 6s.

FERNYHURST COURT. An Every-day Story. By the Author of "Stone Edge." Crown 8vo, 6s.

FIELD'S (GEORGE). The Rudiments of Colours and Colouring. Revised, and in part rewritten, by Robert Mallet, M.A., F.A.S., &c. With Illustrations. Crown 8vo, 4s. 6d.

FITZGERALD'S (PERCY) Proverbs and Comediettas, written for Private Representation. Crown 8vo, 6s.

FRANCIS' (BEATA) Fables and Fancies. With Illustrations by J. B. Zwecker and others. Crown 8vo, cloth gilt extra, 5s.

FRANKLIN'S (JOHN) Illustrations to the Ballad of St. George and the Dragon. Small 4to, cloth gilt extra, 10s. 6d.

FRASER'S (REV. R. W., M.A.) The Seaside Naturalist: Out-door Studies in Marine Zoology and Botany, and Maritime Geology. With Illustrations. Crown 8vo, cloth extra, 3s. 6d.

FRIENDS AND ACQUAINTANCES. By the Author of "Episodes in an Obscure Life." Crown 8vo, 6s.

FRIENDLY HANDS AND KINDLY WORDS.
Stories Illustrative of the Law of Kindness, the Power of Perseverance, and the Advantages of Little Helps. Crown 8vo, cloth gilt extra, 3s. 6d.

GAOL CRADLE (THE). Who Rocks it? Cr. 8vo, 5s.

GARRETT'S (EDWARD) Occupations of a Retired Life. Crown 8vo, 6s.

―――― The Crust and the Cake. Crown 8vo, 6s.

―――― Premiums Paid to Experience. Incidents in my Business Life. Crown 8vo, 6s.

―――― Seen and Heard. Three Vols. Post 8vo.

―――― Crooked Places. A Family Chronicle. With Illustrations. Crown 8vo, 6s.

GEIKIE'S (CUNNINGHAM, D.D.) Life. A Book for Young Men. Crown 8vo, cloth extra, 3s. 6d.

―――― Light from Beyond, to Cheer the Christian Pilgrim. Cloth antique, 2s. 6d.

―――― Life in the Woods. A True Story of the Canadian Bush. With Illustrations. Crown 8vo, cloth extra, 3s. 6d.

GEIKIE'S (JAMES, F.R.S., F.G.S.) The Great Ice Age and its Relation to the Antiquity of Man. With Maps, Charts, and numerous Illustrations. Demy 8vo, 24s.

GERHARDT'S (PAUL) Spiritual Songs. Translated by John Kelly. Small square 8vo, 5s.

GILBERT'S (WILLIAM) De Profundis. A Tale of the Social Deposits. Crown 8vo, 6s.

―――― Doctor Austin's Guests. Crown 8vo, 6s.

―――― The Magic Mirror. A Round of Tales for Old and Young. With Illustrations. Square 32mo, cloth gilt extra, 2s. 6d.

―――― King George's Middy. With Illustrations. Crown 8vo, cloth gilt extra, 6s.

―――― The Little Drummer; or, the Washerwoman's Foundling. With Illustrations. Square 32mo, cloth gilt extra, 2s. 6d.

GILBERT'S (WILLIAM) The Wizard of the Mountain.
Two Vols., post 8vo, 21s.

——————— Shirley Hall Asylum. Crown 8vo, 10s. 6d.

GLADSTONE'S (THE RIGHT HON. W. E.) On "Ecce Homo." Crown 8vo, 5s.

GOSSE'S (PHILIP HENRY, F.R.S.) A Year at the Shore. With Thirty-six Illustrations, printed in Colours. Crown 8vo, 9s.

GOTTHELF'S (JEREMIAH) Wealth and Welfare. Crown 8vo, 6s.

GREENWELL'S (DORA) Essays. Crown 8vo, 6s.

——————— Poems. Crown 8vo, 6s.

——————— Lacordaire. Crown 8vo, 6s.

——————— The Covenant of Life and Peace. Small 8vo, 3s. 6d.

——————— Songs of Salvation. Sewed, 6d.

——————— The Patience of Hope. Small 8vo, 2s. 6d.

——————— Two Friends. Small 8vo, 3s. 6d.

——————— Colloquia Crucis. Small 8vo, 3s. 6d.

——————— Carmina Crucis. Crown 8vo, 5s.

GREGORY'S (BENJAMIN) The Thorough Business Man. Memoirs of Walter Powell, Merchant, of Melbourne and London. With Portrait. Crown 8vo, 6s.

GUTHRIE'S (THOMAS, D.D.) Autobiography; and Memoir by his Sons, Rev. D. K. Guthrie and Charles J. Guthrie, M.A. Vol. I., Post 8vo, 10s. 6d.

——————— The Gospel in Ezekiel. Cr. 8vo, 3s. 6d.

——————— Christ and the Inheritance of the Saints. Crown 8vo, 3s. 6d.

——————— The Way to Life. Cr. 8vo, 3s. 6d.

——————— Man and the Gospel. Cr. 8vo, 3s. 6d.

——————— Our Father's Business. Cr. 8vo, 3s. 6d.

——————— Out of Harness. Crown 8vo, 3s. 6d.

Daldy, Isbister, and Co.'s

GUTHRIE'S (THOMAS, D.D.) Speaking to the Heart. Crown 8vo, 3s. 6d.

—————— Studies of Character from the Old Testament. First and Second Series. Crown 8vo, 3s. 6d. each.

—————— The Parables Read in the Light of the Present Day. Crown 8vo, 3s. 6d.

—————— Sundays Abroad. Crown 8vo, 3s. 6d.

GYPSY SERIES (THE). By E. Stuart Phelps, Author of "The Gates Ajar," "Hedged In," &c. Four neat Vols., with Illustrations, 1s. 6d. each.

Gypsy Breynton.   Gypsy's Sowing and Reaping.
Gypsy's Cousin Joy.   Gypsy's Year at the Golden Crescent.

HACK'S (MARIA) Winter Evenings; or Tales of Travellers. With Illustrations. Small 8vo, cloth gilt extra, 3s. 6d.

—————— Grecian Stories. With Illustrations. Small 8vo, cloth gilt extra, 3s. 6d.; smaller Edition, 2s. 6d.

HARE'S (AUGUSTUS J. C.) Walks in Rome. Two Vols., crown 8vo, 21s.

—————— Memorials of a Quiet Life. Two Vols., crown 8vo, 21s.

—————— Wanderings in Spain. With Illustrations. Crown 8vo, 10s. 6d.

HARE'S (The late AUGUSTUS WILLIAM) The Alton Sermons. Crown 8vo, 10s. 6d.

HÄUSSER'S (LUDWIG) The Period of the Reformation. Two Vols., post 8vo, 18s.

HAWEIS' (REV. H. R.) Music and Morals. With Portrait of the Author. Post 8vo, 12s.

—————— Pet, or Pastimes and Penalties. With Fifty Illustrations by M. E. Haweis. Crown 8vo, cloth gilt extra, 5s.

HAWTHORNE'S (NATHANIEL) Passages from English Note-books. Two Vols., post 8vo, 24s.

—————— Passages from French and Italian Note-books. Two Vols., post 8vo, 24s.

HENRY HOLBEACH : Student in Life and Philosophy. A Narrative and a Discussion. With Letters to Mr. M. Arnold, Mr. Alexander Bain, Mr. T. Carlyle, Mr. A. Helps, Mr. G. H. Lewes, Rev. H. L. Mansel, Rev. F. D. Maurice, Mr. J. S. Mill, and Rev. Dr. J. H. Newman. Enlarged Edition. Two Vols., post 8vo, 14s.

HEROINES OF THE HOUSEHOLD. By the Author of "The Heavenward Path," &c. With Illustrations. Crown 8vo, cloth gilt extra, 3s. 6d.

HERSCHEL'S (Sir J. F. W., Bart.) Familiar Lectures on Scientific Subjects. Crown 8vo, 6s.

HOGE'S (Rev. W. J.) Blind Bartimeus and his Great Physician. Small 8vo, 1s.

HOLBEACH'S (Henry) Shoemakers' Village. Two Vols., crown 8vo, 16s.

HOLMES' (Oliver Wendell) The Autocrat of the Breakfast Table. With Illustrations. Small 8vo, 3s. 6d.

HORNER'S (Susan and Joanna) Walks in Florence, with Illustrations. 2 Vols., crown 8vo, 21s.

HOWE'S (Edward) The Boy in the Bush. With Illustrations. Crown 8vo, cloth gilt extra, 5s.

HOWSON'S (Dean) The Metaphors of St. Paul. Crown 8vo, 3s. 6d.

————— The Companions of St. Paul. Crown 8vo, 5s.

————— The Character of St. Paul. Cr. 8vo, 5s.

HUDSON'S (E. H.) The Life and Times of Louisa, Queen of Prussia; with an Introductory Sketch of Prussian History. Two Vols., post 8vo, 21s.

HUNT'S (Rev. John) History of Religious Thought in England, from the Reformation to the End of Last Century. Three Vols., demy 8vo, 21s. each.

————— Contemporary Essays in Theology. Demy 8vo, 16s.

HUNTINGTON'S (F. D., D.D.) Christian Believing and Living. Crown 8vo, 3s. 6d.

HUTTON'S (R. H.) Essays, Theological and Literary. Two Vols., square 8vo, 24s.

HYMNS FOR THE YOUNG. With Music by John Hullah. 8vo, 1s. 6d. Sewed, 6d.

INGELOW'S (JEAN) Mopsa the Fairy. With Illustrations. Crown 8vo, cloth extra, 3s. 6d.

——————— Studies for Stories. With Illustrations by Millais and others. Crown 8vo, cloth extra, 3s. 6d.

——————— A Sister's Bye-hours. With Illustrations. Cloth extra, 3s. 6d.

——————— Stories Told to a Child. With Illustrations. Square 32mo, cloth gilt extra, 3s. 6d.

IRVING'S (EDWARD) Collected Writings. Five Vols., demy 8vo, £3.

——————— Miscellanies from the Collected Writings. Post 8vo, 6s.

IVAN DE BIRON; or, the Russian Court in the Middle of Last Century. By the Author of "Friends in Council." Post 8vo, 6s. 6d.

JACOB'S (G. A., D.D.) The Ecclesiastical Polity of the New Testament. A Study for the Present Crisis in the Church of England. Post 8vo, 16s.

JACOB'S (P. W.) Hindoo Tales; or, the Adventures of Ten Princes. Freely Translated from the Sanscrit of the Dasakumaracharitam. Crown 8vo, 6s.

JESUS—SAVIOUR. Meditations for Christian Comfort. Cloth antique, 2s. 6d.

JOHNSTONE'S (REV. J. BARBOUR) "It is Your Life." Preaching for the People. Crown 8vo, 2s. 6d.

JONES (AGNES ELIZABETH) Memorials of. By her Sister. With a Portrait. Crown 8vo, 3s. 6d.

JONES' (ARCHDEACON) The Peace of God. Crown 8vo, 5s.

JONES' (REV. HARRY, M.A.) The Regular Swiss Round. With Illustrations. Small 8vo, 3s. 6d.

JOURDAN'S (BEATRICE A.) Chances and Changes. Stories of the Past and Present. With Illustrations. Crown 8vo, cloth gilt extra, 5s.

JUNO STORIES (THE). By Jacob Abbott.
  Four small 8vo Volumes, with Illustrations, 1s. 6d. each.
    Juno and Georgie.   Juno on a Journey.
    Mary Osborne.   Hubert.

KAYE'S (SIR W.) Lives of Indian Officers, illustrative of the History of the Civil and Military Service of India. Three Vols, crown 8vo, 6s. each.

KINGSLEY'S (REV. CHARLES) Madam How and Lady Why. With Illustrations. Crown 8vo, cloth gilt extra, 5s.

————— Health and Education. Cr. 8vo, 7s. 6d.

————— Town Geology. Crown 8vo, 5s.

————— Selections from Writings. With Portrait. Crown 8vo, 6s.

KINGSLEY'S (HENRY) The Boy in Grey. With Illustrations. Crown 8vo, 3s. 6d.

KINGSTON'S (W. H. G.) Foxholme Hall, and other Amusing Tales for Boys. With Illustrations. Small 8vo, cloth gilt extra, 3s. 6d.

————— The Pirate's Treasure, and other Amusing Tales for Boys. With Illustrations. Small 8vo, cloth gilt extra, 3s. 6d.

————— Harry Skipwith. A Tale for Boys. With Illustrations. Small 8vo, cloth gilt extra, 3s. 6d.

KNOLLYS' (MAJOR) Handbook of Field Fortifications. With numerous Illustrations. Crown 8vo, 4s. 6d.

KRILOF AND HIS FABLES. By W. R. S. Ralston. With Illustrations. Crown 8vo, 7s. 6d.

LAUTERDALE. A Story of Two Generations. Three Vols., post 8vo, 31s. 6d.

LEES' (REV. F. G., D.C.L.) The Christian Doctrine of Prayer for the Departed. With copious Notes and Appendices. Demy 8vo, 16s.

LEES' (FLORENCE S.) Handbook for Hospital Sisters. Edited by Professor ACLAND. Post 8vo, 5s.

LEGENDS OF KING ARTHUR AND HIS KNIGHTS OF THE ROUND TABLE (THE). Compiled and Edited by J. T. K. Small 8vo, 1s. 6d.

LEITCH'S (WILLIAM, D.D.) God's Glory in the Heavens. With Illustrations. Crown 8vo, 4s. 6d.

LELAND'S (CHARLES G.) The Egyptian Sketch Book. Post 8vo, 7s. 6d.

LE PAGE'S FRENCH COURSE.

"The sale of many thousands, and the almost universal adoption of these clever little books by M. Le Page, sufficiently prove the public approbation of his plan of teaching French, which is in accordance with the natural operation of a child learning his native language."

French School. Part I. L'Echo de Paris. A Selection of Familiar Phrases which a person would hear daily if living in France. 12mo, 3s. 6d.

N.B. A Key to the above, being Finishing Exercises in French Conversation. 18mo, 1s.

——————. Part II. The Gift of Fluency in French Conversation. 12mo, 2s. 6d.

N.B. A Key to the above: "Petit Causeur; or, First Chatterings in French." 12mo, 1s. 6d.

——————. Part III. The Last Step to French. With the Versification. 12mo, 2s. 6d.

Petit Lecteur des Colléges; or, the French Reader, for Beginners and Elder Classes. A Sequel to "L'Echo de Paris." 12mo, 3s. 6d.

French Master for Beginners; or, Easy Lessons in French. 12mo, 2s. 6d.

Juvenile Treasury of French Conversation. With the English before the French. 12mo, 3s.

Ready Guide to French Composition. French Grammar by Examples, giving Models as Leading-strings throughout Accidence and Syntax. 12mo, 3s. 6d.

Etrennes aux Dames Anglaises. A Key to French Pronunciation in all its niceties. Sewed, 6d.

LILLIPUT LEVEE. Poems of Childhood, Child-fancy, and Child-like Moods. With Illustrations by Millais and others. Square 32mo, cloth gilt extra, 2s. 6d.

LILLIPUT LECTURES. By the Author of "Lilliput Levee." With Illustrations. Square 8vo, cloth gilt extra, 5s.

LILLIPUT LEGENDS. By the Author of "Lilliput Levee." With Illustrations. Square 8vo, cloth gilt extra, 5s.

LIVING VOICES: Selections from Recent Poetry. With a Preface by the Archbishop of Canterbury. Small 8vo, cloth extra, 4s. 6d.

LLOYD'S (Mrs. W. R.) The Flower of Christian Chivalry. With Thirty-four Illustrations by J. D. Watson and others. Crown 8vo, cloth gilt extra, 3s. 6d.

LOCKER'S (Frederick) London Lyrics. Small 8vo, 6s.

LOSSING'S (Benson J.) The Hudson from the Wilderness to the Sea. Illustrated by 300 Engravings on Wood. Small 4to, cloth gilt extra, 21s.

LOVING COUNSEL. An Address to his Parishioners. By the Author of "The Pathway of Promise." Limp cloth, 8d.

LUDLOW'S (J. M.) Woman's Work in the Church. Small 8vo, 5s.

LUDLOW (J. M.) and LLOYD JONES' The Progress of the Working Class from 1832 to 1867. Crown 8vo, 2s. 6d.

LYNCH'S (Rev. T. T.) Memoir. Edited by William White, with Portrait. Post 8vo, 7s. 6d.

———— Sermons for my Curates. Edited by the Rev. Samuel Cox. Post 8vo, 5s.

———— Letters to the Scattered. Post 8vo, 5s.

———— The Rivulet. A Contribution to Sacred Song. New Edition. Small 8vo, 3s. 6d.

———— Tunes to Hymns in "The Rivulet." Edited by T. Pettit, A.R.A.M. Square 8vo, 2s. 6d.

MACDONALD'S (George) Annals of a Quiet Neighbourhood. Crown 8vo, 6s.

———— The Seaboard Parish. Crown 8vo, 6s.

———— Wilfrid Cumbermede. Crown 8vo, 6s.

18   *Daldy, Isbister, and Co.'s*

MAC DONALD'S (George) Dealings with the Fairies. With Illustrations by Arthur Hughes. Square 32mo, cloth gilt extra, 2s. 6d.

——————— The Disciple and other Poems. Crown 8vo, 6s.

——————— Unspoken Sermons. Crown 8vo, 3s. 6d.

——————— The Miracles of our Lord. Crown 8vo, 5s.

——————— The Wow o' Rivven. Sewed, 6d.

——————— At the Back of the North Wind. With Illustrations. Crown 8vo, cloth gilt extra, 5s.

——————— Ranald Bannerman's Boyhood. With Illustrations. Crown 8vo, cloth gilt extra, 5s.

——————— The Princess and the Goblin. With Illustrations. Crown 8vo, cloth gilt extra, 5s.

——————— Works of Fancy and Imagination: being a reprint of Poetical and other Works. Pocket-volume Edition, in neat case, £2 2s.

MAC DONALD'S (Mrs. George) Chamber Dramas for Children. Crown 8vo, 7s. 6d.

MACKAY'S (Charles) Studies from the Antique, Sketches from Nature, and other Poems. Small 8vo, 3s. 6d.

MACKENZIE and IRBY'S (Misses) Travels in the Sclavonic Provinces of Turkey in Europe. With Illustrations. Demy 8vo, 24s.

MACLEOD'S (Norman, D.D.) Peeps at the Far East. With Illustrations. Small 4to, cloth gilt extra, 21s.

——————— Eastward. With Illustrations. Crown 8vo, 6s.

——————— Character Sketches. With Illustrations. Post 8vo, 10s. 6d.

MACLEOD'S (NORMAN, D.D.) The Temptation of Our Lord. Crown 8vo, 5s.

———— Parish Papers. Crown 8vo, 3s. 6d.

———— Reminiscences of a Highland Parish. Crown 8vo, 6s.

———— Simple Truth spoken to Working People. Small 8vo, 2s. 6d.

———— The Earnest Student: being Memorials of John Mackintosh. Crown 8vo, 3s. 6d.

———— The Gold Thread. A Story for the Young. With Illustrations. Square 8vo, 2s. 6d.

———— The Old Lieutenant and his Son. With Illustrations. Crown 8vo, 3s. 6d.

———— The Starling. With Illustrations. Crown 8vo, 6s.

———— Wee Davie. Sewed, 6d.

———— How can we best Relieve our Deserving Poor? Sewed, 6d.

———— War and Judgment. A Sermon preached before and published by command of the Queen. Sewed, 1s.

MACQUOID'S (MRS.) Through Normandy. With Map and 90 Illustrations. Crown 8vo, 12s.

———— Forgotten by the World. Crown 8vo, 6s.

MANSEL'S (DEAN) The Philosophy of the Conditioned: Sir William Hamilton and John Stuart Mill. Post 8vo, 6s.

MARKBY'S (REV. THOMAS) Practical Essays on Education. Crown 8vo, 6s.

MARLITT'S (E.) Gold Elsie. Crown 8vo, 5s.

MARSH'S (J. B.) The Story of Harecourt; being the History of an Independent Church. With an Introduction by Alexander Raleigh, D.D. With Illustrations. Crown 8vo, 6s.

MARSH'S (J. B.) For Liberty's Sake. Post 8vo, 10s. 6d.

——————— Stories of Venice and the Venetians. Crown 8vo, cloth extra, 5s.

——————— The Story of Dick Whittington, the Famous Lord Mayor of London. With Illustrations. Crown 8vo, cloth extra, 3s. 6d.

MARSHMAN'S (J. C.) Story of the Lives of Carey, Marshman, and Ward. Crown 8vo, 3s. 6d.

MARTIN'S (Rev. H.) The Prophet Jonah. Crown 8vo, 6s.

MARTIN'S (W.) Noble Boys. Their Deeds of Love and Duty. With Illustrations. Crown 8vo, cloth gilt extra, 3s. 6d.

MASSEY'S (Gerald) A Tale of Eternity, and other Poems. Crown 8vo, 7s.

MAURICE'S (Rev. F. D.) The Working Man and the Franchise; being Chapters from English History on the Representation and Education of the People. Demy 8vo, 7s. 6d.; crown 8vo, boards, 1s. 6d.

MAZZINI'S (Joseph) The War and the Commune. Sewed, 1s.

MEN OF THE THIRD REPUBLIC. Crown 8vo, 6s.

MERIVALE'S (Charles, B.D., D.C.L.) Homer's Iliad. In English Rhymed Verse. Two Vols., demy 8vo, 24s.

METEYARD'S (Eliza) The Doctor's Little Daughter. The Story of a Child's Life amidst the Woods and Hills. With Illustrations. Crown 8vo, cloth gilt extra, 5s.

MILLAIS' ILLUSTRATIONS. A Collection of Drawings on Wood. By John Everett Millais, R.A. Demy 4to, cloth gilt extra, 16s.

MONRO'S (Rev. Edward) Edwin's Fairing. With Illustrations. Square 32mo, cloth gilt extra, 2s. 6d.

MY MOTHER AND I. By the Author of "John Halifax." Post 8vo, 10s. 6d.

Book List.

MYERS' (Rev. Frederic) Catholic Thoughts on the Church of Christ and the Church of England. Crown 8vo, 7s. 6d.

———— Catholic Thoughts on the Bible and Theology. Crown 8vo, 7s. 6d.

NEILL'S (Edward D.) The English Colonization of America during the Seventeenth Century. Demy 8vo, 14s.

NEWMAN'S (John Henry, D.D.) Miscellanies from the Oxford Sermons, and other Writings. Crown 8vo, 6s.

NOEL'S (The Hon. Roden) The Red Flag and other Poems. Small 8vo, 6s.

NUGENT'S (E., C.E.) Optics; or Sight and Light Theoretically and Practically Treated. With numerous Woodcuts. Enlarged Edition. Post 8vo, 5s.

NUTTALL'S (Dr.) Dictionary of Scientific Terms. Post 8vo. 5s.

ORME'S (Benjamin) Treasure Book of Devotional Reading. Crown 8vo, cloth gilt extra, 3s. 6d.

OSBORN'S (Rev. H. S., M.A.) The Holy Land, Past and Present. Sketches of Travel in Palestine. With Illustrations on Wood and Steel. Crown 8vo, cloth gilt extra, 3s. 6d.

OULITA THE SERF. A Tragedy. By the Author of "Friends in Council." Pocket volume Edition. Cloth extra, 5s.

OUR NEW MASTERS. By "The Journeyman Engineer." Post 8vo, 9s.

PAGE'S (H. A.) Golden Lives. Biographies for the Day, with Illustrations. Crown 8vo, cloth extra, 5s.

———————— Out and All About. Fables for Old and Young. With Eighty-five Illustrations. Crown 8vo, cloth gilt extra, 5s.

PARKER'S (Joseph, D.D.) Pulpit Notes, with an Introductory Essay on the Preaching of Jesus Christ. Post 8vo, 6s.

PARKES-BELLOC'S (BESSIE RAYNER) Essays on Woman's Work. Small 8vo, 4s.

——————————— La Belle France. With Illustrations. Square 8vo, 12s.

——————————— Vignettes. Twelve Biographical Sketches. Crown 8vo, 6s.

PARR'S (MRS.) Dorothy Fox. Crown 8vo, 6s.

——————— How it all Happened, and other Stories. Two Vols., post 8vo, 21s.

——————— The Prescotts of Pamphillon. Three Vols., post 8vo, 31s. 6d.

PARRY (CHARLES, Commander Royal Navy) Memorials of. By his Brother, the Right Rev. Edward Parry, D.D., Suffragan Bishop of Dover. Crown 8vo, 5s.

PATHWAY OF PROMISE (THE). Neat cloth, 1s. 6d.

PAUL GOSSLETT'S CONFESSIONS IN LOVE, LAW, AND THE CIVIL SERVICE. With Illustrations by Marcus Stone. Post 8vo, 2s. 6d.

PEASANT LIFE IN THE NORTH. Crown 8vo, 6s.

——————————————————— Second Series. Crown 8vo, 9s.

PEEPS AT FOREIGN COUNTRIES. With Illustrations. Crown 8vo, cloth, gilt extra, 5s.

PEROWNE'S (REV. CANON) Sermons. Crown 8vo, 7s. 6d.

PERRY'S (REV. F.) Dulce Domum. Essays on Home Life. Crown 8vo, 7s. 6d.

PERSONAL PIETY. A Help to Christians to Walk worthy of their Calling. Cloth antique, 1s. 6d.

PHELPS' (AUSTIN) Man's Renewal. Small 8vo, 2s. 6d.

——————— The Still Hour. Small 8vo, 1s.

PHILLIMORE'S (JOHN GEORGE) History of England during the Reign of George the Third. Vol. I., 8vo, 18s.

PICTORIAL SPELLING-BOOK; or Lessons on Facts and Objects. With 130 Illustrations. New Edition. 12mo, 1s. 6d.

PLUMPTRE'S (PROFESSOR) Biblical Studies. Post 8vo, 5s.

———————— Christ and Christendom; being the Boyle Lectures for 1866. Demy 8vo, 12s.

———————— Lazarus and other Poems. Crown 8vo, 5s.

———————— Master and Scholar, and other Poems. Crown 8vo, 5s.

———————— Sunday. Sewed, 6d.

———————— The Tragedies of Æschylos. A New Translation, with a Biographical Essay, and an Appendix of Rhymed Choruses. Crown 8vo, 7s. 6d.

———————— The Tragedies of Sophocles. A New Translation, with a Biographical Essay, and an Appendix of Rhymed Choruses. Crown 8vo, 7s. 6d.

———————— Theology and Life. Sermons chiefly on Special Occasions. Small 8vo, 6s.

———————— "The Spirits in Prison." A Sermon on the state of the Dead. Sewed, 1s.

———————— Confession and Absolution. A Sermon Preached before the University of Oxford. Sewed, 1s.

POEMS WRITTEN FOR A CHILD. By Two Friends. With Illustrations. Square 32mo, cloth gilt extra, 3s. 6d.

POLITICAL PORTRAITS. Characters of some of our Public Men. Crown 8vo, 6s.

POLLOCK'S (ARCHDEACON) The Temptation and other Poems. Small 8vo, 3s. 6d.

PORTER'S (NOAH, D.D.) The Human Intellect, with an Introduction upon Psychology and the Soul. Demy 8vo, 16s.

PORTER'S (NOAH, D.D.) The Elements of Intellectual Science. A Manual for Schools and Colleges. Demy 8vo, 10s. 6d.

PRESENT-DAY PAPERS on Prominent Questions in Theology. Edited by the Right Rev. Alexander Ewing, D.C.L., Bishop of Argyll and the Isles. One Shilling each; or in Three Vols., crown 8vo, 7s. 6d. each.

 I. THE ATONEMENT.
 II. THE EUCHARIST.
 III. THE RULE OF FAITH.
 IV. THE PRESENT UNBELIEF.
 V. WORDS FOR THINGS.
 VI. PRAYERS AND MEDITATIONS.
 VII. JUSTIFICATION BY FAITH.
 VIII. MOTHER-CHURCH.
 IX. USE OF THE WORD REVELATION IN THE NEW TESTAMENT.
 X. THE CHRISTIAN MINISTRY. Part 1.
 XI. THE CHRISTIAN MINISTRY. Part 2.
 XII. THE ETERNAL LIFE MANIFESTED.
 XIII. SOME LETTERS OF THOMAS ERSKINE OF LINLATHEN.
 XIV. GOD AND THE CHRISTIAN SACRAMENTS.
 XV. ST. AUGUSTINE AND HIS MOTHER.
 XVI. SOME FURTHER LETTERS OF THOMAS ERSKINE OF LINLATHEN.
 XVII. THE FUTURE TEMPORAL SUPPORT OF THE MINISTRY.
 XVIII. THE RELATION OF KNOWLEDGE TO SALVATION.
 XIX. RECONCILIATION

RAE'S (W. F.) Wilkes, Sheridan, Fox: the Opposition under George III. Demy 8vo, 18s.

―――― Westward by Rail. A Journey to San Francisco, and a Visit to the Mormons. With Map. Small 8vo, 4s. 6d.

RALEIGH'S (ALEXANDER, D.D.) The Little Sanctuary. Crown 8vo, 6s.

REED (ANDREW) Memoirs of the Life and Philanthropic Labours of. By his Sons. With Portrait and Illustrations. Crown 8vo, 6s.

RIGG'S (J. H., D.D.) National Education and Public Elementary Schools. Crown 8vo, 12s.

RITCHIE'S (ARCHIBALD T.) Dynamical Theory of the Formation of the Earth. Demy 8vo, 16s.

ROBERTSON'S (JOHN, D.D.) Sermons and Expositions. Post 8vo, 7s. 6d.

ROBINSON CRUSOE. With Illustrations. 18mo, cloth gilt extra, 1s. 6d.

ROGERS' (HENRY) Essays from "Good Words." Small 8vo, 5s.

SACRISTAN'S HOUSEHOLD (THE). By the Author of "Mabel's Progress." Crown 8vo, 6s.

SAINT ABE AND HIS SEVEN WIVES. A Tale of Salt Lake City. Crown 8vo, 5s.

SANDFORD AND MERTON. With Illustrations. 18mo, cloth gilt extra, 1s. 6d.

SAPHIR'S (REV. ADOLPH) Conversion, Illustrated from Examples recorded in the Bible. Small 8vo, 3s. 6d.

SAVING KNOWLEDGE, Addressed to Young Men. By Thomas Guthrie, D.D., and W. G. Blaikie, D.D. Crown 8vo, 3s. 6d.

SEN'S (BABOO KESHUB CHUNDER) Lectures and Tracts. Edited by S. D. Collet. Crown 8vo, 5s.

—— English Visit. An authorized Collection of his principal Addresses delivered in England. Edited by S. D. Collet. Crown 8vo, 9s.

SERBIAN FOLK-LORE. Popular Tales Selected and Translated by Madame Csedomille Mijatovics. Edited, with an Introduction, by the Rev. W. Denton, M.A. Post 8vo, 10s. 6d.

SHAEN'S (MRS. WILLIAM) School Lessons in Household Economy. Sewed, 6d.

SHELMERDINE'S (W.) Selection of the Psalms and other Portions of Scripture, arranged and marked for Chanting. Small 8vo, 1s.

—— One Hundred and Eighty Chants, Ancient and Modern. Arranged for Four Voices, with Organ and Piano Accompaniment. Crown 8vo, 2s. 6d.

Daldy, Isbister, and Co.'s

SHORTREDE'S (Major-Gen.) Azimuth, Latitude, and Declination Tables. Demy 8vo, 7s. 6d.

SIMCOX'S (G. A.) Poems and Romances. Crown 8vo, 6s.

SMEDLEY'S (M. B.) Poems. Crown 8vo, 5s.

———— Other Folk's Lives. Crown 8vo, cloth gilt extra, 5s.

———— Linnet's Trial. Crown 8vo, cloth gilt extra, 5s.

SMEDLEY'S (Frank E.) Gathered Leaves. A Collection of Poetical Writings. With a Memorial, Preface, Portrait, &c. Imp. 16mo, cloth gilt, 8s. 6d.

SMILES' (Samuel) The Huguenots in France, after the Revocation of the Edict of Nantes, with a Visit to the Country of the Vaudois. Crown 8vo, 10s. 6d.

SMITH'S (Alexander) Alfred Hagart's Household. Crown 8vo, 6s.

———— A Summer in Skye. Crown 8vo, 6s.

———— Dreamthorp. A Book of Essays written in the Country. Crown 8vo, 3s. 6d.

SMITH'S (David) Tales of Chivalry and Romance. With Illustrations. Crown 8vo, cloth gilt extra, 3s. 6d.

SMITH'S (Dr. Edward, F.R.S.) Health, a Handbook for Households and Schools. Crown 8vo, 3s. 6d.

SMITH'S (The late Rev. James) The Coming Man. Two Vols., post 8vo, 21s.

SMYTH'S (Professor C. Piazzi) Our Inheritance in the Great Pyramid. With Illustrations. Post 8vo, 18s.

SOME TALK ABOUT ANIMALS AND THEIR MASTERS. By the Author of "Friends in Council." Crown 8vo, 7s. 6d.

SOUTH BY WEST; or Winter in the Rocky Mountains and Spring in Mexico. Edited by the Rev. Canon Kingsley. With Illustrations. Demy 8vo, 16s.

SPEN'S (Kay) True of Heart. Crown 8vo, 5s.

———— Tottie's Trial. Crown 8vo, 10s. 6d.

SPURGEON'S (Rev. C. H.) The Saint and his Saviour. Crown 8vo, 3s. 6d.

STANLEY'S (Dean) Scripture Portraits and other Miscellanies. Crown 8vo, 6s.

——————— The Prospect of Christian Missions. Sewed, 1s.

STAUNTON'S (Howard) The Great Schools of England: an Account of their Foundations, Endowments, and Discipline, with an Account of all the Endowed Grammar Schools of England and Wales. Crown 8vo, 7s. 6d.

STEVENSON'S (Rev. W. Fleming) Praying and Working. Crown 8vo, 3s. 6d.; small 8vo, 2s.

STEWART'S (L.) The Wave and the Battle-field: Adventures by Sea and Land. With Illustrations. Crown 8vo, cloth gilt extra, 3s. 6d.

STIER'S (Rudolf, D.D.) The Words of the Angels. Crown 8vo, 3s. 6d.

STOLBERG (Anna, Countess of) A Story of Our Own Times. Crown 8vo, 5s.

STRACHEY'S (Sir Edward, Bart.) Jewish History and Politics in the Times of Sargon and Sennacherib. New Edition, carefully revised. Demy 8vo, 18s.

STREET'S (Rev. B.) The Restoration of Paths to Dwell in. Essays on the Re-editing and Interpretation of Hebrew Scripture. Post 8vo, 7s. 6d.

STUDIES IN FRENCH PROSE. Specimens of the Language from the Seventeenth Century to the Present Time. With Chronological and Critical Notices, Explanatory Notes, &c. 12mo, 3s. 6d.

STUDIES IN FRENCH POETRY. Specimens of the Language from the Seventeenth Century to the Present Time. With Chronological and Critical Notices, Explanatory Notes, &c. 12mo, 3s. 6d.

SUNDAY EVENING BOOK (The). Short Papers for Family Reading. By J. Hamilton, D.D., A. P. Stanley, D.D., J. Eadie, D.D., Rev. W. M. Punshon, Rev. T. Binney, J. R. Macduff, D.D. Cloth antique, 1s. 6d.

TAINE'S (H., D.C.L.) Notes on England. Translated by W. F. Rae, with an Introduction by the Translator. Crown 8vo, 3s. 6d.

TAIT'S (GILBERT) The Hymns of Denmark. Rendered into English. Small 8vo, cloth gilt extra, 4s. 6d.

TANGLED TALK. An Essayist's Holiday. Post 8vo, 7s. 6d.

TAYLOR'S (BAYARD) Faust. A Tragedy. By Johann Wolfgang Von Goethe. Translated in the original metres. Two Vols., post 8vo, 28s.

————— Lars. A Pastoral of Norway. Small 8vo, 3s. 6d.

THOROLD'S (REV. A. W.) The Presence of Christ. Crown 8vo, 3s. 6d.

————— Parochial Missions. Limp cloth, 1s.

THOUGHTS ON RECENT SCIENTIFIC CONCLUSIONS and their Relation to Religion. Crown 8vo, 5s.

THRONE OF GRACE (THE). By the Author of "The Pathway of Promise." Cloth antique, 2s. 6d.

TOUCHES OF NATURE. By Eminent Artists and Authors. Imperial 4to, cloth gilt extra, 21s.

TREASURY OF CHOICE QUOTATIONS. Crown 8vo, cloth extra, 3s. 6d.

TULLOCH'S (PRINCIPAL) Beginning Life. A Book for Young Men. Crown 8vo, cloth extra, 3s. 6d.

TYTLER'S (C. C. FRASER) Jasmine Leigh. Crown 8vo, cloth extra, 5s.

————— Margaret. Crown 8vo, 6s.

TYTLER'S (M. FRASER) Tales of Many Lands. With Illustrations. Small 8vo, cloth gilt extra, 3s. 6d.

TYTLER'S (SARAH) The Songstresses of Scotland. Two Vols., post 8vo, 16s.

————— The Old Masters and their Pictures. Crown 8vo, 4s. 6d.

TYTLER'S (SARAH) Modern Painters and their Paintings. Crown 8vo, 4s. 6d.

————— Citoyenne Jacqueline. A Woman's Lot in the Great French Revolution. Crown 8vo, cloth gilt extra, 5s.

————— Days of Yore. Crown 8vo, cloth gilt extra, 5s.

————— Girlhood and Womanhood. Crown 8vo, cloth gilt extra, 5s.

————— Papers for Thoughtful Girls. With Illustrations by Millais. Crown 8vo, cloth gilt extra, 5s.

————— Heroines in Obscurity. A Second Series of "Papers for Thoughtful Girls." Crown 8vo, cloth gilt extra, 5s.

————— The Diamond Rose. A Life of Love and Duty. Crown 8vo, cloth gilt extra, 5s.

————— The Huguenot Family in the English Village. With Illustrations. Crown 8vo, 6s.

————— "Noblesse Oblige." An English Story of To-day. Crown 8vo, 6s.

————— Lady Bell. A Story of Last Century. With Illustrations. Crown 8vo, 6s.

VAUGHAN'S (C. J., D.D.) Last Words in the Parish Church of Doncaster. Crown 8vo, 3s. 6d.

————— Earnest Words for Earnest Men. Small 8vo, 3s. 6d.

————— Characteristics of Christ's Teaching. Small 8vo, 2s. 6d.

————— Christ the Light of the World. Small 8vo, 2s. 6d.

————— Plain Words on Christian Living. Small 8vo, 2s. 6d.

————— Voices of the Prophets on Faith, Prayer, and Human Life. Small 8vo, 2s. 6d.

VAUGHAN'S (C. J., D.D.) Half-hours in the Temple Church. Small 8vo, 3s. 6d.

———————— Sundays in the Temple. Small 8vo, 3s. 6d.

———————— Family Prayers. Crown 8vo, 3s. 6d.

———————— The Presence of God in his Temple. Small 8vo, 3s. 6d.

VINET'S (ALEXANDER) Outlines of Philosophy. Edited by M. Astié. Post 8vo, 6s.

———————————————— Outlines of Theology. Edited by M. Astié. Post 8vo, 6s.

WARING'S (A. L.) Hymns and Meditations. Cloth antique, 2s. 6d. Sewed, 1s. 6d.

WARREN'S (JOHN LEICESTER) Searching the Net. A Book of Verses. Crown 8vo, 6s.

————————————————————Rehearsals: A Book of Verses. Crown 8vo, 6s.

—————— Philoctetes. A Metrical Drama after the Antique. Crown 8vo, 4s. 6d.

—————— Orestes. A Metrical Drama after the Antique. Crown 8vo, 4s. 6d.

WATSON'S (FORBES, M.R.C.S.) Flowers and Gardens. Notes on Plant Beauty. Crown 8vo, 5s.

WENTWORTH'S (PAUL) Amos Thorne and other Poems. Small 8vo, 3s.

WHEELER'S (J. TALBOYS, F.R.G.S.) Historical Geography of the Old and New Testaments. Folio, 7s. 6d.

———————— Analysis and Summary of Old Testament History and the Laws of Moses. Post 8vo, 5s. 6d.

———————— Analysis and Summary of New Testament History. Post 8vo, 5s. 6d.

———————— Popular Abridgment of Old and New Testament History. Two Vols., 18mo, 2s. each.

WHITE ROSE AND RED. A Love Story. By the Author of "St. Abe." Crown 8vo, 6s.

WHITEHEAD'S (Rev. H.) Sermons, chiefly on Subjects from the Sunday Lessons. Crown 8vo, 6s.

WHITNEY'S (Adeline T.) Pansies. "—— for Thoughts." Square 8vo, 2s. 6d.

WILBERFORCE'S (Bishop) Heroes of Hebrew History. Crown 8vo, 5s.

WILDE'S (Robert) Poems. Edited by the Rev. John Hunt. Small 8vo, 3s. 6d.

WILKINS' (Professor A. S.) National Education in Greece in the Fourth Century before Christ. Post 8vo, 5s.

WILKINSON'S (Rev. W. F.) Personal Names in the Bible. Small 8vo, 6s.

WILLEMENT'S (E. E.) Familiar Things: their History, &c. Small 8vo, 2s. 6d.

WILLIAMS' (Sarah) Twilight Hours. A Legacy of Verse. With a Memoir by E. H. Plumptre, M.A. Enlarged Edition. Crown 8vo, 5s.

WINDWAFTED SEED. Edited by Norman Macleod, D.D., and Thomas Guthrie, D.D. Crown 8vo, 3s. 6d.

WORBOISE'S (E. J.) Sir Julian's Wife. Small 8vo, 5s.

—————— The Wife's Trials. Small 8vo, 3s. 6d.

—————— The Life of Thomas Arnold, D.D. Small 8vo, 3s. 6d.

—————— Campion Court. A Tale of the Days of the Ejectment Two Hundred Years Ago. Crown 8vo, 5s.

—————— The Lillingstones of Lillingstone. Crown 8vo, 5s.

—————— Lottie Lonsdale; or the Chain and its Links. Crown 8vo, 5s.

—————— Evelyn's Story; or Labour and Wait. Crown 8vo, 5s.

Daldy, Isbister, and Co.'s Book List.

WORDSWORTH'S Poems for the Young. With Illustrations. Square 8vo, cloth gilt extra, 3s. 6d.

YORKE'S (ONSLOW) The Story of the International. Crown 8vo, 2s.

YOUNG'S (JOHN, LL.D.) The Christ of History. Enlarged Edition. Crown 8vo, 6s.

—— The Life and Light of Men. Post 8vo, 7s. 6d.

—— The Creator and the Creation, how related. Crown 8vo, 6s.

PRINTED BY VIRTUE AND CO., CITY ROAD, LONDON.

www.ingramcontent.com/pod-product-compliance
Lightning Source LLC
Chambersburg PA
CBHW030600300426
44111CB00009B/1053